Scepticism

Neil Gascoigne

For Rachel

First published in 2002 by Acumen

Acumen Publishing Limited
15a Lewins Yard
East Street
Chesham
Bucks HP5 1HQ
www.acumenpublishing.co.uk

ISBN: 1-902683-45-5 (hardcover)
ISBN: 1-902683-46-3 (paperback)

British Library Cataloguing-in-Publication Data
A catalogue record for this book is available from
the British Library.

Designed and typeset by Kate Williams, Abergavenny.
Printed and bound by Biddles Ltd., Guildford and King's Lynn.

Scepticism

Central Problems of Philosophy

Series Editor: John Shand

This series of books presents concise, clear, and rigorous analyses of the core problems that preoccupy philosophers across all approaches to the discipline. Each book encapsulates the essential arguments and debates, providing an authoritative guide to the subject while also introducing original perspectives. This series of books by an international team of authors aims to cover those fundamental topics that, taken together, constitute the full breadth of philosophy.

Published titles

Free Will
Graham McFee

Knowledge
Michael Welbourne

Relativism
Paul O'Grady

Scepticism
Neil Gascoigne

Truth
Pascal Engel

Universals
J. P. Moreland

Forthcoming titles

Action
Rowland Stout

Analysis
Michael Beaney

Artificial Intelligence
Matthew Elton & Michael Wheeler

Causation and Explanation
Stathis Psillos

Meaning
David Cooper

Mind and Body
Robert Kirk

Modality
Joseph Melia

Ontology
Dale Jacquette

Paradox
Doris Olin

Perception
Barry Maund

Rights
Jonathan Gorman

Self
Stephen Burwood

Value
Chris Cherry

Contents

Acknowledgements

My fascination with philosophical scepticism began when I was a graduate student in the Department of History and Philosophy of Science at the University of Cambridge. From that period I am indebted to Nick Jardine for encouraging that and other more arcane interests. During our time together at Cambridge I benefited greatly from conversations with Julia Borossa, Mark Collier and Tim Thornton, and have the good fortune of continuing to do so. Tim offered probative comment and criticism on an earlier draft of this work, as did Katerina Deligiorgi and two anonymous readers for Acumen. Jonathan Derbyshire read through several drafts of several chapters, all of which are the better for his philosophically scrupulous attentions. The manuscript was revised and completed whilst I was on sabbatical at the University of Chicago. I would like to thank Robert Pippin, Chair of the Committee on Social Thought, for hosting my visit, and Aaron Lambert and the faculty and graduate students of the philosophy department for making it a pleasurable and stimulating one. The visit to Chicago was suggested to me by a fellow sceptic, Andrea Kern, and made possible through the cooperation of my colleagues in the philosophy department at Anglia, among whom I am grateful in particular to my longstanding partner in departmental crime, Alison Ainley. My former colleague Herr Professor Andrew Bowie has been a source of philosophical stimulation since I first started teaching. Above all I want to thank Rachel for her insightful comments on the (near) final draft and for the support and encouragement that has kept me going during the time it has taken to bring this project to completion.

Introduction: The whimsical condition of mankind

> For here is the chief and most confounding objection to
> excessive scepticism, that no durable good can ever result from
> it; while it remains in its full force and vigour . . . When [the
> sceptic] awakes from his dream, he will be the first to join in the
> laugh against himself, and to confess, that all his objections are
> mere amusement, and can have no other tendency than to
> show the whimsical condition of mankind, who must act and
> reason and believe; though they are not able, by their most
> diligent inquiry, to satisfy themselves concerning the founda-
> tion of these operations, or to remove the objections, which
> may be raised against them.   (Hume 1975: 159–60)

It seems reasonable to open a book such as this with a simple
question: What is scepticism? According to Webster's, it is "an
attitude of doubt or disposition toward incredulity in general or in
regard to something particular". So scepticism relates to doubt;
but what is it to 'doubt' or to have a 'doubting attitude'? Mention
scepticism to anyone who has been subjected to an introductory
course on 'The Problems of Philosophy' and they will probably
recall that there are a number of arguments that seem to show
that we can doubt, and therefore don't know, many if not all of
the things we claim to know. As such, what it is to doubt is
associated with certain sorts of thought-experiments like the
idea that right now you or I might be dreaming, or a disembodied
brain floating around in a vat of nutrients linked up to a supercomputer.

These imagined possibilities, once the preserve of students of philosophy, have entered the mainstream imagination through films like *The Matrix* and *Existenz*, which in turn serve to dramatize how difficult they are to dismiss. As you read this you might find it hard to *believe* that you are asleep or an envatted brain, but do you *know* that you aren't? Are you *certain*? Do you have any evidence to the contrary? Since these possibilities suggest that your sensory experience would be the same as if you were awake, what kind of evidence could convince you that they don't in fact obtain? And if you can't rule them out, can you really claim that you know anything at all about the external world? Once we adopt a certain sort of attitude towards our everyday empirical claims, we view them in a very different light and they start to look very precarious indeed. I'm going to call this particular way of thinking about ourselves – almost as if we were 'outside' our own minds, looking down on ourselves – the 'theoretical attitude'.

Trying to understand how the theoretical attitude relates to scepticism will be one of the main themes in this book, so there's no need to discuss it in detail now. Nevertheless, to get a preliminary feel for how odd it is, imagine the following situation. You the reader have somehow managed to discover that you're neither an envatted brain nor dreaming. Since your sensory experience would be the same even if you were an envatted brain, your discovery cannot be empirical in nature – it can't for example be the case that you've just *seen* that you are embodied. So your discovery must be non-empirical in nature: something that you have arrived at as a result of your philosophical sophistication. Since you know that you're not a brain in a vat, and that you can therefore trust your sensory experience, you know that your friend Tim isn't a brain in a vat either. Tim, however, has never read any philosophy and never goes to the cinema and it has never even occurred to him that he might be dreaming or an envatted brain. Given such an eventuality, can Tim be said to *know* that he's not an envatted brain? If not, can he be said to know what *you* know; namely, that he's got two hands? It's not odd to imagine a situation where you know something about Tim that he doesn't know, but it does seem strange to conclude that *you* know he's got hands but *he* doesn't!

This seems like a counter-intuitive and even rather elitist conclusion to arrive at, but it shows that once one adopts the theoretical attitude, scepticism presents epistemology with a theoretical task: to demonstrate that knowledge of the external world is possible and in general possessed by all, regardless of their philosophical sophistication. Reflecting on the possibility that we might be envatted brains is not the only way to raise sceptical doubts, however; and it is not even the most radical. Consider your most strongly held beliefs or most cherished forms of inference: how do you know that they are dependable? You may have seen the sun rise a hundred thousand times in your life, but does that give you a good reason for thinking that it will rise in the future? Even if you were an envatted brain it would be nice to think that you could rely on the vat-sun rising again, or on vat-beer not suddenly beginning to taste like vat-milk!

The flip-side of this is that when you dismiss such thoughts, leave this book (or dream-book) aside, and re-embrace the contexts of everyday life, you will probably give scant thought to the question of whether or not you can trust inductive reasoning, nor dwell on the thought that you're an envatted brain. When we adopt what I'll call the 'practical attitude', with its encounters and negotiations with the world of objects and other people, theoretical attitude concerns about our dire epistemic situation seem quaint and carry little if any conviction. Indeed, in such contexts, theoretical attitude doubts would appear as invidious attempts to avoid responsibility: 'I can't take you to hospital because I don't know that you or anything else exist!'

So far, then, we have identified two related characteristics of sceptical doubt. On the one hand it involves a peculiar sort of 'reflective withdrawal' from our practical attitude engagements with people and things in the world and the adoption of the theoretical attitude; on the other hand it carries no conviction. But if sceptical doubts really do have no effect on our practices then how do we account for the fact that they arise so naturally when we take up a certain attitude towards those practices? Shouldn't we be able to demonstrate why such doubts carry no conviction, and that there is therefore something unnatural about them? If we can't – if the all-too-human activities of reasoning, believing and acting on those reasons and beliefs cannot be defended against such doubts – do we have the right to our practical attitude insouciance? What does this apparent 'insulation' of the practical attitude from the theoretical attitude tell us about what it is to act, reason and believe?

These questions frame one set of responses to our enquiry into what it is to doubt or have a doubting attitude, and they will recur throughout this book. However, it is important to note that the split between the theoretical and practical attitudes is not as clear-cut as the questions suggest. After all, most people, including philosophers in 'normal' conversation, would also associate scepticism with something much more commonplace. In the way that 'philosophy' itself is often used to vaguely indicate a worldview or reflective standpoint, 'scepticism' in this sense suggests a particular state of mind or attitude towards some issue or other. It may often be negatively associated with expressions of cynicism, and perhaps even of suspicion, but there is also what is referred to as a 'healthy scepticism'. One might not *always* be doubting whether one is in fact really in love, treating others fairly, doing the right job or living the right kind of life, but these practical doubts don't seem nearly as removed from common life as doubting whether or not one is awake or can trust one's basic methods of reasoning. Equally, whereas in the realm of the everyday one might not doubt that one has a body, one might well find oneself being sceptical about a referee's decision or the diagnosis of some illnesses or the claims of a fellow scientist.

Whether they involve moral deliberation, existential speculation, or scientific investigation, these doubts all involve taking up a *reflective* distance on a belief or activity in order to scrutinize it in a broader context that answers to our particular interests and projects. Moreover, whilst it's difficult to imagine what our lives would be like without them and at least the possibility of responding to them, this sort of doubt and its associated reflection does not appear to lead to the kind of disengagement we noted with the theoretical attitude. Practical attitude doubts seem to relate to context in a way that theoretical attitude doubts do not. We might call such an attitude *fallibilistic*: a reflective awareness that although we might have very good reasons for believing some things rather than others, those reasons do not secure an absolute certainty that puts them beyond the possibility of error.

In part, then, the aim of this book is to investigate whether the varieties of sceptical doubt that we've loosely associated with the theoretical and practical attitudes are as remote from one another as at first blush appears to be the case. In addition to being an introduction to the formal problem scepticism presents to contemporary epistemologists, it is therefore also an enquiry into the relationship between philosophical reflection and the sort of reflection we associate with living a life characterized by a degree of critical self-awareness. What is of primary interest here is the history of scepticism, for this constitutes an elaboration of ways in which the relationship between philosophy, critical reflection and practical life has been understood. As such, the history of scepticism presents a focus for reflection that promises to shed a little light on the 'whimsical condition of mankind'.

The task is to balance these two objectives: to get a sense of what importance scepticism has had for different philosophers at different periods, while providing the analytic tools needed to situate the problem as conceived by today's epistemologists. The methodological assumption of this book is that these aims are related – that one can better understand contemporary concerns, and see why various strategies to deal with them take the form they do, when one comes to appreciate how the character and perceived significance of scepticism has changed. At the same time, the genealogical element is not merely a disinterested survey of aged texts; the past takes on the significance it does because of the desire to understand our contemporary concerns, and offers the possibility of new ways of responding to them.

1 Scepticism and knowledge

Introduction

The aim of this chapter is to provide a preliminary introduction to the problem of scepticism as a contemporary epistemologist would see it; namely, as a problem that emerges when one adopts the theoretical attitude towards knowledge claims. In pursuit of this aim, the chapter has three main objectives: first, to enquire into what it is that the sceptic doubts and therefore discover to what aspect of our human self-understanding that doubt poses a threat; secondly, to examine two ways in which the sceptic goes about generating her doubt, the so-called 'argument from ignorance' and the 'Agrippan argument'; and finally, to provide a context from within which the threat of sceptical doubt and the ways in which it is generated can be seen to relate to the concerns of the contemporary epistemologist. In the fulfilment of these objectives I intend to motivate my claim that to understand sceptical doubt more fully we need to know something of its historical development.

The task of epistemology

The central task of epistemology as many philosophers see it is summed up by the American philosopher Barry Stroud:

> We aspire in philosophy to see ourselves as knowing all or most of the things we think we know and to understand how all that knowledge is possible. We want an explanation, not just of this or that item or piece of knowledge, but of knowledge, or knowledge of a certain kind, *in general*.   (1994: 296)

We all claim to know lots of things and presumably aspire to know a lot more. It is important both to our self-understanding and to our understanding of others that knowledge has a value that sets it over and above mere opinion. Whenever we claim to know something or encounter someone making such a claim, we recognize that something is at stake: the claimant has represented himself or herself as satisfying whatever conditions make something a case of knowing. One of the responsibilities that goes along with that representation is to be able to offer reasons why this is a case of knowing and not just one of opinion.

There is nothing mysterious about this; indeed, it is the most common of phenomena. I know that the Sears Tower is in Chicago. If asked how I know this, I might mention that I initially saw a picture of it in a travel guide and then go on to say that I have been to Chicago and seen it for myself. Perception, memory and testimony (I tend to trust the people who write travel guides) all contribute to an explanation of this particular item of knowledge, and there doesn't seem anything unsatisfactory about the reasons I give – certainly nothing that we would look to philosophy to remedy. Contrasting with this, Stroud identifies a much more demanding aspiration. What we want, he suggests, is the assurance that our concept of knowledge is itself *legitimate*; that creatures like us are entitled to think of ourselves as knowers, and that we aren't just deluding ourselves when we claim to know all the things we think we do. This assurance is to be gained by explaining how knowledge (or knowledge of a certain kind) is *possible*.

On Stroud's account, then, the epistemological task is to demonstrate that our concept of knowledge is legitimate by explaining how knowledge is possible. Note that as these things are usually viewed this is a *normative* problem, not a *descriptive* one. It is not going to be answered by giving us facts about how we do or do not use the concept of knowledge; neither is it going to be answered by giving us a scientific account of, say, the nature of perception (since such an account would presuppose that scientific knowledge is possible). Rather, an answer must be in the form of an account that gives us reasons to believe we have a *right* to use the concept. Moreover, since the account is to be general, these reasons will not be tied to specific examples of knowing like those given in defence of my claim to know that the Sears Tower is in Chicago (perception etc.). The reasons that constitute any explanation of how knowledge or knowledge of a certain kind is possible are going to be relevant to *all* such claims to know, irrespective of whether they are about towers, trees or tentacles.

In very general terms we might distinguish three responses to what Stroud identifies as the task of philosophy, what I'll call the *heroic*, the *rejectionist* and the *sceptical*. The *heroic* response is Stroud's own, and it provides a preliminary answer to the question 'what does the sceptic doubt?' What the sceptic doubts is that knowledge (or knowledge of a certain sort) is possible. On the *heroic* understanding of epistemology, scepticism is at the heart of enquiry because it is only by responding to the sceptic's doubts that it can be demonstrated that knowledge is indeed possible. The *rejectionist* response is to deny that showing how knowledge is possible is central to epistemological enquiry, and therefore to deny the centrality of sceptical doubt.[1] To take a well-known example, the proponents of what is called 'naturalized epistemology' proceed on the assumption that knowledge claims are not irreducibly normative, and that knowledge does not in general stand in need of philosophical legitimation. Epistemology is therefore not a normative enquiry but an extension of the methods of the natural sciences.

Despite divergent views on the importance of scepticism, the *heroic* and *rejectionist* responses are both part of the modern epistemological tradition. Indeed, as we'll see below, *rejectionism* can be viewed as a reaction to the perceived failure of epistemological *heroism*. The *sceptical* response derives from a far older tradition, and exhibits a different understanding of what scepticism is. It does not concern the direct question of whether knowledge is possible (although it is clearly related) so much as the question of whether it is possible to offer an account that shows us that knowledge is possible. Viewed from the perspective of the *heroic* response, the sceptic is a philosophical opponent who calls into question the possibility of knowledge by providing reasons for doubt. This sets the task for the *heroic* epistemologist: to give us reasons for thinking that these doubts are unwarranted, thereby entitling us to see ourselves as knowing what we think we know. From the perspective of the *sceptical* response, however, philosophical reasoning is the target – the possibility of philosophical knowledge itself is called into question. In so far as both *heroic* and *rejectionist* epistemologists aspire to the possession of philosophical knowledge (*pk*), then, their theoretical activities attract the attention of the sceptic. To avoid confusion, we'll call this variety of scepticism *pk*-scepticism and reserve the name scepticism for what is of interest in traditional epistemology. We'll turn to the relationship between the *heroic*, *rejectionist* and *sceptical* responses at the end of this chapter. For the time being we'll restrict our attention to the variety of scepticism that presents a challenge to the *heroic* task by questioning the possibility of what we commonsensically understand as knowledge.

The argument from ignorance

How then does the sceptic give us reasons for doubt about the possibility of knowledge? The answer in part depends on what kind of knowledge we're talking about. For most contemporary philosophers the kind of knowledge we'd particularly like to see ourselves as possessing is perceptual knowledge, what is usually referred to as knowledge of the external world. Right now I'm sitting in a library typing – I can see my new computer in front of me, feel the heat from the keyboard, smell the upholstery of the chair I'm in, hear the whirring of the air-conditioning, taste the chocolate in my mouth. I want to say that I *know* that I'm sitting wide awake in the library (or rather, I *say* that I am and that is taken as a claim to know). Here the sceptic casts doubt on the possibility of such knowledge by aiming to undermine my confidence in the cognitive status of my perceptual experiences. She points out that I might be dreaming; or perhaps even a disembodied brain, wired up to a supercomputer and floating around in a vat of nutrients. Both of these sceptical possibilities are seemingly consistent with my having exactly the same perceptual experiences as I'm having now, but in neither case would those experiences be reliable guides to what's really going on in the world.

By invoking possibilities like these, the sceptic presents a challenge to the epistemologist who wants to show how knowledge of the external world is possible. How can it be, if I rely entirely on experience and yet what I experience is consistent with not knowing what I ordinarily take myself to know? And what applies to me, applies equally to you! This particular way of generating doubt can be usefully generalized in the form of an argument. Letting *S* stand for any subject, *q* for any empirical proposition (like 'I'm awake in the library' or 'I've got two hands') and *sp* for any of the sceptical possibilities mentioned (like '*S* is an envatted brain'), we have the following:

> *S* doesn't know that not-*sp*
> If *S* doesn't know that not-*sp*, then *S* doesn't know that *q*

Therefore

> *S* doesn't know that *q*

This is an example of what's called an 'argument from ignorance'. It's often associated with the sceptical arguments Descartes put forward in his *Meditations*, and many philosophers take it to be a definitive statement of the sceptic's challenge to our perceptual knowledge claims. If we can't come up with a philosophical response to the argument from ignorance, the thought goes, the sceptic has exposed the fact that despite our intuitions to the contrary we cannot show how knowledge of the external world is possible.[2]

No-stipulations principle

A great deal of philosophical effort has been expended in the attempt to show that the argument from ignorance is unsound or otherwise uncompelling, and we will consider a number of specific attempts in subsequent chapters. For present purposes it's important to remember that the epistemological task is to show how knowledge is possible. As such, efforts to reject the argument from ignorance frequently focus on offering an analysis of knowledge that links its possibility to an account of where the argument from ignorance goes wrong. To take a simple example, let's imagine that knowing just requires believing that something is possible; that is to say,

(A) *S* knows that *q* iff (if and only if) *S* believes it is possible that *q*

On this account, the argument from ignorance is immediately shown to be unsound, as the first premise is false – I do know that

I'm not for example an envatted brain because I believe it's possible that I'm not. On this analysis the argument from ignorance does not therefore present an obstacle to the possibility of knowledge. The problem with this is that no one thinks that (A) is satisfactory – it fails to capture our intuitive sense of what it is to know something. The moral of this is the 'no-stipulations principle': the epistemologist can't just invent an account of what knowledge is in order to refute the sceptic and show that knowledge is possible. Now consider the following:

(B) S knows that q iff everyone everywhere believes that q, but only on Wednesdays if it's raining

What this suggests is that the no-stipulations principle also cuts the other way: an arbitrary account of knowledge that simply made it unobtainable would cause us to lose no sleep over our cognitive shortcomings. 'If that's knowledge,' we might exclaim, 'who gives two hoots that we don't know anything?' In short, at one extreme stipulation leaves sceptical doubt unintelligible at the cost of making knowledge worthless (A); at the other extreme it makes scepticism unthreatening at the cost of making knowledge impossible (B).

We can draw two related conclusions from this. First, since no one stipulation as to what constitutes knowledge has any greater claim on us than any other, another guide is clearly needed. The knowledge whose possibility the sceptic doubts must be something of which we have an intuitive (perhaps pre-theoretical) grasp. It must be something connected to the way we (at least implicitly) use the concept in everyday life and which captures its importance to our understanding of ourselves as cognitively responsible agents (as creatures who value the distinction between knowledge and opinion). The second point takes us back to (B). The claim was that if this is what knowledge is, we don't care if it's not possible – the sceptic's doubt holds no fear for us. What this suggests is the possibility that it is not knowledge *as such* that we value, and which the sceptic threatens, but a more fundamental feature of our epistemic practices, one that the analysis in (B) fails to capture. Taken together, these point in an obvious direction: we must undertake a closer examination of what knowledge is in order to find out what it is about the sceptic's challenge that threatens our self-understanding;

and in doing so we must allow our intuitions about when we do or do not know something to be our guide.

Varieties of knowledge

Before looking in detail at the concept of knowledge we need to simplify matters. In formulating the argument from ignorance above I indicated that *q* was to stand for any empirical proposition. The knowledge the epistemologist is generally concerned with is *propositional* knowledge. A proposition is what is expressed in a *that* clause. So, for example, my believing *that* there's a chocolate bar over there, my hoping *that* there's a chocolate bar over there and my fearing *that* . . . (etc.) express different attitudes (belief, desire, fear) to the same proposition; namely, 'there's a chocolate bar over there'. The content of the proposition is what makes it the proposition it is – in effect what it 'says'. Propositional knowledge is thus knowledge *that* such and such is the case, where the 'such and such' specifies the content of a particular proposition.

There are of course other kinds of knowledge. One can know Paris or Tim, in the sense that one is acquainted with them or that they are familiar. More importantly, there are the diverse practical abilities sometimes described as varieties of 'know-how': Rachel *knows how* to drive, Tim *knows how* to ride a bike, Jonathan *knows how* to play the bass guitar. In traditional epistemology these varieties of knowledge are viewed as of secondary importance. After all, when we think of a human being, it seems that although no amount of 'knowledge that' (of facts) would provide them with the powers of coordination and balance required to ride a bicycle, they couldn't (know *how* to) do so if they didn't know *that* they had to push down on the pedals to go uphill.

The issue is not clear-cut, however. Consider the case of a trained chimpanzee riding a bicycle round the circus ring. Would we say that it knows *how* to ride a bicycle; and if so, would we claim it's because it knows *that* it has to press down on the pedals? On the one hand, some *rejectionist* ('naturalistic') epistemologists think that an account of knowledge that denies it to animals is simply wrong-headed, but it seems evident that any such account will threaten to undermine the distinction between propositional knowledge and knowledge-as-ability. On the other hand, indicating that a *person* knows how to ride a bicycle may suggest much more than the mere ability to propel him- or herself along. It might imply that they see bicycling as a way of getting themselves efficiently from one place to another, a mode of transport vulnerable to the eccentricities of pedestrians and the thoughtlessness of drivers, but nevertheless a healthy and therefore desirable activity in itself. If these sorts of factors are involved in ascribing such know-how to persons, then there is a strong sense in which chimpanzees, despite the complexity of their behaviour, don't know how to ride a bicycle. This undermines the distinction between knowing that and knowing how in quite a different way from the naturalist.

We'll see more of the *rejectionist* position below, and that alternative account of the relationship between knowing how and knowing that will re-emerge in Chapter 2. Noting that our intuitions, although our guide, are not always entirely clear, we will restrict out attention to propositional knowledge, and review some contemporary thinking on the question of what knowledge is. This will advance our understanding of what it is that the sceptic's doubt really threatens.

The analysis of knowledge

The most familiar approach to the analysis of knowledge is in terms of truth-conditions:

(K) S knows that q iff $(C_1 \,\&\, C_2 \,\&\, C_3 \,\&\, C_4 \ldots C_n)$

$C_1, C_2, \ldots, C_n$ are the separately necessary and jointly sufficient conditions for the application of the concept. If the analysis is correct, then if it's true that S knows that q, $C_1, C_2, \ldots, C_n$ are all true (and if it's false that S knows that q, one or more of $C_1, C_2, \ldots, C_n$ will be false). Whether or not such an analysis is possible, the attempt at one can provide some valuable insights, not least because of the associated method of using imagined examples of knowing to test the analysis against our intuitive grasp of the concept of knowledge.[3]

At the outset it is clear that in order to know that q, S has to believe that q. So we have our first necessary condition:

(C_1) S believes that q

Belief itself is not enough: although one cannot imagine a case of knowing that isn't a case of believing, one can imagine a case of believing that is not one of knowing. What else is needed? One approach has been to regard *certain* belief as knowledge. As it stands, what one means by certainty is in need of further clarification. If one thinks of it in subjective terms, as a sort of *feeling* that one cannot possibly be wrong, the criterion is far too dependent on psychological considerations to provide an insight into knowledge. Viewed in objective terms, however, we begin to move in the right direction. To say that a belief is objectively certain seems to suggest that it is impossible to conceive of its being false. Thus understood, objective certainty would be a property of few of our beliefs: right now I believe that I'm sitting in the library, but I can imagine that the belief might be false; it's just that it isn't. What the talk of objectivity captures is that although any one of your beliefs might be false, in order to qualify as knowledge it must *be* true. So,

(C_2) q is true

We thus have two necessary conditions for knowledge; the question is, are they jointly sufficient? Can one think of an example where one would say of Rachel both that she believes that q and that q is true, but that she doesn't *know* that q? The answer, in short, is 'yes'. Imagine that it suddenly 'pops' into Rachel's head that the bus she's due to take to Boston on Wednesday won't show up (a belief that q); or that she infers the same from having read in her horoscope that travelling on Wednesday is to be avoided. *As it turns out*, the bus doesn't show up: Rachel's belief (that q) was true; but would we want to say that she *knew* the bus wasn't going to show? Every textbook on epistemology has examples like this, but it's worth dwelling on why, although easy to construct, they seem odd.

When we *ascribe* beliefs to people (and that, after all, is what we're doing to Rachel here), we usually do so on the assumption that the way they acquired their belief is linked up in some way with what it's about. In the example we have a *kind* of link: superstition or premonition or what have you, but it doesn't seem 'adequate'. Imagine a conversation with Rachel in which she tries to explain to us why she believes what she does about the bus; or our response when, having failed, she claims in desperation that she just *knows* it won't turn up!

The problem with the 'true belief' analysis is that from *our* perspective, and despite Rachel's protestations, it appears to be a matter of luck that her belief is true – a fortuitous accident. Moreover, we'd be inclined to think that she was an odd fish indeed for believing whatever pops into her head. It's not the sort of thing that the cognitively responsible person – one who values the distinction between knowledge and opinion – does. In short, the relationship of her belief to whatever it is that it is true of doesn't seem adequate:

Belief ————— Adequacy ————— Truth
(Subjective)   (Objective)

The third term of the traditional analysis of the concept of knowledge seeks to address the issue of adequacy (rule out luck and accident) by elucidating a link between the subjective state and its objective truth-conditions. To indicate that a belief is subjective in this context means only that it is a state of a subject S (the putative 'knower'). Similarly, the objectivity of truth means no more than that it is independent of the subject S: her belief that q does not imply that q is true. For much of this century, adequacy has been understood in terms of justification, thus providing us with a third term:

(C_3) S is justified in believing that q

With (C_3) we arrive at the so-called 'justified true belief' (JTB) analysis of knowledge:

(JTB) S knows that q iff (S believes that q) & (q is true) & (S is justified in believing that q)

Scepticism, justification and truth

Adopting to the justified true belief analysis, when a sceptic doubts the possibility of knowledge they are doubting one of the following:

- The sceptic doubts that we have any beliefs
- The sceptic doubts that any of our beliefs are true
- The sceptic doubts that any of our beliefs are justified

On the face of it, it might seem that we can immediately rule out the first possibility as self-refuting: how can anyone doubt that we have beliefs without having beliefs themselves? The case is not quite as simple as it appears, however, but we will put it aside until Chapter 2. Concerning the remaining two options, many (perhaps most) philosophers would argue that our interest in justification is its 'truth-conduciveness', or 'truth-indicativeness': it's truth that we're really interested in, and we think justified beliefs are more likely to be true than unjustified beliefs (more likely in the sense of not being accidentally or fortuitously true). Returning to the example above, what Rachel lacked was a justification for her belief – something that linked her belief that the bus wasn't going to show with the bus not showing. One justification might have been that she knew that there was going to be a strike that day. This would entitle her to her knowledge-claim in the eyes of an audience (including herself) because the reason given links her belief to the conditions of its truth.

It would therefore seem that it is the *truth* of our beliefs that is most vulnerable to the sceptic's doubt; but here are two reasons for thinking that this not straightforwardly the case. First, consider how a sceptic would inculcate such doubts. She is, after all, a *philosophical* opponent, who aims to undermine our confidence in the possibility of knowledge by providing *reasons* for doubt. If the sceptic simply said 'all your beliefs might be false', we would not take it as a serious threat to our epistemic confidence because we are being presented with no reasons to believe this the case. We'd simply shrug it off. The point is that just as we have no direct access to truth, but rely on the truth-conduciveness of justification to get us to it, the sceptic can only get us to doubt the truth of our beliefs by getting us to doubt that our ways of justifying them are adequate. Since we are interested in justification because of its truth-conduciveness, to cast doubt on our methods or practices of justification – our ways of getting at truth – undermines our confidence that they can even be regarded *as* practices of justification. As we saw with the argument from ignorance, the sceptical possibilities lead us to consider that what we normally take to justify our perceptual beliefs – experience – isn't the guide to truth we take it to be, and is therefore no source of justification at all.

There's one reason for thinking that the justification condition is the sceptic's target. Here's another: it's plausible to think that most scientific beliefs held up to the nineteenth century were false, and so didn't amount to knowledge (on the justified true belief analysis). Acknowledging the link between justification and truth, we might conclude that everything that anyone has ever believed that is false is therefore *by definition* unjustified. The problem with this is that we would be unable to make the crucial epistemic distinction between the (false) beliefs that we consider scientists had very good reasons to believe and the (false) beliefs held as a result of sloppy thinking or a belief in the supernatural (believing whatever 'popped' into their heads or what an angel purportedly revealed to them). Again, it's possible – perhaps even probable – that most of what the scientists of our own time believe will turn out to be false, but we still regard some epistemic practices as more reasonable than others. The fact that justification is truth-conducive does not mean that the best available practices of justification guarantee access to the truth, but they do make it more likely that we'll get at it. What is important is that the epistemic distinction between justified and unjustified beliefs is upheld, and it is this distinction that the sceptic attacks.

What the justified true belief analysis suggests is that when the sceptic doubts the possibility of knowledge it is by raising doubts about the justification condition. The argument from ignorance demonstrates one way this can be done. By showing that what we take to justify a certain class of beliefs (perceptual beliefs etc.) is compatible with their falsity, the argument directly undermines the claim that such justifications are truth-conducive (and thus don't count as justifications at all). In the light of our analysis we could therefore rewrite it as follows:

> S isn't justified in believing that not-sp
> If S isn't justified in believing that not-sp, then S isn't justified in believing that q

Therefore

> S isn't justified in believing that q

For completeness we'll call this the argument from ignorance (j), although it will not figure much in what follows for reasons that will now become apparent; namely, because there is a more radical way of raising doubts about the justification condition – one that aims to undermine our confidence that there is *any* sort of reasoned distinction to be made between justified and unjustified beliefs. This relates to another basic form of sceptical argument that I'll call the 'Agrippan argument'.

The Agrippan argument

Although the Agrippan argument[4] is perhaps the most ancient of sceptical arguments, it has undergone a distinct revival in recent years. Since Chapter 2 will deal with Ancient Scepticism in detail, we will begin by restricting our account of the problem to how a modern epistemologist would view it. To see how it arises, consider the following. In the course of conversation, S claims that q. Given the acknowledged and crucial epistemological distinction between knowing (or being justified in believing) that q and merely assuming (or being of the opinion) that q, it seems reasonable to ask S what justifies her in thinking that hers is a case of one rather than the other. Suppose that S now offers some evidence r_1 for her original claim; given the same acknowledged distinction it seems reasonable to ask if r_1 is itself something that she knows or whether she is merely assuming its truth. If this elicits a further source of evidence, r_2, the same question can be repeated (for the same reason). In this way the demand for justification gets passed down along a line of justifying reasons ($q \rightarrow r_1 \rightarrow r_2 \rightarrow r_3 \rightarrow r_4 \rightarrow r_5 \rightarrow r_6 \rightarrow \ldots$) that threatens to regress endlessly. In response, S seems to have to choose one of the following options:

(a) Continue to give reasons indefinitely, opening up the possibility of an infinite regress
(b) Make a dogmatic assumption
(c) Argue in a circle

The problem with (a) to (c) is that each of them threatens to leave the original claim q unjustified in so far as they fail to ground (offer an ultimate or unquestionable source of evidence for) the distinction between knowledge and assumption/opinion. Consider (a): if the giving of reasons or the offering of evidence continues to infinity, there's no point at which one can say that the distinction between assumption and knowledge has been genuinely grounded. It is not the case that for example six iterations yield knowledge as opposed to assumption, because the entire weight of the distinction rests on the final source of evidence (in this case r_6), and that stands unjustified. Similarly, with regard to (b), if S refuses or finds herself unable to give further reasons for her belief, that does not support the distinction. Indeed, it shows that it cannot be made; that since all claims ultimately rest on assumptions, all are equally unjustified. Finally, if S seeks to justify her claim by offering as grounds some reason or other sort of evidence she's already employed, she is implying that certain claims are self-supporting. Let's say r_6 is the same as r_4: if r_5 is offered in support of r_4 and r_6 in support of r_5, r_6 carries the full weight of the justification, and yet it is the same as r_3 (previously considered in need of support by r_4). Since arguing in a circle – or 'begging the question' – is a classic way of demonstrating that someone is reasoning poorly, (c) is not a good basis for sustaining the vital distinction between being justified and merely assuming.

One reaction to this argument is to suggest that there is something contrived about it; and it is indeed reminiscent of the child who responds to every answer with the question 'but why?' Of course, adults tend to end such 'debates' with an exasperated 'because I say so!' or 'that's the way it is!'; and no one doubts that such dialogues with others or oneself (I can ask myself if I know that q, and generate the same problem) *do* come to an end. The problem is that if, when we reflect on it, it is reasonable to ask the original question 'Do I know/am I justified in believing q or am I just assuming that q?', terminating the enquiry through boredom or failure of imagination or with what we imagine would be accepted by anyone is entirely arbitrary. The significance of this is obvious. As we saw above, we are interested in justification because of its truth-conduciveness, and beliefs resting on arbitrary assumptions can give us no confidence that they are justified and thus more likely than not to be true, even if they are accepted as common sense. Since the Agrippan argument confronts us with the apparent impossibility of making sense of the vital distinction between justified and unjustified belief, it undermines the idea that any of our beliefs are so much as justified at all. To put this another way, where the argument from ignorance suggests that our *empirical* beliefs are not in any way constrained by or answerable to the external world (because we can with equal validity consider ourselves awake, asleep or an envatted brain), the Agrippan argument suggests that none of our beliefs – none of our *thinking in general* – is in any way answerable to (adequate to) anything other than itself!

Not surprisingly, philosophers who have recognized the force of the Agrippan argument have been anxious to avoid the sceptical consequences of (a), the threat of an infinite regress. To summarize, this has expressed itself through attempts to show that (b) and (c) do not have the seemingly disastrous consequences the sceptic suggests. On the one hand, the 'foundationalist' denies that all assumptions are dogmatic:

(Fo)   There are some beliefs that do not stand in need of further justification, and which serve as the grounds for other claims.

On the other hand, the 'coherentist' denies that beliefs are justified in a 'linear' manner, and therefore that circularity need be vicious:

(Co)   Beliefs are linked together in a complex system and lend one another mutual evidential support.

If either of these options could be fully realized it would seem that the *heroic* epistemologist could claim to have shown that the Agrippan argument presents no challenge to the task of showing that knowledge is possible. It is not immediately clear what implications this has for the argument from ignorance, but if the justified true belief analysis is correct, the *heroic* epistemologist might be confident that his account of knowledge will also show where the argument from ignorance goes wrong. If that seems to limit the epistemological options, however, consider the following objections:

1.   The presentation of the Agrippan argument presupposes a very specific conception of justification – one that ties it to S's having access to (*knowing*) whatever it is that might justify her claim that q (and hence r_1, r_2, etc.). If we reject that account of justification we could avoid the regress, leaving the being justified/assuming distinction in place.

2. Whatever the Agrippan argument shows, it does not under-
    mine the distinction between knowing and assuming because it
    is a mistake to suppose that justification is even needed for
    knowledge.

Anyone familiar with recent developments in epistemology will
recognize these: they are expressions of what I have called
rejectionism and they clearly bear on our investigation. If the
sceptic is presupposing something unwarranted about the *nature* of
justification (1), we might well have grounds for dismissing the
Agrippan argument (and perhaps the argument from ignorance (*j*)).
Alternatively, if the sceptic is presupposing something unwarranted
about the *necessity* of justification (2), the Agrippan argument and
the argument from ignorance (*j*) are misconceived since their target
has no bearing on our possession of knowledge. The expectation
would be that the analyses put forward as part of (1) and/or (2)
would also provide a response to the traditional argument from
ignorance. Since I've suggested that the Agrippan argument is the
more radical form of scepticism, the remaining task for this chapter
is to begin the enquiry into whether or not (1) and (2) do allow us
to reject it. Before doing so we'll review the recent changes in
epistemology mentioned above. This will support my claim that
rejectionism can be regarded as a reaction to the perceived failure of
heroic epistemology. It will also allow for the introduction of some
jargon that is common currency among epistemologists today.

Gettier

In 1963 a very short paper by Edmund Gettier generated a great
deal of interest and has had an enormous influence on subsequent
developments in epistemology. The purpose of "Is Justified True
Belief Knowledge?" is evident from the title; namely, to question
the adequacy of the traditional analysis of knowledge. In his paper
Gettier offers two counterexamples to that analysis – situations
where our intuitive understanding of knowledge fails to map on to
what the justified true belief analysis suggests it ought to.
Although Gettier had no interest in scepticism, what have become
known generically as 'Gettier examples' have led to major revi-
sions in the analysis of knowledge and, as a consequence, in the

understanding of the significance of scepticism. Consider the following situations:

Example 1

Act 1[5]   Smith and Jones have just been interviewed for the same job. Smith's friend works in the personnel department and informs her that he's just overheard his boss state that Jones is to be offered the job. Smith's passion for numismatics has led her to discover that Jones has 10 coins in her pocket, so she has strong evidence for the following conjunction:

(I) Jones will get the job and Jones has 10 coins in her pocket. This entails:

(II) The person who will get the job has 10 coins in their pocket.

Since Smith has strong evidence for (I), and recognizes that (I) implies (II), she has strong evidence for believing (II) is true.

Act 2   Unbeknown to Smith, it turns out that she and not Jones will get the job after all (maybe the head of personnel got the names confused). It then transpires that Smith herself has 10 coins in her pocket. That being the case, it turns out that Smith's belief (II) is true, but would we want to say that she *knew* that was true? After all, that belief was based on her belief that Jones and not herself had 10 coins in her pocket.

Philosophers anxious to save the traditional analysis were quick to offer a response to this by supplementing the justified true belief conditions. Noting that Smith bases her true belief on a falsity, one might try the following:

(C_4) S's belief that q is not inferred from any falsehood

Unfortunately, others were quick to come up with arguments in the style of Gettier that didn't allow for this quick escape:

Example 2

Act 1[6]   Out (soberly) celebrating her new job, Smith drives along a country road and, spotting a barn in the middle distance and having good eyesight, acquires the justified belief that it is a barn.

Act 2   Unbeknown to Smith, however, she has been driving through barn-façade country, an unusual stretch of road that annually attracts the attention of neo-realist artists competing for the prize of most convincing façade ('As Seen From The Road' section). Had any of the previous or subsequent objects caught her attention she would have equally justifiably judged them to be barns, and would have acquired a false belief. It *just so happens* that her attention is drawn to the one genuine barn in the area (used by the judges as the standard, perhaps) and her belief is true. But would we want to say that she *knew* that she saw a barn?

In this example, there is no inference from a false belief to a true belief (so C_4 is satisfied); indeed, it's reasonable to assume that there is no inference at all – she just sees a barn. Moreover, it would seem that Smith's belief is about as justified as one could hope for. And yet we would not attribute knowledge to her. Why not? Well, as in Example 1, it seems that the connection between her belief and its truth-conditions isn't adequate – it was a matter of epistemic luck that she happened to form a belief about the one real barn in the area. What Gettier examples seem to show is that even if necessary, justification is not sufficient to satisfy the demands of adequacy.

Internalism and externalism

How then have epistemologists responded to the situation, and what implications do their responses have for scepticism? Let's return to the justification condition: what exactly does it mean for a belief to be justified? One response – that of the 'evidentialist' – is to argue that one must have adequate evidence for it. This evidence usually comes in the form of other beliefs that S must be aware of as supporting her belief. In this sense, evidentialism is closely associated with two further doctrines: 'internalism', and the so-called

'KK principle' (or 'KK thesis'; also known as the 'iteration principle').

Internalism, and its contrasting term 'externalism', are used widely in epistemology and not always with clarity. Robert Fogelin (1994: 120) usefully disambiguates two varieties of internalism about justification:

- *Ontological internalism*: for S to be justified in believing that q, the grounds that justify this belief must be contents of S's mind.
- *Methodological internalism*: for S to be justified in believing that q, S must *base* her belief on the grounds that justify it.

What methodological internalism indicates is that in order for S to be justified in her belief that q, the evidence that would normally justify it (the 'grounds' for believing that q) is the evidence that S actually uses to arrive at q. If what justifies Smith believing that there's a barn outside (normally) involves seeing the back as well as the front, and that is the grounds upon which she bases her belief (she gets out of the car to check), then from the perspective of the methodological internalist her belief is justified. To this the onto-logical internalist adds a restriction on what kind of evidence can justify beliefs. To many philosophers it has seemed natural to suppose that the only source of evidence apt to provide grounds for knowledge claims is the contents of one's own mind, because these are things to which we have a privileged and immediate access (my beliefs and experiences are *mine*; I don't infer what's going on my own mind – I just *know*!). Ontological internalism is thus closely associated with a further variety of internalism:

- *Semantic internalism*: the 'content' of S's belief that q – what makes it the belief it is – is entirely determined by what is going on inside S's mind.

We'll discover more about the connections between these varieties of internalism in Chapter 3 when we look at Descartes. What is clear is that both ontological and methodological internalism are evidentialist – they agree that for S to be justified in believing that q, S must recognize what it is that justifies her belief that q; they just disagree about what the acceptable sources of evidence are.

It is this shared commitment that links evidentialism to the KK-principle:

(KK)   If S knows that q then S knows that she knows that q

If knowing that q requires having adequate grounds in the form of evidence that one recognizes *as* evidence, it follows that if you know, you know that you know (you know *that* the evidence is *what* justifies the belief, and thus *that* you know).

Given these definitions, the externalist – anti-evidentialist – alternatives fall into place. Minimally, an externalist denies that S's grounds need be contents of her mind. Most externalists will also deny that S need *base* her belief on the grounds that justify it, and therefore deny that she need be aware of those grounds. More radically, many externalists go so far as to deny that justification is even necessary for knowledge. The rejection of the KK-principle is therefore the hallmark of most varieties of externalism. Finally, the semantic externalist maintains that the 'content' of S's belief that q is at least partially[7] determined by how things are in the world external to her own mind. Henceforward I'll use 'internalism' to refer to the methodological thesis, and 'externalism' to refer to any position that rejects it.

Returning to the Gettier examples, we have seen that these appear to undermine the traditional analysis of knowledge by drawing attention to the apparent inadequacy of the justification condition. We are now in a position to see how, in broad terms, contemporary epistemologists have responded to the challenge:

The internalist options

(In1) Take justification to be internalist (evidentialist) and offer an account that is adequate (immune to Gettier examples).

(In2) Take justification to be internalist (evidentialist) but supplement it with an external condition (a 'fourth clause').

The externalist options

(Ex1) Take justification to be externalist (non-evidentialist) and offer an account that is adequate.

(Ex2) Remain agnostic on the question of whether justification is
internalist or externalist but reject the claim that justification
is needed for knowledge at all.

Heroism, rejectionism and scepticism

With the above classification in place we are in a position to make
good on some earlier undertakings: to address whether or not the
two *rejectionist* objections (1) and (2) above allow the epistemologist
to avoid the Agrippan argument; and to investigate in more detail the
relationship between the *heroic*, *rejectionist* and *sceptical* responses
to the task of epistemology as characterized by Stroud. Seeing how
these two considerations are related will give us an appreciation of
the need for a historical enquiry into the nature of sceptical doubt.

First, it should now be evident that the epistemological theories
most immediately threatened by the Agrippan argument are what we
would now recognize as being internalist–evidentialist. There are
important differences between the traditional approach (In1) and
what are sometimes called 'Indefeasibility Theories' (In2),[8] but for
our purposes these share the assumption that in order for S to be
justified in believing that q, she must be aware that her evidence has
the justificatory force it does. Indeed, the KK-principle to which
internalists share a commitment is an explicit statement of this. Such
internalists are clearly obliged to offer a response to the Agrippan
argument, and given the options, those responses will fall into one of
two classes: they will be either coherentist or foundationalist. Since
the *heroic* epistemologist recognizes the need to demonstrate that
knowledge is possible by refuting the sceptic, *heroic* epistemology will
therefore be either coherentist or foundationalist.

Let's now turn to those two *rejectionist* objections. The first (1)
was to the effect that the Agrippan argument presupposes a certain
conception of justification, which we can now identify as internalist
in character; the second (2) dismisses the argument on the grounds
that justification is not necessary for knowledge. The proponent of
(1) will incline towards the first externalist option (Ex1) and aim to
elaborate an account of justification that does not succumb to the
Agrippan argument; the proponent of (2) will favour the second
externalist option (Ex2) and offer an account of knowledge that
does not involve justification at all.

Lining up internalist and externalist options in this way gives us an insight into the relationship between *heroism* and *rejectionism*. *Heroic* epistemology confronts two major problems. On the one hand, demonstrating that knowledge is possible requires a response to the Agrippan argument; on the other, the justified true belief analysis of knowledge that *heroic* epistemology has come to rely on seems to offer an unsatisfactory account of what knowledge is (in the face of Gettier examples). Since a commitment to internalism seems to underpin both these problems, the *rejectionist*'s key intuition becomes clear; namely, that rejecting the *heroic* demand for a legitimating account of knowledge involves the theoretical formulation of an externalist alternative that avoids *heroism*'s two problems.

It should be noted in passing that even if the *rejectionist* were successful in avoiding these two problems, that would not by itself constitute a solution to our first sceptical problem, the argument from ignorance. Externalist–*rejectionist* responses to this argument will be one of the main topics of Chapter 6, but for now we need to determine whether or not (Ex1) and (Ex2) *really* promise the possibility of an analysis of justification or knowledge that restricts the scope of the Agrippan argument to *heroic*, internalist–evidentialist epistemologies. This will in turn lead to an appreciation of that third, *sceptical* response. I'm going to suggest (Ex1) and (Ex2) do not avoid the Agrippan argument by considering two arguments: the first shows that externalism fails to restrict the scope of the argument; the second explicitly broadens its scope to include externalist theories of justification and knowledge.

The first argument takes us back to the no-stipulations principle. Whatever account of knowledge or justification the epistemologist advances must be one that captures why we value knowledge over opinion or assumption – the feature or features that touch upon our cognitive self-understanding. As we saw with the know how/know that distinction, intuitions are not always clear, but they led us to consider the necessity for justification in the first place. Gettier examples *may* show us that justification is not enough, but they don't as they stand show us that justification isn't important, which is why the two internalist–evidentialist options (In1) and (In2) remain philosophically alive. The fact that an account of justification or knowledge avoids the Agrippan argument is not in itself enough to recommend it to us.

With this in mind, consider a variation on an example used above.[9] It turns out that since we left her, Rachel has become a clairvoyant with entirely reliable powers of prognostication. Rachel has no idea that she has this power and indeed is extremely sceptical about the existence of such a power generally. Now imagine that it suddenly 'pops' into Rachel's head that the bus she's due to take to Chicago on Thursday won't show up. According to externalists, the fact that Rachel has the power she does means that her belief is in fact justified (Ex1) or is in fact a case of knowing (Ex2), whatever she herself thinks about it. In such circumstances, would *we* want to say that Rachel is justified in believing that *q* or that she knows that *q*? Or to put the same point slightly more archly, if in these circumstances Rachel *did* claim to know, would we consider her claim to be a genuine case of knowing?

If this talk of supernatural powers confuses matters, imagine instead that an Amazonian-forest-dwelling and hitherto unassimilated Rachel stumbles upon a telescope. She doesn't know anything about optics or astronomy and absolutely believes that the lights in the sky are the souls of her dead ancestors. Nevertheless, when she observes a planet she decides that it is a solid body and not a twinkling soul. Would we say she *knows* this? The point of the examples is that they present cases where the would-be knower is in some sense irrational in coming to the conclusion that they do – that is to say, they only have the belief they do because *from their own standpoint* (internally) they are willing to live with crazy inconsistencies. From our perspective, this undermines an important feature of whatever the context for knowing is; namely, that a belief has to be reasonable from the knower's own point of view, and not just be objectively reliable. This suggests that justification and knowledge have an irreducibly internalist element.

These examples are mirror images of the Gettier examples: where the latter exploit the weaknesses of internalist theories by pointing to cases of epistemic luck, these exploit the weaknesses of externalist theories by pointing to cases of cognitive irresponsibility. It's worth noting that contemporary epistemologists have gone into less detail than they might have when considering the implications of these cases of cognitive irresponsibility. For example, if (say Clairvoyant) Rachel did indeed maintain that she knew about the bus and we judged her irrational, would we consider her failure in this instance to infect other claims that she makes? Might we contemplate the possibility that she doesn't really know anything at all? As we'll see in Chapter 2, this sort of question resonates with the concerns of ancient Greek philosophers. For present purposes, the conclusion of our first argument is that if *rejectionist* analyses of knowledge and justification do not allow for an internalist element (as neither (Ex1) nor (Ex2) do), they cannot satisfy our intuitions about knowledge and therefore cannot restrict the scope of the Agrippan argument in any sense that makes such a restriction valuable to us as responsibly minded knowers.

Let's now turn to the second argument I mentioned – the one that widens the scope of the Agrippan argument. Imagine that Tim is an externalist of either variety ((Ex1) or (Ex2)). He advances the claim that *S* justifiably believes or knows that *q* because *S* satisfies the appropriate external standard of justification or knowledge (ES), whatever that is. But now imagine his interlocutor Lois. She has two options. She can ask Tim if he *knows* that *S* satisfies the standard or if he is just assuming that it does. If he says he knows, Lois might go on to ask him what his evidence is and off we go again. This response is most immediately problematic for the proponent of (Ex1), as he believes that *something* justifies *S*'s belief, and it seems natural to ask how that *something* could be a justification unless *someone* were aware of the fact. All (Ex1) seems to do is shift the awareness of justification from one person (*S*) to another (Tim), so the Agrippan argument adjusts its target accordingly. It would appear that the second variety of externalism (Ex2) can't easily escape this one either. *S*'s knowing might not require that *she* knows that she knows, but it does seem to require *someone* knowing that she knows, and that can only be Tim. Here the awareness of knowing seems to be shifted from *S* to Tim.

Now consider Lois's second question. Here she asks, not if Tim knows or assumes that ES (the external condition for justification or knowledge) has been satisfied, but if Tim *knows* or is only assuming that ES *is* the appropriate external standard. In other words, Lois addresses herself to Tim's claim to have in his possession a piece of philosophical knowledge. Again, if Tim says he knows, Lois will ask for his evidence and off we go again! Here, we encounter the Agrippan argument with its widest scope, where it leads to *pk*-scepticism – scepticism about the possibility of philosophical

knowledge and therefore about the possibility of offering any justification of our concept of knowledge.

Finally, then, we return to the third response to the epistemological task – what I called the *sceptical* response. Importantly, from
the perspective of this response the *heroic*–internalist attempt to
legitimate knowledge and the externalist–*rejectionist* attempt to
offer an account of knowledge or justification that avoids the
problems this generates are on a par. They both presuppose that
there is such a thing as philosophical knowledge and that it is therefore possible in principle to accomplish one of these tasks. As
already noted, the variety of scepticism that rejects the possibility of
philosophical knowledge is the oldest form of scepticism (what I
called *pk*-scepticism). Part of its legacy is the Agrippan argument,
which remains the most radical challenge to our self-understanding
as knowers even when contemporary epistemologists restrict its
scope to empirical justification. More importantly, it also provides
the resources for the best response to the contemporary epistemologist's sceptical problems.

The last claim will doubtless strike the reader as being somewhat
paradoxical – using scepticism to respond to scepticism! To see that
this is not the case we need to know more about how theoretical
attitude doubt differs from Ancient Scepticism, and consequently
what relation the latter has to the Agrippan argument and to the
argument from ignorance (which many philosophers still take as
the paradigmatic expression of modern scepticism). This will in
turn prepare us for an appreciation of the extent to which themes
from the Ancient tradition have recurred throughout the subsequent history of philosophy. In Chapter 2 we will begin to address
these concerns by returning to scepticism's Hellenistic roots.

2 The legacy of Socrates

Introduction

Hitherto we have encountered scepticism as presenting epistemologists with a certain *theoretical* problem; namely, to show that our empirical beliefs are held on rational grounds by demonstrating that the distinction between being justified in believing that q and merely assuming that q is legitimate. Although the sceptic who uses philosophical arguments to generate doubt about our practices of justification was contrasted with the *pk*-sceptic who challenges the possibility of philosophical knowledge, the latter too was seen as posing a theoretical obstacle, in the form of the radical version of the Agrippan argument with which we concluded Chapter 1. In both cases, then, scepticism was associated with theoretical attitude doubt.

This theoretical picture of *pk*-scepticism and the threat of the Agrippan argument differs from the one that emerges when one looks at the Ancient Sceptics. Like their traditional foes the Dogmatists, these were concerned with the role that philosophy has to play in determining how human beings should live their lives. Principally, the Sceptic's view was that rather than *guide* us in the search for the knowledge that would enable us to live happy lives, philosophy should *cure* us of the disposition to believe that there is any such knowledge. Inspired by the legacy of that most enigmatic of figures, Socrates (*c*. 469–*c*. 399 BCE), they attempted to make sense of his seemingly paradoxical claim that the one thing he knew was that he knew nothing.[1] In part, then, our task is to trace how the Sceptics dealt with this paradox, which leads to what I'll call the *Essential Problem* of Ancient Scepticism. Beyond this, an appreciation of the challenge of Ancient Scepticism will allow us to better understand the subsequent development of sceptical thought, and give us a sense of what the possibilities are for evaluating and responding to it today.

The Essential Problem

Scepticism in the ancient world can be classified under three headings: the Practical Scepticism of Pyrrho (*c*. 360–*c*. 270 BCE) and his pupil Timon (*c*. 320–230 BCE); the Academic Scepticism of Arcesilaus (315–240 BCE), Carneades (*c*. 214–129 BCE), and his pupil Clitomachus (*c*. 187–*c*. 110 BCE); and the neo-Pyrrhonism of Aenesidimus (*c*. 100–40 BCE), Agrippa (*c*. 1st century CE), and Sextus Empiricus (*c*. 160–c. 210 CE). Although little is known of Sextus's life, and he is not regarded as having been an important thinker in his own right, much of what we know about Ancient Scepticism is derived from his surviving works. Of these, the *Outlines of Scepticism*[2] has historically been the most influential, not least because it is the primary source of the Agrippan argument. In its opening sections Sextus describes the ways in which one might conceive of philosophical enquiry:

> When people are investigating any subject, the likely result is either a discovery, or a denial of discovery and a confession of inapprehensibility, or else a continuation of the investigation. This, no doubt, is why in the case of philosophical investigations, too, some have said that they have discovered the truth, some have asserted that it cannot be apprehended, and others are still investigating. (I. 1–2)

These options designate the practitioners of "the most fundamental kinds of philosophy" (I. 4):

- The Dogmatists: those who "think that they have discovered the truth" (I. 3).
- The Academics (or Academic Sceptics): those who "have asserted that things cannot be apprehended" (*ibid*.).
- The Sceptics (or neo-Pyrrhonian Sceptics): those "who are still investigating" (*ibid*.).

For Sextus, the Dogmatist and the Academic present mirror images of each other: where one asserts that knowledge is possible (that things can be apprehended), the other denies it. To put this more precisely, the Dogmatist assumes that we can have the philosophical knowledge that shows that knowledge is possible. Equally, the Academic assumes that we can have the philosophical knowledge that shows that knowledge is not possible. If we take p-knowledge to be a particular kind of higher-order (philosophical) knowledge that justifies lower-order knowledge, this gives us:

- The Dogmatists: we can p-know that knowledge is possible.
- The Academics: we can p-know that knowledge is not possible.

The neo-Pyrrhonian Sceptic aims to rise above this ancient antagonism by showing that neither position is rationally sustainable. He maintains that we cannot assume that we can have the philosophical knowledge that would show *either* that knowledge is possible, *or* that it is not possible. More specifically, the charge against the Academic is that to assert that to p-know that knowledge is not possible is to assume that p-knowing is 'insulated' from the attack that the Academic Sceptic himself wishes to launch against knowing *simpliciter*. If it weren't, then to claim to know that one doesn't know would be contradictory (like asserting that 'there's no such thing as the truth, and that's the truth!'). By refusing to take a stand on the question of whether one can or cannot p-know, the neo-Pyrrhonian response in effect undermines the distinction between the two putative ways of knowing:

- The Sceptics: we can't p-know that knowledge is possible, but neither can we p-know that knowledge is not possible.

The extent to which it is possible to insulate p-knowing from knowing and thereby avoid the seeming paradox of asserting that nothing can be known leads us to what I referred to above as the Essential Problem. To understand this problem aright we need to know a little more about what the Greeks understood by knowledge; and in particular how they conceived of the role of philosophy. It will help if we think about the Ancients' views on philosophy in this period as exemplifying answers to three basic and related questions:

- The 'constitutive' question: what are things like in their essential nature?
- The 'hypothetical' question: what can or cannot we know?
- The 'normative' question: how should we act and what will the outcome be?

It is important to recall that central to Greek philosophy is the concern with living a good, virtuous or tranquil – that is to say, happy – life. The knowledge that the Dogmatist philosopher seeks is not therefore to be equated with the narrowly *theoretical* notion we encountered in Chapter 1. To know that q (that, for example, the world is round) may commit one rationally to other sorts of beliefs (like believing that there is a world), but taken alone it would not change one's *practical* orientation towards the world (what one does; how one acts). When discussing the relationship between propositional knowledge and knowledge as an ability (know-how), I suggested that there were two ways in which the distinction might be undermined. One of them was motivated by the naturalistic desire to ascribe knowledge to animals; the other by the intuition that when the ability to ride a bicycle (for example) is ascribed to a person, that might suggest all manner of related interests (healthy living) and anxieties (safety) as well as knowledge of facts. The sort of knowledge that relates to living a 'good' life is like this – in addition to any strictly cognitive or theoretical element of 'knowing that', it involves the possession of component capacities and abilities.[3]

For the Dogmatist the guiding idea is that philosophical (p-)knowledge facilitates the living of a 'good' life. Through an account of the way things are in their essential nature, and what as a consequence we can know, we are led to an understanding of how we should live. So what does this tell us about the Sceptic and the Essential Problem? Crucially, Sceptics of all varieties (Practical, Academic, and neo-Pyrrhonian) share the Dogmatists' practical orientation. In attacking Dogmatism, then, the aim is *not* to undermine the conviction that there is an ideal sort of life for a human to live. Rather, the general project as conceived by the Ancient Sceptics is to use philosophy to attack the Dogmatic assumption that the good life is to be characterized and attained through the acquisition of knowledge. As a starting-point we'll take it that the three questions above apply equally to the

Sceptic in so far as he is using *philosophy* to attack philosophy. This will change as we get a better understanding of the extent to which Ancient Scepticism develops a different understanding of what philosophy is, but for the time being it gives us a clearer formulation of the Essential Problem. Accordingly, the Sceptic has to offer a response to the constitutive, hypothetical and normative questions that satisfies two conditions:

(TC) It is not self-defeating. However the attack on knowledge proceeds, it cannot leave the Sceptic in the paradoxical position of denying something that their own account requires the assertion of.

(PC) It retains its practical orientation. However the attack on knowledge proceeds, it cannot render unintelligible the idea that there is a way in which one should live one's life (and that this involves acting in the world).

The Essential Problem is a problem for all Sceptics. In our brief exposure to Sextus's thought we saw that he is apt to convict the Academic Sceptic of failing to satisfy the 'theoretical condition' (TC) on the grounds that he assumes that one can justify the claim to *p*-know that knowledge is not possible; that is to say, there is something contradictory about his attempt to use philosophy to attack philosophy. By implication, Sextus would regard the neo-Pyrrhonian as satisfying both the theoretical condition and the 'practical condition' (PC). This evaluation of the relative merits of Academic and neo-Pyrrhonian Scepticism is prevalent to this day, which is part of the reason that Academic Scepticism has generally been neglected as a viable philosophical position. We'll be in a better position to judge whether or not the Academic has a satisfactory response to the Essential Problem by the end of this chapter, and, as a consequence, if this neglect is justified. Before examining the arguments of the Academics and the neo-Pyrrhonian Sextus, however, we'll look at their precursor Pyrrho.

Beyond belief

Although he remains a somewhat shadowy figure, Pyrrho's influence was nevertheless considerable. The little that is known of his views serves as a good introduction to what motivates the Ancient Sceptic, and to the challenge that the Essential Problem presents. Acknowledging that an enquiry into our capacity for knowledge (understood in the broad sense) is critical if we are to arrive at an understanding of what a happy life would be and how to live it, Pyrrho is reported as arriving at the following position:

> Things are equally indifferent, unmeasurable and inarbitrable . . . neither our sensations nor our opinions tell us truths or falsehoods. *Therefore for this reason* we should not put our trust in them one bit, but we should be unopinionated, uncommitted and unwavering, saying concerning each individual thing that it no more is than is not, or it both is and is not, or it neither is nor is not. The outcome for those who actually adopt this attitude . . . will be first speechlessness, and then freedom from disturbance (*ataraxia*); and . . . pleasure.
>
> (Aristocles, 1F. Italics added)

With our taxonomy in mind, this gives us the following:

- Answer to the constitutive question: The things that comprise the world lack any determinate characteristics. Everything in its very nature is incognitive.
- Answer to the hypothetical question: Nothing at all can be known.
- Answer to the normative question: We should not hold opinions, but suspend judgement about everything (*epoche*). The outcome will be a life of tranquillity (*ataraxia*).

As this stands, it is clear that Pyrrho's view possesses the defining feature of Academic Scepticism as Sextus understands it. Where the Dogmatist contends that knowledge constitutes the very possibility of achieving happiness, Pyrrho maintains that what we *p*-know about the nature of things warrants scepticism about such knowledge. As Aristocles points out, this scepticism about the possibility of knowledge is inferred from the assertion about the nature of things. As a result of that inference, the wise recognize that neither the senses nor anyone's opinions are in any way indicators or standards (criteria) of truth, and therefore come to see that they should avoid the mental discomfort that issues from using them to decide what is and is not true. They conclude that living a life in which they do not hold opinions but suspend judgement and remain in a state of equipoise will satisfy the traditional desire for happiness.

From a contemporary perspective this confronts us with a problem. In Chapter 1 we identified three possible targets for the modern sceptic's doubt: truth, justification and beliefs themselves. At that time it seemed absurd to regard the sceptic as doubting that we have beliefs; after all, such doubt would naturally be thought of *as* a belief! Since 'holding opinions' sounds like having beliefs, it appears that Pyrrho is not only rejecting the claim that our beliefs have a normative character (since everything is 'incognitive'), but is advocating living a life without *any* beliefs. It is not surprising that for many years Pyrrho's views were summarily dismissed as viciously self-refuting.

Although this interpretation is misleading, it is instructive, because the rejection of opinion is common to all varieties of scepticism. To defend Pyrrho on this point therefore removes one obvious objection to Ancient Scepticism in general. Given the two conditions that any solution to the Essential Problem must satisfy, the situation appears to be as follows. With respect to the practical condition, any understanding of what it is to 'live a life' suggests people making judgements about how they should act, and yet Pyrrho's answer to the normative question stipulates that we should not make judgements (have opinions) about anything. With respect to the theoretical condition, the argument that we don't know anything (the answer to the hypothetical question), and therefore shouldn't make judgements about things, is advanced on the basis of an answer to the constitutive question; and yet the latter is a judgement (opinion) about the nature of things – a purported item of knowledge. In the first case it would seem that Pyrrho's view is contradicted by the *practical* unavoidability of having to have some sort criterion for action; in the second by the *theoretical* unavoidability of being rationally consistent.

In order to bring these criticisms into focus, we need to relate Pyrrho's talk of 'opinions' to our own all-encompassing concept of belief. Consider the following:

1 People can no more live without beliefs than they can without oxygen. It is *practically* impossible for a person to *function* as a

person – live a life of the morally significant sort – without beliefs. Beliefs are real.

2 Our commonsensical way of understanding the behaviour of people (ourselves and others) – what we call 'folk psychology' – is a theory. It is *theoretically* impossible to understand why people act as they do without ascribing beliefs (and desires) to them. Beliefs are theoretical items (like neutrinos and positrons).

3 Being a person entails being a believer. Beliefs are states of persons: it is *conceptually* impossible to even *be* a person without having beliefs.

In the light of these possibilities, to advocate living a life *without* beliefs suggests one of the following:

1′ An acceptance that beliefs are real, but rejection of the claim that they are guides to action.

2′ An acceptance that beliefs are theoretical, but a rejection of the claim that they are needed to explain how people should and should not act in order to achieve happiness.[4]

3′ An acceptance that beliefs are guides to action, but a denial that to be a person living a life of the desirable sort one need *do* anything at all.

(1′) and (2′) presuppose that (3) is false, since one could only deny that beliefs themselves or the concept of belief are useful if one denied that to be a person one must have beliefs. In other words, the concept of belief must be such that we can detach our grasp of it from our understanding of what a person is; otherwise it would be like saying that it's useful for triangles to have three sides but that they'd still be triangles even if they didn't! (3′) goes even further and detaches the concept of action from our understanding of what a person is. To make sense of Pyrrho's views in terms of contemporary belief-talk, then, he must be presupposing one of the following:

(a) An understanding of persons such that one can make sense of their living a good life but not acting (from 3′).

(b) An account of what beliefs are that warrants the conclusion that they are practically or theoretically useless (from 1′ and 2′).

(c) An acceptance of the everyday sense of the concept of belief in which we use it to understand why people act in the way they do (from 3).

First, there are no grounds for thinking that Pyrrho had any account of what beliefs are that would allow them to be seen as useless in the senses indicated in (b). Secondly, he did not consider that a life without opinions was a life of inaction: although the Sceptic purposefully withholds affirming that things are a particular way *in their very nature*, he can go along with appearances (*phainomenon*: objects as they are perceived) and these provide a criterion for action. Since that leaves only (c), the statement that one should live a life 'without opinion' must amount to something other than a rejection of belief *as such*. What Pyrrho seems to be advocating is that the wise should accept at face value ('go along with') a certain class of beliefs (the apparent), but refuse to assent to beliefs in the non-apparent ('opinions') of the sort that characterize Dogmatic views about the nature of reality.

With respect to the practical condition, then, a life without belief is not unintelligible if it is understood as the rejection of a certain class of beliefs. The acceptable beliefs are not lacking a normative dimension and therefore can serve as criteria for action, but their normativity does not derive from any consideration of their ultimate truth. To see the significance of this, consider the advocate of the justified true belief analysis again. When he says that S believes that q, he indicates that S believes that q is true; and it is this link to truth that is held to give beliefs their explanatory power. Now consider Tracy, an ardent student of Pyrrho. She asks our justified true belief analyst to pass her coat and he ascribes to her the belief that (say) he has her coat – a belief that she must hold to be true if he is to understand her request (even if it is in fact false). If he now asks Tracy if she thinks that her belief is true, she will respond that it *appears* to her that he has her coat in his hand but as to the ultimate truth of the claim she would not like to say, since that would be to assert something about the nature of things (which are unknowable). From her perspective, what he describes as holding true, she describes as going along with appearances. As we've seen, for the modern epistemologist the important contrast is between holding true and knowing (or being justified in believing). For

Pyrrho (and Tracy) the criterion of action derives from the contrast between going along with appearances and assenting to the non-apparent.

On this interpretation Pyrrho's claim that we should avoid holding opinions does not violate the practical condition and leave us without a criterion of action; but what of the theoretical condition? The problem here is more exacting, because it does seem to be the case that the conclusion that nothing can be known is inferred from a judgement about the nature of things; and yet this sort of judgement is precisely what we are enjoined to avoid making on the grounds that we don't know anything. Pyrrho thus seems to be committed to the view that the p-knowing that concerns the nature of things is 'insulated' from the scepticism that it gives rise to. Indeed, this must be the case, because it is our p-knowledge that striving for knowledge is pointless that motivates the conclusion that happiness is to be found by avoiding the search and not by continuing it. Moreover, it is our p-knowledge that knowledge is impossible that underpins the distinction between the apparent and the non-apparent and thus furnishes Pyrrho with a criterion for action (the former). If it weren't for the insulation of p-knowing from scepticism, he would not be able to satisfy the demands of the practical condition.

Unfortunately, this view invites attack from both the Dogmatist and the more thoroughgoing Sceptic. The Dogmatist can point out that since Pyrrho admits that we can p-know at least one ultimate truth, he has given them cause for renewed optimism because he has demonstrated that Dogmatism must be true – there is some philosophical knowledge that provides a guide to the good life and maybe we can come to p-know even more. The Sceptic can remind Pyrrho that leaving open this possibility for further philosophical enquiry is not the way to get us to avoid holding opinions and achieve happiness (*ataraxia*) and then go on to ask him on what basis he claims to p-know that his answer to the constitutive question is correct.

Socratic method

From our discussion of Pyrrho we can draw the following conclusions that relate to Ancient Scepticism in general. First, the rejection of opinions is not contradictory if it is understood as the rejection of a certain class of beliefs. As a corollary to this, it is not senseless to suggest that human happiness depends upon the achievement of a state of tranquillity wherein the search for the truth about the real nature of things is abandoned. Rather than being the essential guide to happiness that the Dogmatist assumes it is, for the Sceptic the search for philosophical truth is the greatest impediment to the living of a good life. Secondly, the rejection of opinions does not leave the Sceptic without a criterion of action: in his tranquil state the Sceptic still goes along with appearances and remains actively engaged in the world. Finally, however, a response to the Essential Problem must satisfy the practical condition and provide a criterion for action without introducing a problematic claim to p-know anything. However the Sceptic comes to the view that he must go along with *appearances* in order to achieve happiness, it cannot be on the basis of a claim to (p-)know what things are *really* like (in their essential nature).

It is not possible to reconstruct any response Pyrrho might have made to this problem, but that need not concern us here as Pyrrho's successors did address it. We can get a preliminary understanding of what this involves by looking briefly at what prompted the emergence of the school of Academic Scepticism. This began around 270 BCE, when Arcesilaus became Head of the Academy, some seventy-five years after the death of its founder Plato. At that time two rival schools dominated Athenian philosophy, Epicureanism and Stoicism. Stoicism developed around 300 BCE when Zeno (*c*. 350–258 BCE) took to frequenting the painted porch (*stoa*) in the Agora;[5] its competitor a few years later when Epicurus (*c*. 341–270 BCE), recently returned to Athens, constituted a kind of alternative philosophical community in the garden of his house. Naturally, the rivals held contrary positions on the most important philosophical issues. First the Epicureans:

- Answer to the constitutive question: all that exists is an infinite number of indivisible atoms and the void through which they move: "Substance is divided" (II. 5).
- Answer to the hypothetical question: we can have knowledge since all 'natural' phenomena can be explained mechanistically, without recourse to a divine plan ("God does not show providence for things in the universe" (*ibid*.)).

- Answer to the normative question: "Pleasure is the beginning and end of the blessed life. For we recognize pleasure as the good which is primary and congenital . . . the feeling [is] the yardstick for judging every good thing" (Epicurus, 21B).

Now the Stoics:

- Answer to the constitutive question: matter is a passive, undivided and unqualified plenum that is pervaded by reason (*logos*), God or cause (sometimes referred to as the 'world-soul') which gives it its determinate characteristics and its historical shape.
- Answer to the hypothetical question: we can have infallible knowledge since "Nature has given the sensory faculty and the impression which arises thereby as our light, as it were, for the recognition of truth" (Sextus, 40K).
- Answer to the normative question: "Being happy . . . consists of living in accordance with virtue . . . in living in accordance with nature" (Stobaeus, 63A), "which is in accordance with the nature of oneself and that of the whole" (DL, 63C).

Despite these rather profound differences, the contending schools shared the conviction that it is philosophy's ability to direct one in the acquisition of knowledge that qualifies it as the guide to living a happy life. To Arcesilaus, this represented a Dogmatic perversion of the Socratic legacy. It was the epistemology of the Stoics in particular that attracted his rancour. As Cicero (106–43 BCE) recounts:

> It was with Zeno . . . that Arcesilaus began his entire struggle . . . because of the obscurity of the things which had brought Socrates to an admission of ignorance . . . So Arcesilaus was in the practice of denying that anything could be known, not even the one thing Socrates had left for himself – the knowledge that he knew nothing: such was the extent of the obscurity in which everything lurked, on his assessment, and there was nothing which could be discerned or understood. For these reasons, he said, no one should maintain or assert anything or give it the acceptance of assent, but he should always curb his rashness and restrain it from every slip . . . He used to act consistently

with this philosophy, and by arguing against everyone's opinions he drew most people away from their own, so that when
reasons of equal weight were found on opposite sides on the
same subject, the easier course was to withhold assent from
either side.   (Cicero, 68A)

On the face of it, Cicero's summary presents us with a position not
dissimilar to that we attributed to Pyrrho. There are, however, two
important differences. First, Arcesilaus is reported as denying
knowledge of the one thing that even Socrates was reported to
know; namely, that he knew nothing. This sounds very much like
the view Sextus used to characterize neo-Pyrrhonian Scepticism,
and thereby distinguish it from Academic Scepticism. At the very
least this suggests that Sextus's taxonomy is overly simplified, and
that the Academic Sceptic cannot be straightforwardly dismissed as
claiming to p-know that things cannot be known.

The second difference relates to the detail we are given of
Arcesilaus's *method*. This suggests a link between the 'way' in which
Socrates arrived at his 'admission of ignorance' and Arcesilaus's
explicit engagement with the opinions of the Dogmatists of his own
time. In Plato's early dialogues Socrates is to be found seeking out
particular interlocutors who claim to possess knowledge of what, for
example, piety, courage or friendship are. In the course of public
discussion, these views and others that are raised along the way are
subjected to criticism, and the conclusion is invariably that none of
those present – Socrates included – can justify their definition of a
particular virtue.[6] The participants are thus led to awareness that they
don't in fact know what the virtue in question 'is', and that this
knowledge of ignorance is preferable to the *ignorance* of ignorance.

As we saw with Pyrrho, this awareness of ignorance can be
thought of as a cognitive achievement, constituting p-knowledge.
Taken in this way it seems to lead the Sceptic to a self-defeating
impasse. As we've also seen, however, knowledge for the Greeks is
not to be understood simply on the model of propositional knowledge – it is better understood as a sort of ability or know-how.
Indeed, even for Pyrrho, going along with appearances equips us
with the ability to act in the world. This suggests a possible response
to the Essential Problem: can we make sense of there being a way of
coming to 'know' that (or of a path to it 'being apparent to us' that)

we know nothing? If the path to – or method by which one could arrive at – such a state can be made intelligible, the Sceptic might be able to respond to the theoretical condition without undermining the distinction between the apparent and the non-apparent, and thus retain the former as a criterion for action.

One influential attempt to move a little in this direction is by offering a 'dialectical interpretation' of Arcesilaus's views.[7] We've already noted that an important aspect of Arcesilaus's approach was the willingness to engage with the Dogmatic theorists of his own time. The defining idea of Dogmatism is the conviction that philosophy can identify a criterion of truth: some indicator or mark that allows for the discrimination between what one should believe and do and what one shouldn't believe and do. As such, a criterion of truth – "something possessing the intrinsic power to convict falsehoods with truths" (Lucretius, 16A) – is the essential guide in the pursuit of the good life.[8] For both Epicureans and Stoics all knowledge (including p-knowledge) is ultimately derived from experience, so the criterion is provided by the senses.

According to the dialectical interpretation, then, the whole point of Arcesilaus's reasoning is not to advance any *positive* thesis about the nature of things, but is exhausted in the entirely *negative* project of 'deconstructing' the epistemological pretensions of the Stoics. To appreciate the dialectical interpretation and the extent to which it is successful in addressing the theoretical condition we therefore need to know a little more about the Dogmatisms that the Academics took such exception to. Before focusing our attention on the Stoics, let's turn briefly to their contemporaries, the Epicureans.

Epicurean empiricism

According to Epicurus, sensation provides us with three criteria of truth: sensation itself, preconceptions and feelings.[9] The first thing to note about sensations is that strictly speaking they are always 'true'; or, since this can sound confusing, they are always 'real'. To take a traditional example, although a barn may appear round from a distance and square up close, each image is – taken *as such* – equally 'real'. In themselves, then, sensations are irrational – passive, mechanical modifications of the body – and it is only judgements on or about them that constitute knowledge claims. These judgements utilize the second criterion of truth, *prolepsis* (precon-ceptions): general concepts that include not only ball, barn and leg, but also more abstract concepts like utility, the desirability of pleasure and even truth. When S judges that the barn is square or that the object is round she goes beyond the sensation itself and utilizes the appropriate concepts.

Now it is evident that reasoning itself requires concepts, and the very possibility of philosophical knowledge is dependent on their having the status of criteria of truth. If they didn't possess the mark of truth the Epicureans couldn't claim to *p*-know that, for example, matter is divided and that pleasure is good. This suggests an obvious question: is the status of concepts as criteria of truth derived entirely from sensation, or does it depend upon non-empirical sources? An example of the latter would be something like Plato's theory of forms, where objective concepts (forms) are grasped by the mind. Since this conflicts with the resolutely empiricist standpoint of the Epicurean, that leaves only the former option: concepts are criteria of truth because they have been abstracted from or otherwise synthesized out of sensations of the appropriate sort.

The sensations from which concepts that are to serve as criteria of truth ought to be abstracted are obviously sensations that are true. However, if *all* sensations are 'true' in the sense that they are real, this is not the sort of 'truth' required to justify the use of the concepts needed for knowledge (particularly *p*-knowledge) claims. It therefore appears that the Epicurean is committed to the view that sensations must incorporate some rational component that would warrant a judgement that things are a certain way. The upshot of this is that some sensations must be representative of their objects. Moreover, since the concept of truth is itself derived from true sensations, these must present themselves as being self-evidently true. That is to say, whatever feature characterizes the sensations that are representative of their objects (true), it must reveal itself *as* the mark of truth.

By way of an illustration consider a book, optimistically entitled *The Philosophical Guide to the Good Life and How to Live It*. It contains a long (perhaps infinite) list of sentences (q_2 to q_n), some of which are true and some of which are false. The book's introduction informs S that if she discovers a foolproof way of distinguishing the true from the false she will get to live the good life. What S wants, then, is a criterion of truth. For the Epicureans, the sensations that are representative of their objects are analogous to the true sentences. When S reads

(q_{901}) Listening to Kylie will ruin your mind, *or*
(q_{119}) Landlord is a fine pint of ale

they will strike her as being self-evidently true. Moreover, she will see what it is about them that marks them out as being self-evidently true. Let's say that in this case it is the fact that they are odd-numbered sentences, allowing her to explicitly formulate the criterion of truth, and complete the book with:

(q_1) All and only the odd-numbered sentences in the book are true.

With this, S's philosophical work would be over and her future fame and fortune assured! Of course, the analogy only works if we can assimilate the Epicurean's sensations to sentences that are *meaningful* to S, and strictly speaking sensations are *irrational*. The closest analogy, then, is for q_2 to q_n to be written in a language S cannot understand. But suppose that in looking at q_{901} and q_{119} S nevertheless still 'sees' that they are true and that they are true because they are odd-numbered, even though she doesn't know what either of them means. The point is that the sentences must be meaningful to S if they are to furnish her with the criterion of truth; which is to say, the Epicurean's sensations must themselves have a rational content such that those that are true reveal themselves as self-evidently true.

Stoic empiricism

The Epicurean formulation of criteria of truth was the starting-point for early Stoic epistemology. However, given the difficulties that issue from trying to make sense of the claim that sensations are irrational in their nature, we can appreciate what motivated their own divergent answers to our three questions. The upshot of the answer to the constitutive question is that where reason (*logos*) or the 'world soul' pervades matter and gives intelligible shape to nature, the individual soul pervades the body and provides *its* rational pattern. The fact that nature and ourselves as part of nature share a common rational structure ensures that the world is as it were *apt* for our knowing.

On this account reason is not external to nature and so sensations are not 'external' to reason. They are not passive (mechanical), uninterpreted modifications of our body but take place in what is called the *hegemonikon* or commanding faculty (the highest part of the soul). Sensations thus have something like propositional content: they indicate *that* things are a certain way. Taking the example of the barn, when S has an impression that it is round, S has a thought with that content: she can say *that* the barn appears to be round or looks round. To undergo an impression is thus to engage in a rational activity; but that still leaves it open to the percipient to assent to the content of the impression or to refrain from doing so. Recalling our book analogy, the fact that impressions are internal to reason means that the propositions q_2 to q_n are guaranteed to be intelligible: we can understand their meaning. Taken in isolation that does not indicate that we should believe what they say. If S reads that the barn is round S can fully understand the claim and still refuse to assent to it.

Of course, this assent is precisely that step beyond appearances and to a claim about how things really are that Pyrrho denied one should take. It does however demonstrate how Stoic epistemology links up with the idea of action oriented towards living the good life. If S assents to an appearance she takes cognitive responsibility for the belief that (say) the barn is round. This application of the term is distinct from the one we associated with Pyrrho, for on the Stoic account this belief will be either true or false (the barn *really is* round or not). Moreover, responsibility to the truth is not to be understood as being merely theoretical. Since knowledge is indeed possible on the basis of the Stoic's answer to the constitutive question, the key to happiness is given by the answer to the normative question. The responsibility at issue amounts to the obligation to shape one's patterns of assent in such a way that one lives in accordance with one's own nature, and with nature as a whole.

To live the Stoic version of the good life is to rationally harmonize one's soul with the world soul, and this requires that one know when to assent and when not to – possesses, as it were, a key to identifying which propositions in the book are true and which are false. In other words, one needs a criterion of truth.[10] For the Stoics this was provided by the 'cognitive impression' (*phantasia kataleptike*). As initially formulated, this had to satisfy two conditions:

(A) It has a real object as its cause: it "arises from what is" (Sextus, 40E).
(B) It represents its object clearly and distinctly: it is "stamped and impressed exactly in accordance with what is" (*ibid.*).

As Arcesilaus is reported to have pointed out, (A) and (B) do not alone constitute a criterion of truth. If S cannot distinguish between a genuine perception of a barn and a barn-hallucination in so far as she is unable to discern which one represents its *real* object (the real object of the hallucination being oneself), the clarity and distinctness of the presentation of an object in an impression is not the criterion of truth. To rescue the concept of the cognitive impression Zeno therefore added a third condition:

(C) The clarity and distinctness of the impression are functions of how things really are: the impression is "of such a kind that could not arise from what is not" (*ibid.*)

What (C) adds is the claim that if I am presented with an impression of a round barn, that impression could only *be* clear and distinct if it were caused by a round barn, and not (say) by myself (as in a dream or hallucination). Arcesilaus remained unconvinced. He deployed a number of examples to challenge (C), seeking to demonstrate that no impression arising from something true ('what is') has a property such that it could be distinguished from one arising from something false ('what is not'). In other words, although an impression *might* clearly and distinctly represent its object, it does not in addition carry a label that provides a subjective guarantee that it does so. It does not as it were carry a passport containing a photo of the object it represents!

In contemporary terms, Arcesilaus is attacking the Stoic's internalist account of justification. The criterion of truth is the basis of any attempt to shape one's life in accordance with reason in pursuit of happiness. In the absence of a criterion of truth the distinction between a justified belief (or action) and an unjustified belief collapses and there is no rational guide to how to live one's life. We'll return to this line of criticism below but it should be noted that the Stoic does have a response. He points out that while S might mistakenly assent to a barn-hallucination, that does not in itself undermine the idea that the cognitive impression serves as a criterion of truth. Rather, it demonstrates that S lacks the discipline-cum-wisdom required to ensure that she only ever assents to impressions that are genuinely cognitive and withholds assent in other cases. So who does have the necessary discipline and wisdom?

Cognition and knowledge

For the Stoic the cognitive impression is our guide to the recognition of truth. Since the cognitive impression arises as a result of our sensory faculty, it is common to human beings – we all have this natural capacity to 'track' the truth. As Sextus also notes, "this impression, being self-evident and striking, all but seizes us by the hair . . . and pulls us to assent" (40K). So we all have the capacity to recognize truths *as* truths – they are the ones that 'pull us to assent' (propositions we read that overwhelm us with their self-evident truth). And this is all as it should be: the good life is the good life for any human being, and Stoic philosophy is the guide to achieving it.

As we saw above, however, the Stoic defence of the cognitive impression – and thus of the distinction between being justified and not being justified in living a certain way – seems to rest on the distinction between the wise (disciplined) and the unwise (undisciplined). What are we to make of this distinction? The answer lies in the fact that the impression 'all but' seizes us by the hair. If it were the case that by definition any and all cognitive impressions literally and absolutely convinced us of their truth, it would be impossible to see how anyone could ever make an erroneous judgement or act in an undisciplined or cognitively irresponsible way.[11] In such a situation, a criterion of truth wouldn't be a criterion at all and the concept of the good (as opposed to any other) kind of life would disappear, along with any role for philosophy (and reflection generally).

The 'all but' indicates that there is a 'gap' between the impression and the assent such that one could fail to assent to even a 'cognitive impression'. To modernize an example used by Sextus

(40K), imagine that S saw a friend die in hospital, and a week later he appears before her in the street (he'd been in a vegetative state, mistaken for death at the time). Here S undergoes a cognitive impression, but, reasoning that her friend can't be alive, withholds assent. In order for the cognitive impression to carry out its criterial function, then, there must be nothing in the context of apprehension that constitutes an impediment to it being taken as such (this includes the mental state of the percipient). This does not exhaust the significance of that 'gap', however. It turns out that *even if S* undergoes and assents to a cognitive impression in a context that presents no impediment to grasping its clarity and distinctness, she *still* does not qualify as wise as opposed to ignorant because this does not amount to knowledge proper (*episteme*), but only to cognition (*katalepsis*).

We therefore have the following hierarchy: *doxa* (opinion), *katalepsis* (cognition) and *episteme* (knowledge). For the Stoics, *doxa* are beliefs that arise from assenting to the 'incognitive' – to what is either false or not 'clear and distinct'.[12] *Katalepsis* refers to those beliefs that result from assenting to a cognitive impression, and therefore approximate to the contemporary epistemologist's justified true beliefs. In our book example *doxa* would be propositions in the book that S assents to and which are false, whereas *katalepsis* would result from assenting to a self-evidently true proposition. To appreciate the distinction between *katalepsis* and *episteme*, recall that cognitive impressions are 'caused' by their appropriate objects (C). The content of the impression – what makes it the kind of impression it is – is thus determined by the way the world is. Assent to any particular cognitive impression does not amount to knowledge in the full sense because *as such* it has no implications for one's responses to other impressions. S might rightly assent to q_{901} but also (erroneously) to (say) q_{1004}. This false belief might in turn cause S to rethink her assent to q_{901}.

To have knowledge proper, then, one must have a stable cognitive economy – there can be no shifting of belief states or re-evaluations of what is held to be the case. To possess knowledge is to be in a state wherein one only ever assents to what is self-evident and thus will never be put into the position of having to re-assess a cognition once made. To possess knowledge in this sense is to exercise the maximal level of cognitive responsibility by having brought one's own nature into accordance with nature as a whole (and as such to have achieved happiness). Only then is the 'gap' between impression and assent fully closed and the person said to be wise as opposed to ignorant. Let's say that anyone who possesses knowledge in this sense satisfies the *Full Competency Requirement*. If S satisfies this requirement she will assent to all and only the propositions in the book that are self-evidently true (the odd-numbered ones).

The dialectical interpretation of Academic Scepticism

For the Stoics, there are only two states of persons: that of the virtuous and wise (the Stoic sage) who satisfies the full competency requirement, and that of the ignorant. Where the latter lack the knowledge (*episteme*) to guide their patterns of assent, the former have trained themselves in such a way that their commanding faculty (the state of their soul) has achieved a perfect rational accommodation with nature. Their patterns of assent-giving are thoroughly integrated in such a way that they never mistake a cognitive impression for a non-cognitive one. They have learned, as it were, to live by the book!

This dualism forms the basis of the dialectical interpretation of Arcesilaus's Scepticism. As we've seen, what makes a cognitive impression the kind of impression it is, with the kind of content it has, is fixed by the way things are with the world. Imagine, then, two persons, A (ignorant) and B (wise). Both are placed in front of a barn under ideal circumstances (no impediments), and both assent to the relevant impression. Arcesilaus argues that while B's assent is by definition knowledge (*episteme*), since he is wise, A's assent cannot by definition amount to anything other than opinion (*doxa*), because he is ignorant. In other words, although cognitive impressions are supposed to be the universal criterion of truth, they don't *as such* seem to do any work at all. Either a claim is fully justified and amounts to knowledge, because it is made by a wise man, or it lacks any justification at all and is mere opinion.

Of course, the Stoic has to hold that the ignorant (more or less all of us) have some cognitive impressions, and that knowledge is the state of someone who satisfies the Full Competency Requirement. But this returns us to the earlier problem; namely, Arcesilaus's

objection that although an impression *might* clearly and distinctly represent its object, it does not in addition carry a label that provides a subjective guarantee that it does so. The Stoic response to that was that the wise man will never assent to the incognitive and that Arcesilaus's concern was therefore not well founded. But this suggests that only the wise man is in a position to know that an impression carries that subjective guarantee (because he has trained himself in accordance with nature).

Unlike *B*, then, *A* has no grounds for thinking that *his* impression is a cognitive one, and therefore for thinking that *he* has cognitions as opposed to mere opinions. If he follows the advice of the Stoic sage *B* he should therefore withhold assent in *all* cases. But now what of *B*? How does *B* know that *he* has satisfied the Full Competency Requirement and so qualify as a wise man? If it's possible to raise doubt; if, for example, he has ever made – or even thinks he might have made – a mistake; then even the *aspiring* sage cannot rule out that a clear and distinct impression might *not* have come from something existent. Since the Stoic sage will never assent to what is not self-evident, he ought by his own lights to similarly suspend judgement on all matters!

On the dialectical interpretation, then, the Academic Sceptic does not argue that one should withhold assent/suspend belief (*epoche*) on the basis of a contradictory metaphysical thesis, as appeared to be the case with Pyrrho. Instead the suspension of belief (*epoche*) is a natural result of the Stoic's own presuppositions. If the Stoic is pursuing knowledge in order to achieve virtue, then by his own standards he should accept that *epoche* results from it. Arcesilaus is not himself vulnerable to the theoretical condition. He does not need to 'insulate' a claim to *p*-know from a claim not to know anything because the assumption that one can *p*-know is the Dogmatist's own and not the Sceptic's. Since the method involves bringing his Stoic interlocutors to the recognition that the state of *epoche* is what the *p*-knowledge of their own ignorance commits them to, the dialectical process takes place in the 'space' of the Dogmatist's own beliefs. Without a dogmatic opponent there is nothing for the Sceptic to do.

In spite of its appeal, however, the dialectical interpretation leaves the issue of Arcesilaus's own philosophical views untouched. Because the dialectic engages the Dogmatist in the 'space' of their own beliefs, it seems natural to ask if, in addition to his dialectical ingenuity, he offered any substantive responses to the constitutive, hypothetical and normative questions. Was he satisfied to force his Dogmatic opponents to suspend belief, or did he positively argue for *epoche* himself; and if so, was it on the grounds that everything is incognitive? From Cicero's summary of Arcesilaus's position it seems plausible to conclude that he did indeed actively endorse *epoche*, and most contemporary scholars agree. The reasoning seems clear enough. If Arcesilaus is a 'merely dialectical' thinker he is in no position to offer an answer to the normative question or provide a criterion for action. But Sceptics share the Dogmatist's orientation towards action, recognizing the force of the practical condition. As we saw with Pyrrho, actively endorsing *epoche* by maintaining that things are incognitive by their very nature serves two related ends: it motivates the claim that happiness is to be found by relinquishing a futile search for knowledge, and grounds the distinction between the apparent and the non-apparent that provides Sceptics with their criterion of action.

It is not surprising that the dialectical interpretation of Arcesilaus's method is supplemented with the claim that he actively endorsed *epoche* himself. It thus presupposes that his method involves two discrete modes. The dialectical mode is purely *negative*: it leads the Dogmatist to an awareness of the inconsistency of his own position. In addition to this there is a *positive* mode when the Sceptic advances his own account of how things are. The suggestion is that nothing of significance connects the two activities, and in the absence of the second nothing would be achieved but a moment of Socratic self-awareness on the part of the Dogmatist. Unfortunately, this does not take us very far towards resolving the Essential Problem. On the one hand, although the Stoic has come to embrace *epoche* without the Sceptic himself being caught in a contradiction, he has been left with no criterion for action; on the other hand, the Sceptic seems to have to advance some *positive* but question-begging response to the constitutive question in order to arrive at *epoche* himself. That may lead to the conclusion that he should go along with appearances, but it does so at the cost of violating the theoretical condition again.

This re-emergence of the Essential Problem fits neatly with the assumption that in order to do philosophy one must offer positive answers to the constitutive, hypothetical and normative questions.

When I originally introduced the theoretical condition and the practical condition I indicated that, as our understanding of the thought of the Ancient Sceptics developed, we would begin to see that they were advancing a different understanding of what philosophy is. In the next section I shall suggest that there is a way of understanding the negative dialectical mode that does not make it obvious that it needs to be supplemented by a positive mode in order for the Sceptic to satisfy the practical condition, while avoiding violating the theoretical condition. According to what I'll call the *Therapeutic Interpretation*, the Academic Sceptic is trying to elaborate a non-Dogmatic understanding of what philosophy is.

The Therapeutic Interpretation of Academic Scepticism

So far we have seen (with Pyrrho) that the failure to resolve the theoretical condition undermines the distinction between the apparent and non-apparent that grounds the Sceptic's account of how action is possible in the absence of assent (the practical condition). The dialectical interpretation resolves the theoretical condition but, regarding Sceptical opposition as taking place in some 'insulated philosophical space', fails to give an account of what implications this has for the Sceptic. The response was to suggest that the Sceptic is obliged to advance a positive thesis after all (thus potentially reintroducing the theoretical condition). To this we can add our specifically modern concern: even if a distinction between the apparent and the non-apparent could be sustained, that would not do justice to *our* epistemic intuitions. Establishing the apparent as the criterion of action is not sufficient to account for the fact that *we* hold some everyday beliefs to be better justified than others.

As we saw above, Sextus is keen to classify the Academics as 'negative dogmatists' who claim to *p*-know that we cannot know. Accordingly, Arcesilaus is held to have positively advocated *epoche* on the grounds that everything is incognitive. Having done so, he recognized that if he was to avoid the Stoic counter-charge that a life without assent made action impossible, he had to come up with an alternative criterion for action:

> Since after this it was necessary to investigate the conduct of life too, which is not of a nature to be explained without a

> criterion, on which happiness too, i.e. the end of life, has its
> trust dependent . . . one who suspends judgement about every-
> thing will regulate choice and avoidance and actions in general
> by 'the reasonable'.   (Sextus, 69B)

Sextus records a similar observation about Arcesilaus's most famous
successor, Carneades, a figure of near-legendary brilliance whose
influence overshadowed that of Plato and Socrates at the time.
Carneades is reported as extending Arcesilaus's attack on the criterion of truth to cover not only the Stoics' 'cognitive impression' but
the alternatives put forward by their empiricist and rationalist opponents. For Sextus, this decisive attack on the idea that a mark of
certainty can guide us in our everyday lives means that Carneades is
"virtually compelled" to seek some alternative criterion "for the conduct of life and the attainment of happiness". This is, he goes on to
say, "both the 'convincing' (*pithanon*) impression and the one which
is simultaneously convincing, undiverted, and thoroughly explored"
(69D). If, as Sextus implies, Carneades indeed claims to have shown
that *any* criterion of truth is impossible (that everything is incognitive
and we should therefore refrain from assent), there is no *objective*
standard to guide judgement. Such a negative dogmatism would
therefore necessitate the formulation of an alternative criterion for
judgement. According to Sextus, this addresses the *subjective* conditions of judgement. This allows us to distinguish between those
impressions that are apparently true (convincing) and those that are
apparently false (unconvincing). Moreover, of those that are apparently true, some are confused and indistinct, whilst others are clear
and distinct. The general criterion of judgement is the convincing
impression that is clear and distinct (or 'fully manifested').

   Since this criterion is compatible with the falsity of the impression,
it is fallible, and not a criterion of truth. Similarly, since the truth of
an impression cannot be an *explanation* of why it is convincing, the
occasional error should not lead us to distrust its general applicability. This generic fallibilism is then reinforced by two further 'criteria'
of convincingness. In recognition of the holistic character of impressions, the first of these refers to the 'undiverted' nature of an impression, or what we might call its 'contextual consistency'. In our usual
example, if S believes there's a barn in the distance, that belief must
not be obviously contradicted by anything associated with it (its

appearing to have no sides etc.) and is more credible for not being so 'diverted'. Finally, a belief is more credible still if it is 'fully explored', or what we could call 'contextually justified'. In this case, rather than just assume that it is sufficient that all the associated beliefs that could bear on the impression in question do not obviously appear false, we investigate them using the best available methods drawn from experience (get out of the car and look around the sides of the barn). As with the general criterion, truth does not come into play with either of these further criteria, and which one is appropriate is dependent on our interests: "In matters of no importance we make use of the merely convincing impression, but in weightier matters the undiverted impression is a criterion, and in matters which contribute to happiness the thoroughly explored impression" (Sextus, 69E). This fallibilistic, contextualist approach to epistemological questions is a far cry from the Stoic idea of knowledge satisfying the full competency requirement. Dropping talk of impressions, although the *truth* of beliefs plays no role in the evaluation of their normative character, we are nevertheless cognitively empowered to make responsible discriminations between beliefs on the grounds of their differential justificatory status. If *S* has no reason to believe that her barn might be a barn-façade, *S* has no responsibility to *prove* that it isn't: the possibility of its being one isn't relevant to her belief that it isn't, and her belief doesn't lack justification even if it isn't.[13]

Setting aside contemporary considerations, we need to know if this appealing picture of our cognitive situation requires a new criterion for action as Sextus suggests. If not, it is important to discover if there is an interpretation of Academic Scepticism that satisfies the practical condition and doesn't fall foul of the theoretical condition. If it does, we have a familiar problem; namely, how the Sceptic advances such a criterion without falling back into Dogmatism. After all, *epoche* seems inconsistent with the very idea of promulgating any criterion. As we've seen, the temptation to respond in the affirmative derives from the supposition that the *positive* mode of the dogmatic is opposed to the *negative* mode of the dialectic, and as we'll see in the next section this is Sextus's own diagnosis of the Academic's commitments. There is no need for such an opposition, however. The dialectical engagement with the Stoics shows that by their own lights all they are entitled to is the criterion of the convincing, but at the same time this operates positively to illuminate what we do in fact do: that is to say, not search for certainty, but test our beliefs against one other to the extent that we consider challenges to them reasonable or important. This is what the Stoics *would* be doing if they abandoned their distracting and *philosophically unwarranted* fixation with certainty. For the Academic Sceptic, like Socrates himself, engaging with those that claim to know is a vital propaedeutic to making them aware of what they can in fact have: not certainty, but fallibility. When the Academic 'withholds assent', then, it is 'philosophical assent': assent to the unconditional truth of how things are. When he acts, it is because he gives 'weak assent': guided by the convincingness of the appearances, which convincingness extends to systematic testing of concurrent appearances where that is deemed appropriate. Since convincingness is never itself a criterion of truth, there is nothing question-begging about the idea of 'increased convincingness': it is, as it were, a justificatory standard internal to and arising from reflection on our practices, and not an inappropriate philosophical ideal that is externally imposed upon them.

On this interpretation it would appear that a 'dialectical' rejection of a criterion of truth does not necessarily commit the Sceptic to having to advance an alternative criterion dogmatically. Going back to our original taxonomy, the question now is, did Carneades *assert* that nothing could be apprehended – that he p-knew that knowledge is impossible? According to Cicero, this was not a dogmatic claim but one that emerged from the same dialectical engagement with the Stoics; namely, that if what apprehensibility amounts to is p-knowledge that one knows (through the criterion of certainty), then everything is inapprehensible. But that in itself does not mean that one's beliefs might not be true: appearances might in fact coincide with/be an apprehension of 'reality'.[14]

This shifts attention back to the criterion of truth itself. The Academic Sceptic claims that no impression can be cognitive because no impression carries with it a subjective marker of objective truth. The need for such a marker to underpin assent derives from the Stoics' distinction between appearance and reality. The rejection of the idea of a cognitive impression could therefore be regarded as a theoretical diagnosis and rejection of this underlying metaphysical distinction. The question then is, are the Academics any better placed to reject that distinction than the Stoics are to presuppose it? Is the assertion of the impossibility of a criterion of truth not only dogmatic but self-refuting and therefore a failed response to the theoretical condition?

On this interpretation it would appear that while the practical condition can be satisfied without dogmatically imposing a new criterion, asserting the non-existence of a criterion of truth raises a familiar problem. In response, one might place the emphasis on the Academic Sceptic's demonstration that the conditions for a cognitive impression are difficult to resolve. Since this leaves the proponent of the criterion unable to 'assent' by their own lights, they should (in their own practical interests) be open to reformulating assent in another way – one that connects it to convincingness rather than certainty. In this way the Dogmatist might himself come to think of his underlying metaphysical commitment as the cause of the problem in the first place. Now the Sceptic would not have made the dogmatic claim that he p-knows that he doesn't know so much as rendered problematic the distinction between p-knowing and knowing. By using philosophy to attack the Dogmatic assumption that the good life is to be attained through the pursuit of knowledge, this version of pk-scepticism promises to change our understanding of what philosophy is.

According to the Therapeutic Interpretation no formal rejection of the criterion of truth is necessary, and no dogmatic assertion of a criterion for action need be made. Whether or not this is what the Academics intended, the Therapeutic Interpretation presents a version of pk-scepticism that is a live option and we will encounter it again in subsequent chapters. For the time being, it should be noted that such a sceptic has to acknowledge that since no *decisive* rebuttal of the existence of a 'criterion of truth' is possible, someone (perhaps even oneself) might still find themselves inclined to go beyond appearances and claim for their beliefs a status as truths about reality. This raises an intriguing question: is the desire to transcend appearances derived from a tradition of dogmatic search for truth, or does it answer to something deep inside us? If the latter, can that striving be satisfied, as the dogmatist hopes, or does it dictate a task unachievable by finite creatures like us? If the former, the sceptic's task can never end while there is a dogmatism to oppose.

This sense of the open-endedness of the sceptic's task takes us to our final 'variety' of Scepticism, that of the neo-Pyrrhonist. In contrast with the Therapeutic Interpretation, on Sextus's reading the Academics' rejection of the criterion of truth necessitates the dogmatic assertion of an alternative. For the neo-Pyrrhonist, no such criterion can be sustained, and going along with appearances is our only option. If this radical version of *pk*-scepticism is correct, it is not just that philosophy has nothing to say about appearances and thus cannot guide us in pursuit of the good life. The consequences are devastating for our commonsense epistemic intuitions: no normative discriminations can be made among appearances – none of our beliefs is justified at all!

The end of philosophy

In the *Outlines*, Sextus maintains that: "Anyone who holds beliefs on even one subject, or in general prefers one appearance to another in point of convincingness or lack of convincingness, or makes assertions about any unclear matter, thereby has the distinctive character of a Dogmatist" (I. 223). Sextus regards the Academic Sceptic as proceeding "in a sceptical fashion" in so far as he recommends withholding assent from the non-apparent. Nevertheless, he views any attempt to discriminate criterially between appearances on the grounds of their relative convincingness as constituting an abandonment of the "distinctive character of Scepticism" (I. 222) and a lapse back into Dogmatism. For Sextus, then, the Academic Sceptic's need for a criterion like the 'convincing' constitutes his shared commitment to the Dogmatist's idea that philosophy provides some *positive* and *critical* guidance to what the good life is and how to live it (answering the normative question). That is to say, Sextus takes the Academic as a negative Dogmatist who positively advances *epoche* on the grounds that he *p*-knows that knowledge is impossible, and who positively advances an alternative criterion of action.

This view of the Academic Sceptic shares much with the contemporary 'dialectical interpretation', and we considered an alternative interpretation in the preceding section. What we must now consider is the neo-Pyrrhonian response to the Essential Problem. From Sextus's perspective *epoche* cannot be positively recommended as good, in so far as it leads to tranquillity (*ataraxia*), the goal of life. Since there is no criterion, even of convincingness, all appearances are equal. Not only can he *not* assert (the truth of) high-order philosophical beliefs like 'tranquillity is the aim of life', 'all things are incomprehensible', and '*epoche* will lead to tranquillity'; he cannot even find such claims more convincing than any rivals. For Sextus the *objective* criterion of truth and the *subjective* criterion of convincingness (or Arcesilaus's 'reasonable') are equally insupportable.

So what is the alternative? As Sextus envisages it,

> Scepticism is an ability to set out oppositions among things which appear and are thought of in any way at all, an ability by which, because of the equipollence (*isostheneia*) in the shared objects and accounts, we come first to suspension of judgement (*epoche*) and afterwards to tranquillity (*ataraxia*). (I. 8)

The idea that scepticism is an ability is key here: it is not conceived as an item of *p*-knowledge but as a dialectical ability to contrast any argument that an interlocutor puts forward with another that is equally convincing (equipollent). Suspension of judgement is not therefore warranted by an appeal to the incognitive nature of things, for as Sextus argues, "the Sceptic expects it to be possible for some things actually to be apprehended" (I. 26). Indeed, to assume otherwise is the hallmark of the negative Dogmatism Sextus attributes to the Academic Sceptic; although until that apprehension actually occurs one *should* suspend judgement. Similarly, tranquillity is not guaranteed by the withholding of assent: again, it would be silly to withhold assent in the (albeit unlikely) case of a genuine apprehension, for no lack of tranquillity could derive from knowledge of the truth. The desire to know which things one should assent to (to distinguish between truth and falsity) was originally motivated by the Dogmatic philosophical assumption that tranquillity would ensue. It is, as it were, a *contingent* discovery of the Sceptic that tranquillity follows from withholding assent to the equipollent, and not from the Dogmatic pursuit of knowledge. It is this discovery that gives the 'should' in 'one should suspend judgement' its normative force.

On this account Sextus can be regarded as addressing the shortcomings we identified with the dialectical interpretation of the Academic position. Of course, if no criterion of truth emerges (even contingently) from the exchange of dialectically opposed alternatives, what are we to say about the practical condition? Since Sextus maintains that invoking the reasonable or convincing simply reaffirms the Dogmatic assumption that *p*-knowledge is the guide to the good life, there is no lesser form of 'belief' that falls short of the criterion of truth but which nevertheless could be distinguished from the non-apparent. Given what we saw of Pyrrho, the standard for action is unsurprisingly "what is apparent, implicitly meaning by this the appearances" (I. 22). Sextus is more forthcoming about the 'content' of the apparent, which consists in: "guidance by nature, necessitation by feelings, handing down of laws and customs, and teaching of kinds of expertise" (I. 23). In Chapter 3 we'll see this advertence to the norms of tradition re-emerge; for the time being we have something like the following. Seeking tranquillity (freedom from falsity), the reflective individual leaves behind the standards of action that are apparent to her (those found in 'common life') and begins a philosophical investigation in order to discover the knowledge that she believes will lead her to it. Encountering dissent everywhere (Stoics and Epicureans, for example – dissent more troubling that anything to be found in common life) she comes to see that in the realm of philosophical reasoning all speculation is on a par with respect to convincingness. Given this equivalence, the suspension of judgement is natural: if no one theory is any more convincing than another it would be arbitrary to assent to *any*. Fortuitously, the enquirer discovers that this withholding of assent actually issues in the sort of tranquillity that she'd originally been seeking. Philosophy discovers its self-negating justification in its failure to achieve the end it set itself: the pursuit of tranquillity. When she 'returns' to common life, then, our reflective individual finds that its standards provided all the motivation required for action. Moreover, if any investigation of the legitimacy of these standards is suggested in the future (by herself or some other) by the invocation of a new standard (the 'reasonable', say, or 'convincing'), she re-enters the realm of philosophical debate and counterposes it with an equally reasonable or convincing alternative. Tranquillity is restored.

This is the extreme form of *pk*-scepticism. In the absence of any criterion, what is 'apparent' in common life is the standard and it is entirely 'insulated' from philosophical speculation. In other words, philosophical reflection cannot issue in a critique, illumination or even a legitimation of what nature, feeling and tradition tell us. If the Sceptic poses any theory that seeks to undermine the authority of appearances, that is merely to counterbalance one that seeks to legitimate or justify them. This insulation of common life from philosophy is a fundamental challenge to the very idea of critical reflection. If the neo-Pyrrhonian is 'correct', moving away from the fixedness or givenness of the apparent leads one to a 'philosophical space' in which nothing can be settled. Reflection on our practices is a senseless distraction: no p-knowing makes itself evident (although the Sceptic is happy to acknowledge that it might) and thus none of our beliefs is justified (at least as an internalist would understand justification).

Of course, to talk about the neo-Pyrrhonian being 'correct' cannot indicate going beyond appearances and making a claim about how things really are. There is no standard of correctness here, just the situation as one finds it once one has acquired the ability ('expertise') that Scepticism is. Where the Stoic has to achieve the state that constitutes satisfaction of the full competency requirement in order to become a sage, the would-be Sceptic has to be able to field oppositions in the 'dialectical space' of philosophical argument when the need arises. Sextus's work is primarily a handbook containing guidance on how to do this. Just as being able to ride a bicycle is not itself reducible to propositional knowledge, and cannot be achieved just from reading about it, there is no p-knowing that knowledge is impossible that constitutes the state of being a Sceptic, although the availability of certain standard forms of argument (like the instruction to push down on the pedals) can help one on one's way.

The majority of book I of the *Outlines* is turned over to a discussion of the ten modes of Aenesidimus and the five modes of Agrippa,[15] general strategies for the generation of opposing points of view that will lead to *epoche*. The ten modes are essentially different ways of emphasizing the relativity of appearances: the fact that how things appear depends on the perceiving subject, the object perceived, and the relations between them. For example, a bird sees in black and white and we see in colour; honey tastes sweet to me, but sour to someone else; a barn appears small in the distance, but tall close up; we see things differently when we're asleep to when we're awake. Given such variation, "we shall be able to say what the existing objects are like as observed by us, but as to what they are like in their nature we shall suspend judgement" (I. 59). The real danger in the Sceptic's armoury is the distant progenitor of what we encountered in Chapter 1 as the Agrippan argument. It occurs in its purest form in the five modes of Agrippa (I. 164–177): Dispute, Infinity, Relativity, Hypothesis and Circularity. The modes of Dispute and Relativity can be thought of as dialectical preliminaries that foreground the question of justification. Relativity shows that, as in the above examples, appearances are given to enormous variation; Dispute is the equivalent among ideas, be they arguments in common life or the disagreements among philosophers. As appearances these give rise to no conflicts here: *that* the telephone box appears red to one person but grey to another – or *that* Stoics think this and Epicureans that – does not generate a dispute. However, when *S* says that the box *is* red and *R* that it *is* grey, or when a Stoic says that matter is one and an Epicurean that it is divided, I am entitled to ask them to justify their views: to tell me what the criterion is that allows them to distinguish between what is real/true/knowledge and what is appearance/false/opinion. We have already seen both examples of the use of a criterion (Stoics and Epicureans) and criticisms of it (Academics). The neo-Pyrrhonian response is more general. With the invocation of a criterion, the Dogmatist enters the realm of philosophical debate, hotly pursued by the Sceptic who now asks him how he justifies his choice of criterion. At this point he has three choices, to each of which one of the remaining modes corresponds.

- Mode of Infinity: he offers another criterion, in response to which the Sceptic asks him how that is justified and the process goes on indefinitely, or chooses another option.
- Mode of Hypothesis: he refuses to give further reasons and make a dogmatic assumption, which as such is as lacking in justification as any other assumption.
- Mode of Circularity: he gives the same criterion or justification as before, thus reasoning in a circle.

Consider our book example once more. Its opening sentence is

(q_1) All and only the odd-numbered sentences in the book are true.

If I decided to live my life and dispense advice to others on the basis of this book, someone might rightly ask how I know that (q_1) is true, and hence that I am justified in believing that the odd-numbered sentences in the book are true? I might of course respond that (q_1) is itself odd-numbered and therefore true, but that would clearly be to argue in a circle (mode of Circularity).

Now imagine a different book, otherwise identical but whose second sentence is

(q_2) All and only the even-numbered sentences written in this book are true.

How would we know which if either of the books were correct? We could of course dogmatically assert that one or the other is correct (mode of Hypothesis), but we wouldn't be able to further justify our choice. Alternatively, we might continue our search and discover a third book, containing one proposition only:

(r_1) q_1 is true.

We now have a justification for distinguishing between the first two books, and a way of escaping from the charge of circularity that comes from asserting (q_1) alone; but what are our grounds for believing (r_1)? Perhaps another book will assert that:

(s_1) q_2 is true.

This will leave us having to look for yet another book to resolve the matter, threatening an endless search through a limitless pile of books (mode of Infinity).

Ancient Scepticism and the theoretical attitude

Sceptics and Dogmatists agree that any value accruing to philosophical enquiry derives from its practical role in guiding human beings towards achieving happiness. Their disagreement concerns whether or not philosophy has a positive role in bringing about that aim through the theoretical identification of a criterion of truth. The neo-Pyrrhonian Sceptic wants to relieve himself and others of the distress that comes from being burdened with the responsibility of discovering such a criterion. It is only if we abandon the quest for knowledge of how to live happily that we will achieve happiness!

The striking difference between the concerns of the Ancient philosophers and those of contemporary dogmatists is that an explicitly practical interest in human happiness is absent from the work of the latter. As we saw in Chapter 1, epistemology is oriented towards a theoretical understanding of knowledge, not a consideration of its relation to the practical pursuit of the good life. True, the contemporary dogmatist thinks that knowledge is a good thing and that people with knowledge are in a better position to make rational judgements than people with just opinions; but they don't think that epistemology *per se* will make us any happier and professional epistemologists are no happier than the rest of us!

Ironically it is this very disengagement of epistemology from the practical that makes it susceptible to *pk*-scepticism. Since epistemologists already suppose that practical ends play no role in the elaboration of a philosophical theory of knowledge, they grant from the outset what the *pk*-sceptic wishes to establish; namely, that philosophical theory and common life are 'insulated' from one another. It is because of this insulation that the Agrippan argument has the seemingly devastating consequences it does. Since the epistemologist's philosophical ambitions involve adopting the theoretical attitude, only a theoretical solution will suffice. However, once the attempt is made to justify taking an appearance or belief as anything more than the way it is presented in common life, the sceptic and the dogmatist enter a realm of argument in which a theoretical-philosophical justification of beliefs seems impossible to achieve. The Agrippan argument appears to undermine our sense that the discriminations we make among our beliefs on the basis of their relative justificatory status is legitimate. Accordingly, we lose our grip on the idea that *any* belief is justified, and consequently that we can be cognitively responsible at all.

We have now seen how the Agrippan argument emerged historically as part of a philosophical assault on the idea of *p*-knowledge. We have also seen what sort of challenge it poses for the contemporary dogmatists who hope to acquire *p*-knowledge and among whom we must consequently include both *heroic* and *rejectionist* epistemologists. Finally, we've noted that the project of contemporary epistemology breaks with that of the Ancients in so far as it is not oriented towards a practical concern with the good life but involves adopting the theoretical attitude. This determines that what it is to be a knower and thus what it is to be cognitively responsible are different. For the Ancient, knowledge relates to an overall state of the person who is happy, and their responsibility extends as far as the achievement of that state. For the contemporary epistemologist knowledge relates to whether or not someone's attitude (belief) towards a particular proposition (q) satisfies the appropriate conditions, and their responsibility is restricted to ensuring where possible that those conditions are satisfied.

The change from a practical to a theoretical orientation in epistemology is associated with Descartes. As we noted in Chapter 1, Descartes is also customarily associated with the argument from ignorance. In Chapter 3 we will thus turn our attention to this change in orientation, and look at how it relates to both the Agrippan argument and the argument from ignorance. Before we leave the Ancients, however, it is important to note that we have identified two distinct form of pk-scepticism. Like the neo-Pyrrhonian, the Academic Sceptic has nothing to fear from the Agrippan argument because he too can use it dialectically against any dogmatist who tries to take up the theoretical attitude. Where he differs is that he allows that the engagement with philosophical theories might illuminate some of the features of common life and give us a better understanding of the nature and extent of our justificatory practices. Philosophical enquiry is therefore not completely 'insulated' from common life; combating dogmatism is a way of elucidating or clarifying the realm of the practical–apparent rather than a prelude to offering an alternative dogmatism.

This Therapeutic Interpretation runs somewhat counter to Sextus's own reconstruction of the Academic's position, but that need not necessarily trouble us. Sextus was writing some 300 years or so after Carneades, and the sources are incomplete and contradictory. He was also well aware that the Academic Sceptics offered a competing account of the nature and purpose of philosophy (as Scepticism). More importantly, there is a significant strand of Academic thought running through the subsequent history of scepticism. Although these versions of scepticism do not share the same degree of orientation towards the living of a good life that characterizes the thought of the Ancients, they do suggest a way of thinking about knowledge and ourselves as knowers that allows us to resist the complete insulation of theoretical reflection from practical activity. Indeed, as I suggested at the end of Chapter 1, if the attachment of *heroic* and *rejectionist* epistemologies to the theoretical attitude necessarily makes them vulnerable to the Agrippan argument, a Therapeutic–Academic *sceptical* response to such epistemological theorizing might be the best way of dealing with traditional sceptical problems – using a version of *pk*-scepticism to cure us of the thinking that leads to scepticism. In Chapter 3 we will therefore extend our understanding of what a contemporary Therapeutic–Academic position might be by counterbalancing an account of Descartes's thought with an evaluation of the naturalism of David Hume. As we will see, this too has implications for what it is to be a knower and what the consequent limits of cognitive responsibility are.

Demons, doubt and common life

Introduction

For most philosophers, the *Meditations on First Philosophy* (1641) marks the beginning of a new phase in the long history of scepticism. As we saw in Chapter 1, foundationalism is one attempt to respond to the Agrippan argument, which threatens the idea that any of our beliefs are justified. Descartes's 'First Philosophy' is the original systematic attempt to formulate such a response. Crucially, he uses scepticism in a methodologically constructive way to advance his foundational project and in doing so gives rise to another sort of sceptical problem, which we have associated with the argument from ignorance. The task for the first part of this chapter is to examine how the emergence of this new form of scepticism relates to the disengagement of epistemology from a practical concern with the good life and with the theoretical attitude. As we saw in Chapter 2, the idea of cognitive responsibility for the Ancients is linked to the achievement of a practical goal and thus with a certain idea of what sort of thing the responsible knower is. Part of this task will therefore be to investigate what cognitive responsibility amounts to when practical concerns are eliminated, and what new concept of the knowing subject emerges as a result.

The association of Descartes's philosophical method with a response to the Agrippan argument is not arbitrary. The works of Sextus and other Ancient Sceptics were rediscovered in the sixteenth century and had a profound influence on the direction of European thought and culture in the hundred or so years before the *Meditations* appeared.[1] This period threw up more than just an opposition between neo-Pyrrhonians and dogmatists, however; it presaged the return of a more moderate, 'mitigated', scepticism. Resembling the thought of the Academics more than that of the neo-Pyrrhonians, this 'therapeutic' scepticism seeks to undercut theoretical attitude doubt by attacking the unbounded use of reflection/reason but without denying it any role whatsoever. As such it articulates a different understanding of human capacities – of what we are – and a different appreciation of what philosophy can achieve. In the English-speaking philosophical tradition the most influential of these 'mitigated sceptics' is David Hume, and an evaluation of Hume's scepticism is the task for the second part of this chapter. Before turning to Descartes and then Hume, we'll look briefly at the crisis that the rediscovery of Ancient Sceptical thought brought about.

The *crise pyrrhonienne*

As Popkin notes, "The problem of finding a criterion of truth, first raised in theological disputes, was then later raised with regard to natural knowledge, leading to the *crise pyrrhonienne* of the early seventeenth century" (1979: 1). The original disputes to which Popkin refers took place during the Reformation, when theologians such as Luther contested the spiritual authority of the Catholic Church and argued that the criterion of religious knowledge is what strikes each individual conscience upon reading scripture. With the Agrippan mode of Dispute already much in evidence, this prompted a typically neo-Pyrrhonian question from the conservative Erasmus; namely, how does Luther know that he has hit upon the correct interpretation of scripture? To offer another criterion in response raises the further question of how *that* is to be justified, threatening an infinite regress (mode of Infinity). Similarly, invoking conviction or conscience again involves arguing in a circle (mode of Circularity). Finally, a dogmatic avowal that that is just the way it is (mode of Hypothesis) simply reinforces the fact that here is a disagreement standing in need of a criterion (mode of Dispute).

In the absence of a reasoned response to this dispute, the *pk*-sceptical lesson was clear to Erasmus: one should 'go along with appearances'; and in this context going along with appearances meant conforming to the traditional authority of the Church. This sceptical insouciance appalled Luther: "A Christian ought to be certain of what he affirms, or else he is not a Christian . . . Anathema to the Christian who will not be certain of what he is supposed to believe, and who does not comprehend it. How can he believe that which he doubts?"[2] Since no question could be more pressing than one's relationship with God, one can perhaps appreciate Luther's desire for certitude. The Greek concern with living a good life was now transformed into a concern for one's immortal soul. In the context of eternity, seeking 'tranquillity' in the form of an uncritical faith in an external authority must have seemed unbearable once one was seized by doubt. When certainty is only available to enquirers who can discover in themselves no reason to doubt, the idea of a subjective warrant derived from personal encounters with the legitimate word of God becomes compelling.

The problem of a criterion for religious knowledge thus set the scene for the debate between conservative and reformist elements. If, on the one hand, one could only look to oneself for the criterion of certainty, how could one distinguish between a genuine encounter with the truth and a merely psychological disposition to believe? The mere fact of disagreement about the meaning of scripture threatened to undermine the idea that there is such a criterion at all. On the other hand, the Church's external authority was itself derived from a long series of other people's claims to have discovered (often incompatible) truths for themselves. What grounds were there for favouring their beliefs over the reformist's own?

Calvin's response to the problem of the criterion is particularly revealing: if a truth were to be recognized as such, then it must be on the basis of an overwhelming encounter that was not based on any rational criterion, and was not therefore susceptible to the threat of a regress. Indeed, such a self-evidencing 'inner persuasion' must be so overwhelming that the very idea that a criterion might be needed could never arise. In such a cognitive context doubt would be simply inconceivable. Of course, the neo-Pyrrhonian might point out that while S claims to be persuaded by q, R claims to be equally persuaded by not-q, in which case 'inner persuasion' cannot be sufficient for truth and some other criterion is required. Calvin's response to this line was brutal: only the 'elect' will recognize the truth *as the truth*. On this account what I called the Full

Competency Requirement is given its Christian apotheosis. Where the Stoic sage is required to discipline himself to achieve a perfect rational accommodation with nature (and so assent to all and only cognitive impressions), his Christian counterpart has been chosen to be a knower by God.[3]

With Ancient Sceptical arguments being used to fuel both sides of the debate, it soon became apparent that they were applicable to not only theological but also scientific and philosophical claims to knowledge. The stage was thus set for the rapid unravelling of much of what remained of the medieval worldview as humanists and freethinkers attacked the morals and Aristotelian science of their day. Throughout the early seventeenth century, 'mitigated' sceptics like Mersenne and Gassendi tried to set limits on the destructive effects of the *crise pyrrhonienne* and open up a conceptual 'space' for the emerging experimental sciences to develop in. As Popkin notes, however "a new dogmatism had to develop and be demolished before this new solution to the *crise pyrrhonienne* could be accepted" (1979: 129). We'll examine one strain of this 'new solution' when we turn to Hume in the latter sections of this chapter. First we need to look at the philosopher who provided that dogmatism by teaching his age "the art of making Scepticism give birth to philosophical Certainty".[4]

The quest for certainty: from the book of the world to the book of the mind[5]

Descartes's first published work, the *Discourse on Method*, appeared in 1637. Structured in the form of an intellectual quest, Descartes's narrative draws heavily on the related themes of cognitive responsibility and methodological internalism. It begins by charting the author's progress from an unquestioning faith in the possibility of scientific knowledge to a moment of Socratic self-awareness:

> From my childhood I have been nourished upon letters, and . . . was persuaded that by their means one could acquire a clear and certain knowledge of all that is useful in life . . . But as soon as I had completed the course of study . . . I completely changed my opinion. For I found myself beset by so many doubts and errors that I came to think I had gained nothing

from my attempts to become educated but increasing recognition of my ignorance . . . This made me feel free to judge all others by reference to myself and think there was no knowledge in the world such as I had previously been led to hope for.
(*AT* VI: 4–5)

The general disillusionment extended to the claims of philosophy: "It has been cultivated for many centuries by the most excellent minds and yet there is still no point in it which is not disputed and hence doubtful" (*ibid.*: 8). The awareness of his own state of ignorance leads Descartes to conclude that it would be unwise to assume that others actually do possess the knowledge they claim to. Indeed, he finds that among the sciences it is only mathematics that does not disappoint "because of the certainty and self-evidence of its reasonings" (*ibid.*: 7).

In the next stage of his journey in search of truth, Descartes turns away from the pursuits of the learned and towards the wider world of practical experiences and activities:

For it seemed to me that much more truth could be found in the reasonings which a man makes concerning matters that concern him than in those which some scholar makes in his study about speculative matters.   (*Ibid.*: 9)

In common life, however, scarcely less contradiction was to be found than among the philosophers: what one nation, tribe, cultural group or person found acceptable, another found distasteful. Reflecting the conclusion drawn from his enquiries in the realm of the theoretical, the diversity of such beliefs showed that in practical life too the reasonings of others could offer no infallible guide to the truth. Here too, then, he would have to 'judge all others' by the standards he set for himself. Since Descartes acknowledges that his own beliefs are in all likelihood also held on merely customary grounds, "which may obscure our natural light and make us less capable of heeding reason", he concludes that his task is to purge himself of these. To that end he resolves to set aside his studies in 'the book of the world' and "to undertake studies within myself too and to use all the powers of my mind in choosing the paths I should follow" (*ibid.*: 10).

This section of the *Discourse* introduces an important variation on a sceptical theme. Reminding us that in theoretical-philosophical life opinions differ introduces the mode of Dispute. At this point we would anticipate the neo-Pyrrhonian trying to draw the dogmatist into committing himself to the identification of a criterion, and then subjecting him to the embarrassment of the Agrippan argument. In response the neo-Pyrrhonian would recommend going along with appearances; that is to say, with traditional views. As Descartes implies, however, this 'solution' is not available to the cosmopolitan inhabitant of the seventeenth century: there is just as much dispute in the realm of the practical as there is in the realm of the theoretical. It is no longer at all clear what 'going along with appearances' could signify.

Setting aside the 'book of the world', then, Descartes turns to what one might call the 'book of the mind' and asserts the cognitive priority of the subject's self-scrutiny. Knowing that others don't know leads to the only apparent alternative, the ontological internalist's conviction that the contents of one's own mind provide the source of justification.[6] Although not confident at this stage of actually discovering anything, Descartes nevertheless has the 'certainty and self-evidence' of mathematical reasoning to encourage him. As one of the outstanding mathematicians of his time, Descartes was aware that trust in such reasoning did not constitute a violation of the decision 'to judge all others' by reference to himself. Moreover, reflection on it provides Descartes with the guide to discerning the method that he will use to pursue his (methodologically and ontologically) internalist enquiry. It consists of four precepts:

1. "Never to accept anything as true if I did not have evident knowledge of its truth . . . to include nothing more in my judgements than what presented itself to my mind so clearly and so distinctly that I had not occasion to doubt it."
2. "To divide each of the difficulties I examined into as many parts as possible."
3. "To direct my thoughts in an orderly manner, by beginning with the simplest and most easily known objects in order to ascend . . . to knowledge of the most complex" (*AT* VI: 18).
4. "To make enumerations so complete . . . that I could be sure of leaving nothing out" (*ibid.*: 19).

The metaphysical 'results' of Descartes's study are sketched in the *Discourse*, but it is to his subsequent masterpiece that we must turn to see the full impact of his thought and its implications for contemporary scepticism.

Cartesian scepticism

The first of the six *Meditations*[7] begins with a pithy reminder of the autobiographical theme of the *Discourse*: "Some years ago I was struck by the large number of falsehoods that I had accepted as true in my childhood, and by the doubtful nature of the whole edifice that I had subsequently based on them" (*AT* VII: 17). As we saw above, Descartes's response to the sceptic suggests a methodological reorientation towards the thinker investigating the powers of his own mind. He links this turn 'inwards' with the possibility of providing knowledge with the support required to avoid any future sceptical attack: "I realized that it was necessary, once in the course of my life, to demolish everything completely and start again right from the foundations if I wanted to establish anything at all in the sciences that was stable and likely to last" (*ibid.*: 17). With the assumption that the search for foundations will involve the thinker's self-scrutiny, Descartes states something like methodological precept (1): "Reason now leads me to think that I should hold back my assent from opinions which are not completely certain and indubitable just as carefully as I do from those that are patently false" (*ibid.*: 18).

Although none of the other precepts are introduced formally, they are nevertheless applied in what follows. Descartes recognizes that the task of subjecting each and every individual belief to inspection is impossible. If, however, we can identify the principles that justify beliefs of a certain sort, any doubts raised about the legitimacy of those principles will suffice to show that we should withhold assent from them all. If we alight on one or more general principles that cannot be doubted, then we have hit those epistemic 'foundations' of knowledge. Posing and then answering a radical form of scepticism promises a 'First Philosophy' that puts science beyond the reach of any subsequent doubt.

Descartes begins his implicit dialogue with the sceptic by suggesting that the senses are customarily taken to be our criterion of truth. Although we do on occasion make mistakes these can nevertheless be corrected on the basis of more immediate experiences. A barn may look round from a distance, but close up we can assure ourselves that it is square. At this point we can well imagine the Stoic attempting to identify the conditions for a criterial impression. Similarly, we could anticipate an Academic Sceptic's response: nothing in the nature of such an experience guarantees that it represents its object (comes from what 'is' as opposed to what 'is not'). Rather than draw attention to the possibility of error in this piecemeal way, Descartes exploits the ontological internalist's standpoint to offer an alternative description of our epistemic situation:

> How often, asleep at night, am I convinced of just such familiar events – that I am here in my dressing-gown, sitting by the fire – when in fact I am lying undressed in bed! . . . As I think about this more carefully, I see plainly that there are never any sure signs by means of which being awake can be distinguished from being asleep. (*AT* VII: 19)

This is often taken to be an example of – indeed, the inspiration for – the argument from ignorance, which we examined in Chapter 1. The problem is that if we do not have a criterion for distinguishing waking experiences from dreaming experiences we cannot eliminate a possibility (dreaming) that on the face of it is incompatible with our claim to know things about the external world. We cannot demonstrate that we do know what we think we know.

In terms of Descartes' enquiry, then, if science is to have an epistemic foundation it cannot be one that relies on the senses alone. Nevertheless, as Descartes goes on to note, the fact that I do not know that any of my beliefs about the external world are true does not rule out other candidates for truth. There are, for example, the very truths that Descartes never doubted when he entertained his scepticism about philosophy and common life: the mathematical reasonings that kept alive faith in certitude. Surely, even if I am dreaming it is impossible to doubt that $2 + 3 = 5$ or that a square has four sides! According to Descartes's methodology, if one cannot doubt them they must be true. It is in response to this position that he introduces his second sceptical possibility.

He begins by noting that he has rooted in his mind the idea of an omnipotent God who could, should he so desire, ensure that certain things appeared to him as indubitable even if they were not true. Indeed, since some people make mistakes about even the most basic calculations, how does one know that every time one adds 2 to 3 one does not arrive at a falsehood? Doing the sum over and over again does not give us the possibility of rectifying an error since there is no check on truth independent of the feeling of assurance that comes from doing the calculation the first time (this might not be the case when doing a more complex sum). Alternatively, imagine that as a result of some particular cultural circumstance or odd evolutionary process human beings found certain beliefs impossible to doubt. Here we would have a sort of psychological indubitability that is entirely consistent with the falsity of what is believed.

If this were possible, then it would seem that the search for certainty requires that one withhold assent from even these beliefs. As Descartes remarks, however, doubting them seems far less reasonable than assenting to them, and this is particularly the case after years of habitual and confident assent. Given the foundational nature of the enquiry, however, the very possibility of falsity has to be ruled out, and this requires extending the realm of doubt to even these beliefs. But how do we make ourselves doubt that $2 + 3 = 5$ – a belief that we have assented to without question for most of our lives – in order to rule out the possibility that we are merely psychologically disposed to believe it? Descartes's solution is that one must break the bonds of custom and habit by *willing* oneself not to believe – make oneself deceive oneself. To aid us in this task of training the mind he suggests that henceforth he will imagine not a benevolent God, but a malevolent demon whose task is to ensure that all our beliefs are false, even those that by their very nature seem to demand assent.

The idea of the *malin génie* thus generalizes the most extreme level of doubt by driving a wedge between our strongest criterion of justification and truth. Not only do we have no criterion for distinguishing between veridical and non-veridical experiences of the external world, but now no criterion that presents itself in terms of psychological indubitability will suffice for discriminating truths from falsehoods. The *malin génie* extends the attack on epistemic foundations to metaphysical foundations, thus fully elucidating the task confronting a 'First Philosophy'. Is there any belief whose indubitability could not be merely apparent? After summarizing the findings of the first *Meditation*, Descartes famously finds one:

> there is a deceiver of supreme power and cunning who is delib-
> erately and constantly deceiving me. In that case I undoubtedly
> exist, if he is deceiving me; and let him deceive me as much as
> he can, he will never bring it about that I am nothing so long as
> I think that I am something. So after considering everything
> very thoroughly, I must finally conclude that this proposition, *I
> am, I exist*, is necessarily true whenever it is put forward by me
> or conceived in my mind.   (*AT* VII: 25)

The *cogito* (I think) becomes the basis for Descartes's 'First Philosophy' – the rational foundation upon which science can build.
Having established it he quickly goes on to perceive that since one
cannot doubt that one exists when one contemplates the question
of one's existence, thinking itself constitutes the essence of that
existence. Moreover, since I can continue to doubt that the external
world exists (I still don't know that I'm not dreaming or that there
isn't a *malin génie*), the sceptical possibilities reaffirm the ontological internalist view that it is to the contents of my mind alone that I
must turn in order to pursue the project of justification.

Having established a datum of certainty – the *cogito* – Descartes
proceeds to establish the metaphysical foundations of our knowledge: the existence of a non-deceiving deity, the so-called 'real
distinction' between mind and body, and the existence of the external world. By the end of the *Meditations* we have bought back our
epistemic warrant: "[we] should not have any further fears about
the falsity of what [the] senses tell [us] every day; on the contrary,
the exaggerated doubts of the last few days should be dismissed as
laughable" (*AT* VII: 89). The influence of Descartes's great work
cannot be overstated, but it is his sceptical arguments and not his
positive metaphysical picture that contemporary philosophers
continue to find of *explicit* interest. (The *implicit* influence is more
complicated.) Nevertheless, the idea of using a sceptical method to
reaffirm the possibility of a dogmatic metaphysics is important,
and invites comparison with the varieties of scepticism we have
encountered so far. In the next section we'll look more closely at
Descartes's sceptical strategy with an eye to doing precisely that.

The *cogito* and the theoretical attitude

First, it should be noted that Descartes does not envisage that his scepticism will have any effect on how one lives one's life. Contemplating the extreme doubt required to overcome the psychological disposition to believe, he notes that "no danger" will result from his plan "because the task now in hand does not involve action but merely the acquisition of knowledge" (*AT* VII: 22). What we are asked to do, then, is to take a particular standpoint on our beliefs that insulates them from their ordinary contexts of evaluation – those in which they provide reasons for action.

This account of 'insulation' recalls to mind the Ancient Sceptics. For Sextus, the insulation of philosophical reflection from common life is achieved by training oneself in (for example) the modes of Agrippa. This renders one immune to the disquiet that derives from reflecting on appearances in order to justify them as reasons (criteria) for action. As we saw, the neo-Pyrrhonian restriction on reflection extended to a rejection of even the 'mitigated' Academic Sceptics' criterion of 'conviction'. The point is that for the neo-Pyrrhonian the insulation of common life from philosophical reflection takes place from *within* the realm of the practical.

For Descartes the situation is reversed. In order to radicalize doubt to the point of achieving certain knowledge, the enquirer has to train his mind to *bracket out* any thoughts relating to the practical realm of common life. Only in this way will he be able to overthrow the influence of custom and habit and contemplate all possible sources of error. This is the purpose of the dreaming and *malin génie* thought-experiments. Here philosophical enquiry is insulated from common life and rendered purely theoretical from within enquiry itself. When one adopts the theoretical attitude one takes up the standpoint of the pure enquirer who has eliminated all thoughts of the practical from his reflections on knowledge. As such, the knower is no longer like the Stoic, who regards himself as responsible for the practical life he lives. Instead the knower is 'pure' and disinterested *cogito*, responsible only to the demands of theoretical reflection.

At the end of Chapter 2 I remarked that the theoretical attitude leaves the epistemologist particularly vulnerable to the Agrippan argument. I have now associated the emergence of that attitude with Descartes's use of doubt in pursuit of certain foundations. The question now is how Descartes's attempts to uncover some guide to truth using indubitability. Aware of the Agrippan argument, Descartes knows that 'the way of the criterion' is self-defeating, since to suggest one as a justification for believing that q invites the plausible question how one knows that this form of justification is adequate. How then to establish a foundation for knowledge *without* a criterion? What the *malin génie* possibility presents is a challenge to any criterion: one has no reasons for holding that any of one's beliefs are true. Even the apparent unavoidability of belief is deemed insufficient as a guide to truth. If, however, there is something that I *cannot* doubt – if I cannot even conceive the possibility that the indubitability attending it *is* merely psychological – then what I have encountered is a primitive truth.

For Descartes the 'I am, I exist' constitutes this primitive truth. Unlike the cognitive impression of the Stoic, there is no sense here of a logical gap between the belief and the assent I give it. I do not recognize the presence as it were of a criterion of truth and *as a result* assent to the thought. Consider the book example from Chapter 2. The idea was that I should assent to (say) q_{119} because it satisfies the criterion of truth (being an odd-numbered sentence). This suggests a deduction along the lines of a syllogism:

All odd-numbered sentences are true
(q_{119}) is an odd-numbered sentence

Therefore

(q_{119}) is true.

Descartes's primitive truth does not function like this. As he notes in a reply to Mersenne, "When someone says 'I am thinking, therefore I am, or I exist', he does not deduce existence from thought by means of a syllogism, but recognizes it as something self-evident *by a simple intuition of the mind*" (*AT* VII: 140, emphasis added). The parallel is rather with the following:

(q_1) All and only the odd-numbered sentences in the book are true.

When I read this, I don't note that the sentence is odd-numbered and thereby *deduce* that it is true. After all, it is only if I understand that the sentence is true that I know that being odd *is* the criterion of truth. To claim to know that q_1 is true on the grounds of its oddness would be to argue as follows:

All odd-numbered sentences are true (q_1)
(q_1) is an odd-numbered sentence

Therefore

(q_1) is true.

This is the sort of circular reasoning that the Agrippan argument is intended to bring about. To operate as a datum of certainty, then, q_1 must be something that we recognize as self-evidently true 'by a simple intuition of the mind'. To understand it is to understand that it is true. This is how the 'I am, I exist' is to be understood: the awareness of the necessity of my existence in the thought of my existence is grasped intuitively in the act of thinking itself.

The upshot of this is that since no criterion is being invoked, the Agrippan argument does not threaten. Descartes then goes on to inspect this simple, self-grounding belief for some criterion that will serve as a guide for expanding his knowledge (cf. precept 3): "I now seem able to lay it down as a general rule that whatever I perceive very clearly and distinctly is true" (*AT* VII: 35). Descartes acknowledges that since this did not serve *as* the criterion for the basic belief it would not be sufficient if it ever turned out that something he perceived with that property were in fact false.[8] This naturally reminds us of those beliefs that stood the test of the dream possibility and for which the idea of the *malin génie* was introduced. If I now turn to the consideration of, for example, $2 + 3 = 5$, I discover that it is in fact attended by the same clarity and distinctness as the *cogito*. Indeed, I am so convinced by its truth (and the truth of propositions like it) when I focus my attention on it there remains only a "very slight and so to speak, metaphysical" doubt (*ibid.*: 36).[9]

The following might therefore be a response to the neo-Pyrrhonian. It is indeed the search for a criterion of truth that leads us astray. The mistake is to think that our enquiry has anything to do with *practical* life, and that this has to be insulated from the unsettling effects of philosophical reflection. Once we appreciate that our enquiry is from the start *theoretical* we see that the failure to find a criterion does not necessitate a return to appearances. Rather, when we clear our minds of prejudice and contemplate indubitable truths without distraction we see that they stand in no need of a justificatory criterion because they are self-evidencing. The *malin génie* reveals this by making us focus on the simplest of those beliefs: one cannot be distracted from an awareness of the existence of oneself while entertaining the thought with that content. Where the *Outlines* was a training manual to help us resist philosophical distractions, the *Meditations* trains us to block the demand for a criterion that may arise within our everyday lives as a result of the disputes one sees all around. It arms us against any subsequent threat of the Agrippan argument by providing a 'First' – true – philosophy.

Scepticism unbound

Whatever the appeal of Descartes's approach, a number of problems present themselves, most of which relate to the character of ontological internalism. The most fundamental is the charge that Descartes does not in fact establish *any* datum of certainty. As Schelling (and before him Leibniz) noted, objective thinking goes on even when I am not aware of it, so the thinking and the 'I' that reflects on it are two different things and not an immediate identity. Maybe I'm wrong in thinking that the thinking that was going on is my thinking, in which case 'I think, I exist' has no more force than 'I walk, I exist'.[10] This might sound rather convoluted, but it offers possible support to another (more modern) claim: that Descartes *presupposes* a particular theory of mind in order to be able to formulate his sceptical arguments.[11] If that could be demonstrated it would not only bring into doubt the apparent naturalness of those arguments, but would leave the field open to the redeployment of the Agrippan argument, for the sceptic can readily ask what criterion one would employ to demonstrate the truth of such a theory.

Even if we accept the *cogito* argument, the problem remains of how far 'clarity and distinctness' can take us. The human condition ensures that it does not apply to our empirical experiences: "The nature of man as a combination of mind and body is such that it is bound to mislead him from time to time" (*AT* VII: 88). In the

Meditations Descartes relies on proofs of the existence of God to ultimately remove the sceptical possibilities and assure us that, although we are capable of error, most of our beliefs are nevertheless true. Since God also underwrites the testimony of memory we are similarly assured that, even when not *attending to* the 'clarity and distinctness' of ideas and demonstrations, our belief in their truth remains justified. The problem is that these very proofs, and a number of other metaphysical conclusions that Descartes draws, are not experienced as indubitable. Of course, it is always open to Descartes to claim that we are not convinced by the proofs because we are distracted from their 'clarity and distinctness', but that comes dangerously close to something the Stoic sage could say; namely, that we don't possess 'knowledge' in the sense of being in the right 'state' (satisfying the Full Competency Requirement). At this point the *pk*-sceptic might intervene to direct our attention to all the beliefs that people have claimed as indubitable but which are no longer taken to be so. If this were sufficient to undermine one's faith in the veracity of clear and distinct ideas, the conclusion might be that one should withhold assent from all one's beliefs. Indeed, Descartes's method of doubt would appear to commit him to this conclusion. Alternatively a request for a criterion of truth might follow, and we find ourselves once again in the clutches of the Agrippan argument.

As we have seen, Descartes's motivation was to resist the scepticism of his day and to provide a philosophical foundation for the sciences. In an obvious sense, then, he was motivated by the threat to *p*-knowing represented by the Agrippan argument. His response to this involves showing that the 'certainty' required for such a foundation is not to be achieved by specifying a criterion of truth, but by removing sources of distraction that prevent one from seeing the truth *as* the truth. This removal of distraction involves two related elements. Distraction from the claims of others requires a turn inwards towards the operation of one's own mind; distraction from one's own habits of thinking requires the resolute and methodical application of doubt. The result is a new sort of epistemological enquiry and a new sort of sceptical problem. When one adopts the theoretical attitude one takes up the standpoint of the pure enquirer whose reflections on knowledge have been purged of any relation to the practical.

Descartes's ontological internalism promises to rescue the idea of cognitive responsibility by emphasizing each subject's ability to identify for themselves the foundations of knowledge, but at the cost of changing the subject of knowledge. It is our essential nature as thinking beings that enables us to re-establish contact with the world through the rational scrutiny of that nature. Descartes's enquiry is 'insulated' from ordinary life because *in our essence* we too are insulated from it. This claim should not be misunderstood, however. Descartes does not think that *we* are disembodied minds: "I am not merely present in my body . . . I am very closely joined and . . . intermingled with it" (*AT* VII: 81). Nevertheless, "my essence consists solely in the fact that I am a thinking thing . . . And accordingly, that it is certain that I am really distinct from my body" (*ibid.*: 78). On Descartes's account the retention of cognitive responsibility requires an alternative view of the knowing subject. In the stead of the practically oriented, embodied self, immersed in the world and seeking the path to happiness, we find a disembodied, self-knowing, theoretically reflective mind: "Knowledge of the truth about things seems to belong to the mind alone, and not to the combination of mind and body" (*ibid.*: 82–3). If this is the price of certainty, not everyone has proven willing to pay it. We have seen that there are good reasons for thinking that Descartes's foundationalist response to the Agrippan argument does not succeed; but even if one accepted its legitimacy his attempt to answer his own sceptical possibilities has convinced few. Turning to the subject's awareness of the operations of its own thinking in order to answer the *pk*-sceptic still leaves us with the argument from ignorance, and thus with an apparent inability to see how knowledge of the external world is possible.

At this point we are left with two possibilities: on the one hand a radical sceptical challenge to the very idea of justification; on the other a dogmatic claim that human beings are capable of obtaining certain knowledge. As we saw in Chapter 2, however, there is another option in the form of Therapeutic–Academic Scepticism. This aims to place limits on the extent to which reason can leave behind the practical standpoint of common life while acknowledging that it nevertheless has a legitimate realm of application. Along with this goes a different understanding of what human beings are. In the remainder of this chapter we will be concerned with David Hume's account of human cognition, and with his use of 'mitigated' scepticism to offer a 'naturalistic' account of the limits of theoretical reflection.

Hume: between naturalism and scepticism

In his (originally anonymous) 'Abstract' of the *Treatise of Human Nature* (1739–40),[12] Hume notes that while the author "proposes to anatomize human nature in a regular manner, and promises to draw no conclusion but where he is authorized by experience" (*T*: 646), "the philosophy contained in this book is very sceptical, and tends to give us a notion of the imperfections and narrow limits of human understanding" (*ibid.*: 657). These two facets of the *Treatise* – the 'naturalism' and the 'scepticism' – have tended to dominate interpretations of Hume's work.[13] In the immediate aftermath of its publication, and for many years thereafter, Hume was taken as the sceptical nemesis of John Locke's philosophy. Locke took the basic framework of Descartes's ontological and methodological internalism and adapted it to his own empiricist ends. According to his representative realism, 'reality' possesses certain properties independently of our cognitive constitution. Locke aimed to establish that some of our beliefs about the world have objective purport (external content) because they accurately represent those properties through a relation of resemblance. The task was to find which ones, and Hume-the-sceptic was seen to have demonstrated the futility of this endeavour. More specifically, he demonstrated that on this empiricist supposition the 'imperfections' of the human understanding are such that we are unable to justify our beliefs in inductive inference, the external world and even the self.

More recent interpretations have emphasized a different aspect of Hume's work, and Hume-the-naturalist has emerged.[14] 'Naturalism' is a much-contested term in contemporary philosophy, and it is not always clear what the many philosophers who now call themselves naturalists have in common. Nevertheless, the shape of Hume's naturalism is clear enough on this interpretation. He is embarked upon the project of developing a general theory of the mind. Rather than identify a priori principles through speculative thought like Descartes and his rationalist successors, Hume aims to elucidate the principles of human nature in an experimental[15] manner, and thereby show how we come to hold certain beliefs and make the sorts of judgements we do. Like all experimental reasonings, the guide and – more importantly – the limit in such enquiries is determined by experience: "We must . . . glean up our experiments in this science from a cautious observation of human life, and take them as they appear in the common course of the world" (*T*: xix). In this mode Hume concludes that beliefs are "nothing but a peculiar sentiment, or lively conception produced by habit" (*ibid.*: 657) and not the result of reasoning.

Is Hume a naturalist or a sceptic? To a first approximation the answer is both. The passage just quoted immediately succeeds the reference to the 'imperfections of human understanding' and Hume's 'naturalistic' account of belief extends to our most fundamental convictions regarding inductive inference, and the existence of the external world and the self. These too are held to be both unjustifed and unjustifiable. Only the sceptic, then, can be a naturalist. It is by using scepticism to demonstrate the frailty of human understanding and reveal the *hubris* of philosophical attempts to legitimate such beliefs that we can come to see that the experimental method is the right approach for elucidating the principles of human nature.

In suggesting that Hume is both a sceptic and a naturalist, we should remind ourselves that scepticism comes in many varieties. Hume gives us a guide to identifying his own in the *Enquiry Concerning Human Understanding*.[16] He describes Descartes's method as an *antecedent* scepticism, which assumes that no scientific or philosophical enquiry can take place until our beliefs and reasoning faculties have been subjected to a universal doubt from which some original principle can be deduced and serve as a foundation. Since it is part of Hume's naturalistic experimentalism to suppose that one begins with the phenomena of common life, this doubt is rejected as either unattainable or incurable. In contrast with antecedent scepticism, *consequent* scepticism subjects the phenomena of common life to scrutiny. Among the *consequent* sceptics, Hume distinguishes the *excessive* scepticism of the neo-Pyrrhonians from the *mitigated* scepticism of Academics and others. His description of the relationship between the two is illuminating:

> Another species of *mitigated* scepticism which may be of
> advantage to mankind, and which may be the natural result of

the Pyrrhonian doubts and scruples, is the limitation of our enquiries to such subjects as are best adapted to the narrow capacity of human understanding. The *imagination* of man is naturally sublime, delighted with whatever is remote and extraordinary ... A correct *Judgement* observes a contrary method, and avoiding all distant and high enquiries, confines itself to common life, and to such subjects as fall under daily practice and experience ... To bring us to so salutary a determination, nothing can be more serviceable, than to be once thoroughly convinced of the force of the Pyrrhonian doubt, and of the impossibility, that anything, but the strong power of natural instinct, could free us from it.   (*E*: 162)

For Hume, Descartes's philosophical quest for certainty (for *p*-knowledge) constituted a failure to respect the limits of human understanding and a submission to the imagination's delight in the 'remote and extraordinary'. Since Locke inherited and adapted much of Descartes's internalist framework, he too had neglected those limits and given in to dogmatic speculation. Pyrrhonian doubt undermines the very idea that any of our beliefs are justified. By attacking *all* the claims of the understanding, not just those of the dogmatist, it does not so much 'narrow' the legitimate realm of the understanding as completely erase it.

Hume's objective is not to eradicate judgement, however, but to confine it to common life, and this is the position of the *mitigated* sceptic. Our task in the rest of this chapter is thus to examine what Hume means when he says that a *mitigated* scepticism may be the 'natural result' of Pyrrhonian doubt. In other words we'll examine how Hume aims to advance the claims of his naturalism (the 'contrary method') by employing sceptical reasoning against the dogmatist and then confronting that scepticism with 'the strong power of natural instinct'. In the process we'll come to see that Hume's *mitigated* scepticism shares two key features with that of the Therapeutic-Academic. First, he is dialectically engaged with the detail of his opponents' theories, and with their internalist framework in particular. Secondly, his method hinges on an understanding of the nature of belief – in this case one that takes issue with the dogmatist's view of what kind of thing the subject of knowledge is (and thus challenges the intelligibility of the theoretical attitude). We'll conclude by observing that if Hume's naturalism does not cure us of either scepticism or dogmatism, that is because it does not by itself fix the limits of human understanding.

Causation, induction and belief

As I sit here in the library thinking about Hume, I find my mind wandering towards thoughts of the coming evening's arrangement to meet Aaron for a drink in the bar; a dog howls in the distance; I feel hungry and reach for a bar of chocolate. Suddenly I find myself wondering *why* I think Aaron is around; *what* leads me to conclude that it's a dog out there; *how* do I know that the chocolate will ease my hunger-pangs? Turning back to Hume I read the opening of section 4 of the *Enquiry* ('sceptical doubts concerning the operations of the understanding'):

> All the objects of human reason or inquiry may naturally be divided into two kinds, to wit, *Relations of Ideas*, and *Matters of Fact*. Of the first kind are the sciences of Geometry, Algebra, and Arithmetic; and in short, every affirmation which is either intuitively or demonstratively certain ... Propositions of this kind are discoverable by the mere operation of thought ... Matters of fact are not ascertained in the same manner; nor is our evidence of their truth, however great, of a like nature with the foregoing. The contrary of every matter of fact is still possible; because it can never imply a contradiction, and is conceived by the mind with the same facility and distinctness, as if ever so conformable to reality. (*E*: 25)

Relations of Ideas are like Descartes's clear and distinct ideas: their truth is made evident to thought. Logically, to entertain the negation of such an idea is to contemplate a self-evident falsehood (I cannot envisage a triangle without three sides). Hume calls the kind of reasoning we use when we contemplate relations of ideas 'demonstrative' (or a priori) reasoning. *Matters of Fact* are initially characterized by the absence of self-evidence, and the logical possibility of their negation (I *can* contemplate the sun not rising tomorrow). Hume calls the kind of reasoning that concerns matters of fact ('and existence') 'moral' or 'probable' reasoning.

My thoughts about the plan for the evening, the dog and the chocolate clearly fall into the class of matters of fact and existence; I can easily imagine that Aaron is not around, for example. The question Hume goes on to pose is the following: if self-evidence is the criterion of truth for relations of ideas, what is it that justifies my claims concerning matters of fact and existence? When S contemplates the dog howling in front of her, experience itself warrants her claim that the dog is howling, but what is it that allows her to associate a distant howling with an as yet unseen dog? The answer, says Hume, lies in *the relation of cause and effect*. When we 'anatomize' all such reasonings we find that causal links of differing degrees of directness are being presupposed. A dog is taken as the *cause* of the howling and chocolate assumed to *satisfy* my craving for sustenance (albeit temporarily). My belief that Aaron is in town is based on the fact that he rang me to tell me so, set against the backdrop of his general reliability. Beliefs of this sort are never attended with the certainty that we associate with relations of ideas (because we can contemplate their negation without contradiction) but they are absolutely central to our practical lives. It's impossible to imagine how we could act if we did not go beyond our immediate experiences in this way. But if the relation of cause and effect is the criterion for our reasoning concerning matters of fact, a further question naturally arises: what is the criterion of cause and effect? In other words, what justifies us in invoking cause and effect as a justification for our beliefs?

Hume's initial response to this question is to rule out the possibility that there is a rational link between a cause and its effect that can be ascertained by a priori reasoning. If S is presented with a unique event *c*, she will not be able to deduce its effect *e* just by thinking hard about *c*. Hume acknowledges that when S has repeatedly witnessed *c*-type events being followed by *e*-type events she will find herself thinking that there must be some necessary connection between the two, and that it is through a priori reasoning that she identifies this connection; but this is a mistake. If S isolates *c*'s occurrence from *e*'s occurrence and treats it as if it were a unique event, she will see that there is no such necessary connection: the thought that *c* might not be followed by *e* does not give rise to a self-evident falsity. Since we cannot deduce an effect from its cause (a priori), Hume concludes, the relation must be based on experience (a posteriori).

So the criterion of reasoning concerning matters of fact and existence is cause and effect, and the relation of cause and effect is not based on some rational criterion according to which we 'grasp' the effect in the cause, but is grounded in experience. The question now is how does experience serve as a criterion for the relation of cause and effect? How *does* experience justify the claim that *c*-type events cause *e*-type events? What is it about my chocolate-eating experiences that warrants the claim that the chocolate bar in front of me will keep me going until lunch? Recalling the Stoics, one suggestion might be that a chocolate-bar-eating impression reveals to me the truth of the claim that chocolate bars ease one's hunger pangs; but as we have seen, nothing in the *idea* of a chocolate bar as *cause* warrants that conclusion about its *effect*. All experience can teach me, then, is that in the past examples of chocolate-bar-eating have been succeeded by the alleviation of hunger. According to Hume it is on this basis alone that I reach for the one at hand. In doing so, then, I make something like the following inference:

1 This is a chocolate bar
2 All chocolate bars in the past have tasted delicious

Therefore

4 This chocolate bar will taste delicious

When we view the matter in this way it seems that everyone naturally makes such inferences in the course of reasoning concerning matters of fact. The question is how, on the basis of past experiences, one is warranted in drawing conclusions about the course of future experience.[17] What we appear to need is something like the following:

3 Future chocolate bars will taste like those in the past

This is the criterion for a genuine induction from experience. It is an example of a more general metaphysical principle:

3′ The future will be conformable with the past (in relevant respects)

According to Hume, if our warrant for (3′) is to be rational, it must proceed according to some argument. If, on the one hand, (3′) is a relation of ideas, it will be justified through demonstrative reasoning (concerning relations of ideas). If, on the other hand, it is a matter of fact and existence it will be justified through moral/probable reasoning. Considering the former, I can easily imagine someone changing the recipe of the chocolate[18] and therefore contemplate without contradiction the thought that chocolate might not satisfy my hunger. If (3′) is not a relation of ideas, it must consequently be a matter of fact and existence, and reasoning about the future on the basis of the past must be founded on moral reasoning. But we have already seen that reasoning concerning matters of fact and existence relies on cause and effect. Since the relation between cause and effect is grounded in experience, which only justifies is in so far as the truth of (3′) is *presupposed*, a probable justification of (3′) turns out to completely circular!

Given this application of what is recognizable as the Agrippan argument, Hume's conclusion is predictable enough: an attempt to offer a methodologically internalist justification for one's everyday beliefs leads to a regress of justification which comes to an end with the discovery that the ground (3′) is in fact of a kind with the beliefs it is supposed to justify. Since the regress ends with circularity, the sceptical conclusion appears to be that neither our beliefs in, nor reasonings about, matters of fact and existence are justified. It seems that although we cannot avoid believing (3′), it is not in fact 'reasonable' to do so. (3′) is not the ultimate justification of our empirical beliefs and it does not constitute a piece of *p*-knowledge.[19] From the standpoint of the theoretical attitude it is just a dogmatic assumption.

What are we to think about these beliefs and this reasoning if they are not amenable to justification? It is at this point in Hume's account that a dialectical reversal takes place. The conclusion is that "there is a step taken by the mind which is not supported by any argument or process of the understanding" (*E*: 41). None of our practical beliefs are rationally justified. Nevertheless, this lack of rational warrant confronts the basic psychological fact that we continue to reason in exactly the same way. What, then, is the nature of that 'step', upon which this reasoning is based? The answer, in brief, is Custom or Habit:

It is that principle alone which renders our experience useful, and makes us expect, for the future, a similar train of events with those which have appeared in the past . . . Without [it] . . . there would be an end at once to all actions, as well as of the chief part of speculation.   (*E*: 44–5)

When I stared down at my bar of chocolate my mind was placed in such a context that thoughts of its deliciousness simply arose through expectation based on customary conjunction. Similarly, when *S* hears a howl she associates some recalcitrant canine with the noise. This process, extending to 'the chief part of speculation', is a species of 'natural instinct', no different in kind from when a dog cowers at the sight of its master's raised arm. Beliefs are not egregiously rational items, then. The assent that characterizes them does not follow from the identification of a criterion of truth but is merely the *feeling* that accompanies them when the imagination, as a result of repeated experiences of the conjunction of *c*- and *e*-type events, is led from one thought or object to another.

This analysis clearly has a salutary effect on our understanding of the concept of causation itself. The claim is that our expectation that a *c*-type event will be succeeded by an *e*-type event is not based on some demonstrative relation (a priori) between *c* and *e*. It is simply that where *e*-type events (fallings-to-the-floor) follow *c*-type events (releases-in-the-air) the imagination becomes habituated to expect an *e* when confronted with a *c*: the connection is something "we *feel* in the mind" (*E*: 75). Causation is not therefore an *objective necessity* – a metaphysical concept, identifiable by reason and expressive of relations between objects in the world – but an idea we form as a result of that feeling. It is a *subjective necessity* projected on to the world as a result of the peculiarities of our psychological constitution (a necessary fiction).

Humean, all-too Humean

Much criticism has been made of Hume's distinction between relations of ideas and matters of fact, and the history of empiricism is in part the history of attempts to justify it.[20] With our Therapeutic Interpretation of Academic Scepticism in mind we might offer the following defence. Doing so will allow us to return to our standing question: how Hume thinks that a *mitigated* scepticism may be the 'natural result' of Pyrrhonian doubt. So let us imagine a dogmatic, methodologically internalist philosopher who wishes to demonstrate that there is *p*-knowledge, which provides our empirical beliefs with a rational foundation (shows *heroically* how knowledge is possible). Going back to Hume's distinction, there might be some disagreement about where exactly to draw the line between one sort of belief and reasoning and the other, but the primary concern is with the status of philosophical beliefs or reasonings. Any sort of justification of empirical knowledge claims will require beliefs or reasonings of this type.

The dogmatist begins with the assumption that since *p*-knowledge is supposed to justify matters of fact it must involve relations of ideas and be arrived at through demonstrative reasoning. So on our interpretation the dogmatist is initially granted Hume's distinction. Following the 'Pyrrhonian doubts and scruples' that the Agrippan argument generates, the dogmatist finds that his attempt to adopt the theoretical attitude towards common life in order to justify his 'moral' beliefs and reasonings leads to circularity. The *demonstrative* conclusion is that one's beliefs are not justified and that one therefore cannot *p*-know that knowledge is possible.

At this point the neo-Pyrrhonian would have the dogmatist *discovering* that tranquillity follows from withholding assent. For Hume, rather than issue in tranquillity, at the moment where he becomes 'thoroughly convinced of the force of the Pyrrhonian doubt,' a 'natural instinct' intervenes to remind the dogmatist that he never needed a *demonstration* in the first place. It is a *feeling* – something that the theoretical attitude cannot accommodate – that rescues him from scepticism. This discovery leads to the awareness that custom and habit have obscured a general feature of our practically oriented beliefs: feeling and not the cognition of some indicator of truth is the mark of assent. Moreover, the dogmatist comes to see that the problem (the *need* for justification) that seemed to demand a theoretical-philosophical solution is actually 'unreal'; it arises because the imagination exploits the fact that transitions (from thoughts of causes to thoughts of effects) take place so quickly in our minds. Finally, since it is feeling – that is to say, experience – that has led to this discovery about the nature of belief the dogmatist finally realizes that it is experimental reasoning itself that has provided this insight and not demonstrative reasoning. Indeed, it is only by abandoning the theoretical attitude with its vulnerability to the Agrippan argument that this feature of common life can be elucidated.

This, then, is how *mitigated* ('therapeutic') scepticism becomes the 'natural result' of Pyrrhonian doubt. The dogmatist's assumption that relations of ideas provide the basis for philosophical reflection on matters of fact (common life) turns out to undermine itself. When the impossibility of offering a demonstrative response to the Agrippan argument encounters the natural instinct that belief is, the experimental method is validated. The discovery is that there is no greater justification to be had than when we merely reason 'probably'. Moreover, since the arguments that have led to this discovery cannot themselves be demonstrative (since such reasoning leads to circularity), this understanding of common life has been achieved by probable reasoning. The capacity of human understanding has been narrowed by showing that its dreams of demonstrative justification are a fantasy; but that capacity has not been negated – it is restricted to moral reasoning, and hence so is philosophy.

On this interpretation, Hume's attack on methodological internalism and the subsequent validation of common life is akin to the Academics' attack on the Stoics, updated to suit the dogmatisms of his day.[21] There is of course one important difference: although Hume de-intellectualizes justification, his version of the 'convincing' – feeling – is still a subjectivist account of assent. The problem is that his philosophical context is now one in which Descartes's sceptical thought-experiments (and the argument from ignorance) are available to the sceptic. In other words, the backdrop is not only methodologically internalist but also ontologically internalist. The question thus 'naturally' arises about where this leaves us in relation to the objective world. If belief is a species of feeling and causation (like the conformability of the future to the past), a subjective necessity generated by the workings of the mind (and only fictively applicable to the world), then is it not possible that our beliefs might be wholly inadequate to the world?

This takes us to Hume's view of the 'problem' of the external world. His fullest account, 'Of scepticism with regard to the senses', runs to some thirty or so pages in the *Treatise*. A shorter version in the *Enquiry* omits much of the dialectical detail but still gives the flavour of Hume's approach. He begins by describing what he calls the 'vulgar' view of perception:

> It seems evident, that men are carried, by a natural instinct or prepossession, to repose faith in their senses; and that, without any reasoning, or even almost before the use of reason, we always suppose an external universe, which depends not on our perception, but would exist, though we and every sensible creature were absent or annihilated . . . It seems also evident, that, when following this blind and powerful instinct of nature, they always suppose the very images, presented by the senses, to be the external objects, and never entertain any suspicion, that the one are nothing but representations of the other. This very table, which we see white, and which we feel hard, is believed to exist, independent of our perceptions, and to be something external to the mind, which perceives it.
>
> (E: 150)

The 'vulgar' view comprises two commitments, which are taken to be the result of the same natural instinct. One expresses our simple intuition about objectivity – the feeling that the world is the way it is independently of our thoughts about it. The second captures the feeling that when we have an object-experience it is the object itself that we experience. What S sees when she looks at the chocolate bar in front of her is just that – *the* chocolate bar. When you look down at this book what you're seeing is *the* book, an object that like the chocolate bar is part of the objective world and does not depend on you for its existence.

In the *Treatise* Hume begins his discussion by noting that although we may ask "*What causes induce us to believe in the existence of body?*" we cannot ask "*Whether there be body or not?*" because we must take that for granted in all our reasonings (T: 187). So why do we believe in an external world? Let's return to the chocolate bar again. When S turns away from her bar and then looks back again, she takes it that what she sees is the same (independently existing) bar. However, she believes that her perceptions are of independently existing objects and the second perception is clearly distinct from the first; after all, she looked away for a moment. Given that S has here two distinct perceptions, neither of which reveals that it is the external object, what *reason* has she for thinking that there is an independently existing object at all?

Hume's answer is that there is a natural propensity of the imagination to bestow an identity on perceptions that *resemble* one another. When *S* looks back at the chocolate bar the imagination as it were notes that the second perception resembles the first and gives rise to the belief that they are in fact the same. The overall result is that this propensity produces the fiction of a continued and independent existence. On this causal account of the 'vulgar' belief there is no reason to believe in the existence of the external world. As with the concept of causation itself, the concept of the external world is a metaphysical fiction imposed on us by the all-too-human workings of the imagination.

At this point Hume proceeds to note that despite the appeal of the vulgar view, as soon as we start to reflect on it *philosophically* it seems obvious that we don't perceive objects in this naively realist way. If, staring at this table, I press my eye, the *perception* changes but I don't regard the *table* as having changed. If you are sitting across from me, the table must look different from where you are; but what is that 'looking' other than a different perception of the same object? When we adopt the theoretical attitude in this way it seems obvious that the perception is a representation in the mind of an object that exists external to it. It is the object that persists, while our perceptions undergo the change.

As we've seen, *something* along the lines of this representational theory of perception goes back to the Greeks, but it is Locke's ontologically internalist version that Hume has in mind: "the opinion of a double existence and representation" (*T*: 202). The by now familiar problem arises when we are asked which of our representations (beliefs) adequately represent their objects. Once the distinction between (external) object and (internal) representation is made, it is incumbent upon the philosopher to identify some criterion that would allow us to distinguish, for example, waking experiences from those we have when we are dreaming. From a Humean perspective, any argument that aims to justify our empirical beliefs in this way will be either demonstrative or moral. However, if the dogmatic philosopher attempts to demonstrate that our empirical beliefs are on the whole true (represent objects), the *mitigated* sceptic can apply the Agrippan argument and press for a criterion. Descartes's attempt to respond to his own sceptical arguments shows how difficult it is to discern philosophical principles that have the degree of self-evidence of the *cogito*, even if one accepts the latter. In the absence of a demonstration, then, any argument must be moral: it must be a question of fact whether or not our perceptions accurately represent objects (whether our empirical beliefs amount to knowledge). As we've already seen, such reasonings are dependent on experience; but by hypothesis the only things we do experience are objects of perception: we cannot 'get outside' our own minds to compare a representation with its object: "This is a topic, therefore, in which the profounder and more philosophical sceptics will always triumph" (*E*: 153).

Hume pushes the point against the empiricist even further. Developing a distinction originally suggested by Descartes, Locke distinguishes between an object's primary and secondary properties. The former inhere in objects and are represented in our perceptions of them (like extension and solidity). The latter are subjective properties of our sensory experiences (colours, odours etc.) and are not found in objects themselves, although they are *caused* by their primary properties. Applying arguments elaborated by Berkeley in his attack on Locke's metaphysical realism, Hume argues that any concept we form of a primary property is through the senses. The concept of extension, for example, central to an understanding of the 'external' world, is acquired by seeing and touching things and is therefore, strictly speaking, subjective. It cannot be the result of *abstraction* from our experiences, for an invisible, intangible extension (as opposed to, say, a hard black one) is impossible to conceive of.

The philosophical conclusion is that arguing from cause and effect leads us to conclude that we can neither explain how any connection between our perceptions and their putative objects could be possible, nor give the concept of the external world any more content than that of an "unknown, inexplicable *something*; a notion so imperfect, that no sceptic will think it worthwhile to contend against it" (*E*: 155).

When we depart from the vulgar view of perception and take up the philosophical view of the theoretical attitude we are thus led to abandon our 'natural instinct' to place trust in our senses. Without Descartes's veracious deity, then, the ontological internalism that

Locke inherits from him renders us incapable of justifying the view that some of our perceptions (or beliefs) resemble things external to our minds (have empirical content). So what is its appeal? Why did it convince – and continue to convince – many philosophers? According to Hume the reason is that the 'double existence and representation' view of perception is nothing less than a "monstrous offspring" (*T*: 215) of two contrary principles. The first derives from *reason*'s discovery that our resembling perceptions are interrupted and differ from each other. The second derives from the *imagination*'s propensity to believe that our resembling perceptions have a continuous and uninterrupted existence (as external objects). The philosophical doctrine of double existence of perceptions and objects is an attempt to overcome this contradiction through the invention of yet another, peculiarly philosophical, fiction. It convinces many philosophers only because it is parasitic upon the 'natural instinct' that the vulgar view expresses; although, as we have seen, the attempt to makes sense of the doctrine proves destructive to that very instinct.

The Humean Paradox

One might expect the concepts of an objective world and causation to feature in any account of the metaphysical foundations of our knowledge. On Hume's account, however, the imagination and not reason is the source of these (and other) beliefs, and they have no objective realm of application. If we suppose that they have then we "either contradict ourselves, or talk without a meaning" (*T*: 267). We *must* reason concerning matters of fact and existence, and we cannot shake the view that we experience objects that comprise an external and independent world; and yet it is instinct alone that moves us to do so. Any attempt to justify these beliefs philosophically from the theoretical attitude (*p*-knowing) gives way to the most unnerving scepticism.

The Humean Paradox is most in evidence in the conclusion to Book I of the *Treatise*. The imagination is described as the foundation of all the faculties (memory, understanding etc.). It makes us reason from cause and effect and it convinces us of the existence of the external world; and yet as we have just seen, reasoning from cause and effect leads us to the conclusion that our beliefs in causation and the external world are fictional. Although reason and the imagination are both parts of our nature, then, they stand in conflict. But then what are we to do? Simply assenting to everything that the imagination suggests to us undermines any possibility of distinguishing between our beliefs in terms of their degree of convincingness and leaves us prey to the most outrageous fantasies. At the same time, succumbing to the temptation of the dogmatist and seeking a criterion that will justify our reasoning invites the Agrippan argument and leads to the equally unappealing conclusion that none of our beliefs are justified. Finally, we cannot even advocate the rejection of all reasoning, for, as we saw in Chapter 2, this negatively Dogmatic position rests on the assumption that we can p-know that knowledge is not possible, and that leads us to "the most manifest absurdities . . . We have, therefore, no choice left but betwixt a false reason and none at all" (*T*: 268). Fortunately, when such doubts assail us, "Nature is always too strong for principle . . . the first and most trivial event in life will put to flight all [the sceptic's] doubts and scruples" (*E*: 160).

The key to the Humean Paradox is that even if beliefs are a species of feeling, reflection (understanding) is nevertheless a natural feature of our nature. The *mitigated* scepticism that derives from the encounter of Pyrrhonian doubt with instinct does not thereby presage a return to a common life without reflection. It is intended to be one in which our cognitive limitations are embraced rather than glossed over by the imagination's flights of philosophical fancy. For Hume, however, exposing such limitations does not set a priori restrictions on reflection: "Very refin'd reflections have little or no influence upon us; and yet we do not, and cannot, establish it for a rule, that they ought not to have any influence; which implies a manifest contradiction" (*T*: 268). We cannot establish for a rule that they ought not to influence us because it is *instinct* that opposes them, not the *understanding* itself. Since neither one can ultimately checkmate the other, reflection will be driven by the imagination into self-destructive bouts of scepticism when the theoretical attitude is adopted, only for instinct to check it at the moment of action. We can no more cease to reflect on our beliefs than we can cease to believe. That means of course that we cannot *justify* our everyday epistemic concepts, only *use* them.[22] Strictly speaking the sceptic is correct.

Of course, if we *could* show that these "refin'd reflections" ought not to have any influence – that at some specifiable point they lead to 'contradiction' or 'meaninglessness' – we could set limits on reflection without confining ourselves to neo-Pyrrhonian denial or exposing the understanding to radical scepticism. If we could resist the sceptic about understanding in this way it might even be possible to justify some substantive p-knowledge claims (including, perhaps, claims about causation and the external world). We will begin Chapter 4 by examining one attempt to do precisely that; namely, to resist pk-scepticism by setting limits on the understanding and thereby justifying p-knowledge.

4 Transcendental meditations

No worries!

In Hume's hands it turns out that if Descartes's sceptical possibilities ultimately don't worry us, it is not because we have a *reason* not to worry; rather, it is simply that confronted with the exigencies of life away from the study our natural 'instinct' to believe reasserts itself. This limitation on reason is double-edged, however, for it is also why we can't show *as a rule* why we *ought not* to be worried. As a result we cannot vindicate what we otherwise take to be uncontentious features of our experience – that they are of an external world of causally related objects, for example. The lesson seems to be that whilst untrammelled speculation leads reason (when adopting the theoretical attitude) to make philosophical claims it cannot justify, 'naturalizing' reason to the point where it can only trace relations of ideas and matters of fact deprives it of the resources to sustain any normative reflection on the epistemic practices of common life or to see key features of our experience as anything other than illusory. The upshot of the Humean Paradox is that we have to concede victory to the sceptic.

In this chapter we'll examine approaches to sceptical problems that set less onerous limits on reason in order to show that we do have a *right* not to worry. Our starting-point will be Immanuel Kant. Where Descartes's 'First Philosophy' was a response to the *pk*-scepticism of his own time, Kant's 'Transcendental' philosophy is similarly motivated. His concern is to defend the possibility of metaphysical (*p*-)knowledge in the face of Hume's sceptical attack, while acknowledging the force of the latter's critique of reason's attempt to justify itself. Hume pits reason's self-destructive tendency against the power of the imagination and a (dumb) unjustifiable instinct (experience). Kant aims to show that experience itself is not a non-rational barrier against scepticism that threatens to undermine our ability to act, but instead serves as the self-validating criterion for metaphysical knowledge-claims (experience justifies reason). As long as these claims are restricted to what makes experience possible, and experience is taken as a given, the Agrippan argument cannot arise. As we'll come to see, everything here turns on what experience is. In the second part of the chapter we'll see how Kant's anti-sceptical insights develop when philosophers turn away from a concern with the mind and focus instead on language.

The contest of the faculties

In the Preface to the first edition of the *Critique of Pure Reason*[1] Kant paints a striking picture of the problem that confronts the philosopher: "Human reason, in one sphere of its cognition, is called upon to consider questions, which it cannot decline, as they are presented by its own nature, but which it cannot answer, as they transcend every faculty of human reason" (A: vii). As he continues, a familiar image of the Humean Paradox[2] emerges. In the experience of common life we use certain concepts (say, cause and object) unproblematically. We also find it natural to reflect on these to find out if and when their use is legitimate. This enquiry carries us to increasingly higher levels of abstraction, further and further removed from the contexts in which we *use* the concepts. Something must be wrong, we conclude, because although common sense affirms their applicability, such 'refin'd' reflections lead to "Confusion and contradictions" (*ibid.*). At this point we cannot use experience as a criterion to distinguish between rival philosophical claims because, having adopted the theoretical attitude, we find that reflection has carried us so far away from where it has an obvious bearing on them. As we saw in Chapter 2, the Stoics and the Epicureans agreed that experience was the criterion of truth and yet we still found them arguing for contradictory theses, such as that our actions are free or determined by laws of nature, and that an absolutely necessary being does or does not exist.[3] Indeed, it was the existence of these 'Disputes' among the Dogmatists that allowed the Ancient Sceptic to employ the Agrippan argument. As Kant puts it,

"The arena of these endless contests is called *metaphysics*" (*ibid*.). In among them we encounter an equally familiar "embarrassment to philosophy and to the general human reason"; namely, that we're "obliged to assume, as an article of mere faith, the existence of things external to ourselves (from which, yet, we receive the whole material of knowledge . . .) and not to be able to oppose a satisfactory proof to anyone who may call it in question" (B: xxxvii, fn).

Despite the 'embarrassment', the challenge of external world scepticism is ancillary to what Kant regards as a much more pressing need. His main aim is not to show how empirical knowledge is possible but to legitimate *metaphysical* (*p*-)knowledge itself. As he describes this in the *Prolegomena*, "The special problem upon the solution to which the fate of metaphysics wholly rests" (1977: 377) is to show *how metaphysics is possible*. The task of what Kant calls "transcendental philosophy, which necessarily precedes all metaphysics" (*ibid*.: 279), is thus to demonstrate that we can have a form of knowledge that although non-empirical (a priori) in nature does not succumb to *pk*-scepticism. If successful, it would prove that when we reflect on the concepts we use in common life we do not leave ourselves vulnerable to the destructive power of the Agrippan argument, and thus are not led to the Humean conclusion that these concepts are just 'contentless' fictions. In other words, Kant aims to buy us the *right* to use these concepts by putting them beyond the reach of the *pk*-sceptic.

Kant's work is complex and difficult, but three objectives relate to our general enquiry:

1. To demonstrate that the general framework of concepts that form the basis of our knowledge claims about the world (causation etc.) is legitimate by showing that metaphysics is possible.
2. Building on Hume's sceptical attack on traditional metaphysics, to diagnose why reason makes contradictory claims, and show that although natural these are nevertheless illusory.
3. To end the 'embarrassment' to philosophy and prove the existence of things external to ourselves.

Objectives (1) and (2) are central to Kant's 'Critical' project, and work together to resist Hume's version of *pk*-scepticism and offer a response to the Humean Paradox. (1) would show that the concepts that comprise our fundamental epistemic commitments are *objective* features of our experience *of* the world, and not *subjective* features we impose *on* it. (2) would demonstrate that the 'Disputes' about *p*-knowledge that invite a demand for a criterion (and *pk*-scepticism) are not 'real'. Recall that for Hume these metaphysical illusions are the fantasies of the imagination. Since the imagination is the basis of all reasonings about matters of fact, Hume has no standpoint from which to dismiss them completely, and hence cannot show *for a rule* that 'refin'd reflections' *ought not* to influence us. Kant's objective in (2) is to show that since these illusions are in fact the work of reason there is a *reason* why they ought not to influence us.

We'll look at (1) and (2) in the next three sections. Objective (3) – the 'Refutation of Idealism' – was included in the second edition of the *Critique* in response to the charge that Kant's own philosophical position was a form of 'subjective' idealism like Berkeley's. Although of peripheral interest in the context of Kant's transcendental enquiry, it is nevertheless regarded by some contemporary philosophers as offering the model for a new form of argument whose anti-sceptical force survives in isolation from Kant's overall project. We'll postpone a discussion of these so-called 'transcendental arguments' until the second half of this chapter.

Metaphysics, experience and transcendental idealism

According to Kant, the mistake that empiricists make is to insist on regarding the mind as essentially passive, and therefore knowledge as an accommodation to the objects presented to it. The Epicureans provide one example of the sceptical implications of this: if the concepts ('preconceptions') by which we judge the objectivity of sensations are themselves derived from 'passive' sensation, some sensations have to be self-revealing of their objects. As we saw, only a problematic criterion of truth can close the gap between appearance and reality by determining which sensations the concepts that can legitimately be used in making judgements about reality can be derived from. Hume's adaptation of Berkeley's attack on Locke's distinction between primary and secondary properties is another example. Here the assumption that the mind passively 'represents' the primary properties of objects gives rise to the most extreme form of scepticism, leaving us with Hume's description of the world as an 'unknown, inexplicable *something*'.

Hume's sceptical reasoning proceeded on the assumption that since all beliefs relating to experience/the world are based on the relation of cause and effect ('nonrationally' founded on habit), the only truths that are necessary and knowable a priori are relations between ideas (or what we would now call concepts). Kant amended Hume's division of truths in the following way:

HUME
Relations of ideas   Matters of fact and existence

KANT
Analytic judgements   Synthetic judgements
A priori truths   A posteriori truths

These distinctions have been much debated in philosophy since Kant's time, so it's worth clarifying them. Kant draws the analytic–synthetic distinction in a number of different ways, but the basic idea is that in an analytic judgement the subject concept 'contains' the concept that is predicated of it, whereas in a synthetic judgement it does not. For Kant, then, an analytic judgement is *explicative* – it makes apparent a connection between the subject- and predicate-concepts that is implicit in our grasp of the concepts. A synthetic judgement is *ampliative* – it goes beyond what we already understand to affirm a new connection between the concepts. 'A bachelor is a man' is regarded as analytic because to grasp the concept of bachelorhood is to understand its relation to gender, whereas 'Tim is a bachelor' is synthetic because there is nothing in the concept of Tim that indicates his marital status. Analytic judgements are based on the principle of contradiction; synthetic judgements are not.

The a priori–a posteriori distinction relates to the different ways in which truths are known. The former are known independently of experience and are both necessarily true and universally applicable; the latter are known only through experience and are contingent.[4] The important point is that if it is the case – as Hume in effect supposed – that all analytic judgements concern a priori truths and all synthetic judgements a posteriori truths, the only genuine (ampliative) knowledge claims are those that derive from experience. Metaphysical (p-)knowledge of the world is impossible (and such claims entirely fictive). For Kant, then, the future of metaphysics as a science rests with the possibility of a new class of judgements: those that are synthetic and a priori. Such judgements would be genuine contributions to our knowledge (as the predicate is not contained in the subject), and since they would be knowable independently of experience and necessarily true they would constitute p-knowledge of the world. The question is, how are these possible? If Hume had demonstrated the sceptical consequences of the passive model, the first step towards a solution is to

> assume that the objects, or, which is the same thing, that *experience*, in which alone objects, as given, are known, conform to my conceptions – and then I am at no loss how to proceed. For experience itself is a mode of knowledge which requires understanding. Before objects are given to me, that is, *a priori*, I must presuppose in myself laws of the understanding which are expressed in concepts *a priori*. To these concepts, then, all the objects of experience must necessarily conform.   (B: xvii)

This account of experience is what Kant calls 'transcendental', 'formal', or 'critical' idealism (1977: 375) and it is the key to his response to pk-scepticism. Accordingly, the objects of experience are given to us *in* experience *as* empirical knowledge. Being necessarily linked to experienc*er*s, the objects of this knowledge-experience are appearances (phenomena) and not what Kant terms things-in-themselves (noumena). Because knowledge requires rules or norms (criteria) of judgement and because the objects of this knowledge are appearances, these objects are subject to criteria provided by the understanding and not the other way round (not criteria dictated *by* the objects *to* the understanding). Finally, since "we only know in things a priori that which we ourselves place in them" (B: xvii), the limit of what can be known a priori of experience is restricted to the legitimate application of these criteria (concepts of the understanding) in the world of appearances (experience as empirical knowledge). These criteria do not apply to things-in-themselves, and consequently nothing can be known (experienced) of the latter.

Kant's suggestion that knowers play an *active* rather than merely *passive* role in cognition allows him to draw a significant contrast between phenomena (appearances) and noumena, and thus resolve a world that we can know out of Hume's sceptical 'unknown, inexplicable *something*' – the world of appearances. Given the truth of transcendental idealism, the task of (1) – showing how metaphysics (*p*-knowledge) is possible – becomes clearer. If Kant can show that the norms or criteria that comprise the framework within which we make our empirical judgements (as appearances) are precisely those that we actually contribute to experience, then two things follow. First, the question of the legitimacy of these norms cannot be raised as it makes no sense to ask of these norms as described whether or not they are the *right* ones for justifying knowledge claims. The sceptic cannot therefore use the Agrippan argument. Secondly, since they are knowable a priori, these norms constitute the content of *p*-knowledge. Put together, Kant's approach promises to make *p*-knowledge immune to *pk*-scepticism.

The transcendental deduction

Kant begins his search for a priori knowledge by drawing a distinction between the 'form' of our experience and its 'content'. The former is a result of our *active* 'spontaneity' and is contributed by the mind; the latter is a result of our *passive* 'receptivity' – our openness to the impact of things-in-themselves on our senses. Since we are looking for the contribution of the mind, candidates for a priori knowledge must relate to the *form* of experiences and not their *content*. What is it about the form of experience that cannot be detached from its status *as* experience? Kant's answer is 'Space' and 'Time'. When we remove all 'content' from experience of the world we are left with the idea that it takes place in a spatiotemporal framework. Our ideas of space and time cannot be derived from experience because a non-spatiotemporal experience of an object is impossible. They are the 'purest' formal conditions of the possibility of experience and are contributed to experience by the mind.

The account of the 'ideality' of space and time furnishes Kant with some synthetic a priori propositions,[5] but for our purposes the most important point is that it is said to provide a 'clue' to solving the problem of how metaphysics is possible. To see the clue, imagine that S claims that snow is white. Since this involves a judgement it invites a sceptical challenge to S to justify her criterion and threatens the Agrippan argument. Imagine now that the sceptic tries to raise an objection to S's claim that a particular experience is in space and time. S cannot make sense of such an objection because that is just the way experience is presented to her. She can't imagine something being an experience if it is not spatiotemporal. The clue is that experience itself blocks any attempt to generate the Agrippan argument in this way. It is no more than a clue, however. Although the formal necessity of space and time for (external) experience is immediately demonstrable because the latter is *unthinkable* without the former,[6] philosophers have been disputing for millennia about which concepts are knowable a priori and therefore provide the basis for legitimate metaphysical claims. To make any real headway against the *pk*-sceptic we need to know which concepts are knowable a priori and can be used to make synthetic propositions, and demonstrate that these are immune to the Agrippan argument.

The crux of the problem is that even if we can show that we must apply certain concepts in our judgements – that they are 'subjectively' necessary – this is clearly *not* the right kind of necessity for dealing with the *pk*-sceptic. First, as Kant points out, there are some ('usurpatory') concepts like 'fortune' and 'fate' that are both universally used and contributed by the mind, but that we do not expect objects of experience to express (in the way we *do* expect them to express relations of cause and effect). Such concepts can easily lead to irresolvable metaphysical speculation about the nature and purpose of human existence. Secondly, although we consider concepts like cause and object to play a central role in justifying empirical claims, this is no guarantee that they are *the* concepts that determine truth in the realm of appearances ('objectively real') – that they themselves are legitimate. As we saw, Hume offers an account of the origin of the concept of cause that shows that it is both psychologically unavoidable and objectively illegitimate. Finally, Descartes's attempt to purge our thinking of any psychological necessities or habitual commitments through the thought-experiment of the *malin génie* offers a methodological lesson. Since it leads at best to an awareness of our own existence as a thinking being, it is ill suited to establish the *objectivity* of our thinking.

The task, then, is to demonstrate that the concepts we find ourselves having to think with when we evaluate our empirical claims (experiences) are objectively applicable to those claims. The test of the legitimacy of these concepts will be their immunity to the Agrippan problem. That is to say, when S suggests as an explanation of a particular event that it was *caused* by another event, the *pk*-sceptic will be unable to generate doubts about the objectivity of the concept of cause by driving a wedge between what S *thinks* and what occurs in the world. To this end Kant distinguishes between two questions regarding concepts, each suggesting a different methodological approach. The "question of fact (*quid facti*)" (A: 84/B: 116) proceeds on the empiricist assumption that since we find ourselves having to think with certain concepts, their origin must be traced back to experience. According to Kant, Locke invented this approach and it had led to a familiar *impasse*. To the left stood the Scylla of dogmatism: with nothing to restrain his enquiries Locke had been led to the wildest metaphysical "extravagance". To the right stood the Charybdis of scepticism: Hume's response had been to abandon the quest for p-knowledge and to give "himself up entirely to scepticism" (A: 94/B: 127). In order to "safely . . . conduct reason between these two rocks" (*ibid.*) and ensure that the concepts are 'objectively' valid (legitimate), Kant holds that a different question has to be addressed: the "question of right (*quid juris*)" (A: 84/B: 116). This requires "a far different certificate of birth from that of a descent from experience" (A: 85/ B: 118). Adapting juridical jargon, according to which to deduce something is to prove its legitimacy, Kant claims that what we need is a (transcendental) *deduction* of the relevant concepts.

The 'inspiration' for the deduction comes from Kant's view of space and time. As we saw, these turned out to be formal conditions of the possibility of appearances a priori. The question is, are there any concepts without which the objects of experience cannot be thought? In other words, when we examine our experience of the world (of 'common life'), can we find any concepts without which it would not be possible? "If this question be answered in the affirmative, it follows that all empirical knowledge of objects is necessarily conformable to such concepts, since, if they are not presupposed, it is impossible that anything can be an object of experience" (A: 93/B: 125). In other words, objects must conform to the conditions of thought because it is only through these conditions that they can *be* objects of experience. Take for example the concept of a material object: *contra* Locke, I cannot have derived this from experience. Imagine trying to teach the concept of a car to a child by pointing out different cars; now imagine trying to teach the concept of an object by pointing out different . . . objects! Unlike the concept of a car, it is not a norm or criterion that can be *mis*applied to an object in experience because it is the condition of possibility of such experiences.

This, then, is the purpose of the transcendental deduction: to distinguish subjective necessities from objective necessities by identifying those concepts that are the conditions of possibility of experience. To demonstrate that a certain concept X is a necessary condition of experience (of external objects) is *not* to show that without it one could not have particular beliefs (thoughts) about the world; rather, it shows that X is an objectively valid feature of the world-as-experienced. To put it another way, these concepts – the so-called categories – do *not* relate to features that objects of experience must exemplify if they are to be *thinkable* by us. That would suggest that if these features were lacking, the objects of experience might still exist even though creatures like us could not know them (they would be like noumena). On the contrary, the categories relate to features that objects of experience must have if they are to *be* the objects of experience they *are*. It is a necessary condition of a feature or concept being applicable to an object in thought (the 'subjective' necessity) that it is exemplified in/by the object: "If by these categories alone it is possible to think any object of experience, it follows that they refer by necessity and *a priori* to all objects of experience" (B: 126).

Transcendental deductions thus answer Kant's *quid juris* by showing that it is only "by means" of such concepts as cause and effect that "experience is possible, in which experience they become objects and alone knowable to us" (Kant 1956: 53). If the *pk*-sceptic tries to generate the Agrippan argument by drawing our attention to the existence of certain (usurpatory) concepts or beliefs which although universally held seem to lead to disputes among the metaphysicians, he can (purport to) show that, unlike these, the categories and the constitutive (synthetic a priori) principles of the understanding that govern their use are necessary for experience. The Agrippan argument poses no threat because the question of how we know or are justified in believing that these categories and principles are the right sort for justifying our empirical claims cannot be raised without begging the question. What makes them claims (experiences) in the first place is that these categories and principles are formally contributed by the mind. Recalling Hume's sceptical attack on the justification of matters of fact and existence, Kant's response is that cause and effect is not a *criterion* for such claims, and so no regress of justification threatens. Rather, these claims are the empirical judgements that comprise experience and they just come structured in this way (e.g. they are always in space and time).

Transcendental illusion and the Humean Paradox

Kant aims to show how metaphysics is possible and satisfy (1) by demonstrating that the categories find legitimate employment in experience. With Hume, nature rescues us from scepticism in the form of dumb belief. For Kant, once we understand experience aright (that is to say, transcendentally), we understand that it legitimates *p*-knowledge (synthetic a priori) by blocking the challenge to justify the categories and principles we use to justify our empirical claims. Indeed, without experience the categories are said to be "without *sense*, that is, without meaning" (A: 239/B: 298). Kant's idealism is therefore a kind of verificationism – let's call it 'transcendental verificationism'. Experience verifies the categories because they only become meaningful *in* (that is to say, through *constituting*) experience.

We'll return to the issue of verificationism in later sections, but for the time being it should be noted that although the categories are without significance ('empty') when not expressed in experience, they nevertheless can be 'thought' independently of it. If they couldn't, Kant wouldn't be able to reason philosophically, which employs the categories 'outside' experience (the transcendental deduction). This independence is also the key to the second part of Kant's response to the sceptic and to the Humean Paradox – the task of showing that sceptical doubts *ought not to* have any influence on us by explaining how they arise (2).

At the end of Chapter 3 we noted that for Hume reflection is part of the imagination. Since the only check on reflection is instinct, we cannot show that the sceptical conclusions we arrive at when reflection drives us to adopt the theoretical attitude ought not to influence us (we cannot show that sceptical problems are unreal or meaningless). For Kant, however, reflection derives from reason and not the imagination. Accordingly, both questions that can be answered and questions that cannot be answered – both real problems and unreal problems – are presented to reason by its own nature. Thus, while he acknowledges that it might amount to "extravagant boasting and self-conceit" to "avow an ability to solve all problems and to answer all questions," (A: 475/B: 503), nevertheless, "the peculiarity of transcendental philosophy is, that there is no question relating to an object presented to pure reason, which is insoluble by this reason" (A: 477/B: 505). Central to (2) and Kant's response to the Humean Paradox is the identification of what he calls "*transcendental illusion*". This "leads us, in disregard of all warnings or criticism, completely beyond the empirical employment of the categories" (A: 294/B: 350) and to make *p*-knowledge claims about a realm of objects that we can never encounter in experience:

> There is indeed something seductive in our concepts of the understanding which tempts us to a transcendent use – a use which transcends all possible experience . . . understanding inadvertently adds for itself to the house of experience a much more extensive wing which it fills with nothing but beings of thought, without ever observing that it has transgressed with its otherwise legitimate concepts the bounds of their use.
>
> (1977: 315–16)

When confronted with an 'unreal' philosophical problem, then, the answer does not lie in a dogmatic metaphysical solution that would serve to generate the sort of disputes that attract the attention of the *pk*-sceptic. It is only "by means of a transcendental reflection" (A: 294/B: 350) that we can steel ourselves against what is "*natural* and unavoidable" (A: 296/B: 352) and which "does not cease to exist, even after it has been exposed, and its nothingness clearly perceived" (*ibid*.). The 'solution' is thus to alert us to the fact that the object of the (unreal) problem is solely in our own minds (a 'being of thought') and not to be encountered in experience.

We are now in a position to see how (1) and (2) work together against the *pk*-sceptic and constitute a response to the Humean

Paradox. If the sceptic tries to motivate doubt about the status of our empirical knowledge by questioning the legitimacy of the basic features of our epistemic practices, Kant indicates that the deductions that ground them show that they stand in need of no criteria because no meaningful question about their applicability to experience can be raised. It is not a case of asking whether or not this experience is adequate to reality, because it is always and already a cognition in which the appropriate categories have been deployed (to make it an experience). In response to Hume, Kant can point out that the reason that 'refin'd' reflections have little influence on us is that we are conceptually (understanding) and not merely habitually (imagination) 'at home' in experience. Similarly, if the sceptic tries to generate doubt by deploying the mode of Dispute, Kant can insouciantly explain that the reason metaphysicians have disagreed is because they have misemployed the very categories that he has patiently demonstrated are legitimately applicable only to experience. They *ought not* to carry any conviction because although it is entirely natural for us to think that the categories apply to things-in-themselves, transcendental reflection shows that when we do there is no *object* adequate to our idea that can "be given by any possible experience" (1977: 317).

Transcendental idealism and the linguistic turn

Although impressive, it will not have gone unnoticed that the condition of possibility of Kant's own solution to the problem of *pk*-scepticism is the doctrine of transcendental idealism. One way to evaluate the significance of this is to recall an earlier attempt at epistemology. In Chapter 2 we noted that the Stoics held that sensations are not 'external' to reason but have something like propositional content. It was on this basis that we drew the analogy with the book to the effect that the propositions q_2 to q_n are guaranteed to be meaningful. Following that analogy, for Kant the key to *p*-knowing is not the identification of a criterion of truth applicable to particular propositions, but the discernment of the underlying conditions of possibility of meaning applicable to all propositions in the book (including the false ones). We can still doubt the truth of particular propositions, but what we cannot doubt is what constitutes them *as* propositions. It is Kant's version of the Stoic claim that *logos* pervades matter – transcendental idealism – that assures us of the objectivity of appearances (the meaningfulness of q_2 to q_n).

Another way to evaluate Kant's idealism is by reconsidering Descartes's ultimate sceptical thought-experiment. We *could* regard the *malin génie* as co-extensive with things-in-themselves. In both cases we cannot *know* anything about the underlying cause, or ground, of what we experience. Where Descartes requires the existence of a God who is not a deceiver, Kant assures us that "appearances constitute objects that are wholly in us" (A: 129). As a result, the idea of being 'deceived' is, when related to the idea of objects as appearances, incoherent, because there are no other objects to be known. Kant's idealism thus redefines the concept of objectivity to *give us the world*, one whereby no gap can exist between subject and object because what is *thought* possible circumscribes the (empirically) real.

The conclusion seems to be that transcendental idealism is required to rescue *p*-knowing. But if the 'truth' of this somewhat troubling doctrine really is the only way of proving that metaphysical knowledge is possible, the *pk*-sceptic might well conclude that (as with Hume) they have been awarded a technical knockout. On the other hand, many 'realist' philosophers in search of a more full-blooded concept of objectivity than Kant appears to deliver (one that does not simply assure us of the world but makes it a bit of struggle to ensure that our concepts are the right ones!) have chafed at the thought that we can know nothing of the world in itself, concluding that if this is indeed the price for rebutting the sceptic it is too high to pay.

Nevertheless, there can be no doubting the long-term (often unconscious) influence of Kant's work on subsequent philosophy, and a great deal of energy has been expended on disentangling what has been taken to be his crucial insight – the distinction between 'passive' receptivity and an 'active', experience-constituting spontaneity – from its association with the phenomena–noumena distinction of Kant's idealism.[7] If this task can be given a specific focus, it is on the related issues of 'constitution' and the a priori. Due in part to philosophical criticisms (like Hegel's) and developments in logic, geometry and physics, but no doubt also to the impetus given to naturalism by the spread of Darwinism, the idea that there are 'ahistorical', 'apodictic' concepts in the 'mind' that somehow 'constitute' phenomena came to lose its appeal. Philosophers became increasingly convinced that language and not mind was the proper subject of enquiry, and Kant came to be seen as having failed to distinguish questions of fact (the realm of experience/knowledge) from questions of meaning (the realm of sense). From this perspective, attention to the semantic distinctions at play in our *uses* of language promised a new way of formulating Kant's innovation that was seemingly free of his idealism. The transcendental method thus came to be regarded as a concern not with the constitution of what there *is* but of how we *mean* – how we come to speak with objective purport. Rather than mysterious features of the mind, the a priori came to be seen as relating to the deepest structures of the language we use – to the conditions of possibility of our meaning what we say.

This so-called 'linguistic turn' is the distinctive feature of twentieth-century philosophy. Evolving from the critique of Kant, it has developed two somewhat antagonistic schools of thought, each regarding itself as a variety of naturalism. The first of these allies itself with 'scientific' language and the methods of formal logic, and continues to hold sway over much contemporary thinking in epistemology and the philosophy of language in the United States. The second looks to our uses of 'ordinary' language in the search for philosophical clarity, and has had the greatest influence in the United Kingdom. Each has a characteristic range of approaches to scepticism, which will be dealt with in detail in Chapters 6 and 5 (respectively). In the remainder of this chapter we will examine how they developed 'linguistic' versions of distinctively 'Kantian' anti-sceptical themes. The two most influential proponents of scientific naturalism are Rudolph Carnap (1891–1970) and Willard Van Orman Quine (1908–2000). Although there are marked differences between them, Quine was influenced by Carnap and other members of the 'Vienna Circle'.[8] We'll look briefly at logical positivism and Carnap's quasi-Kantian response to epistemological scepticism, and Quine's recommendation to 'naturalize' epistemology by eliminating the normative element from it. We'll then return to (3) above and examine what are taken to be the contemporary heirs of Kant's transcendental deductions, transcendental arguments.

Naturalism and verificationism

Although many philosophers accepted that Kant's receptivity–spontaneity dualism was the basis for epistemological enquiry, it was not at all clear how one was to understand the related notions of 'constitution' (with its mysterious suggestion that the mind somehow 'made up' or 'created' reality) and the a priori. In his *Der Logische Aufbau der Welt*[9] of 1928, Carnap offered a semantic solution. For an object or concept[10] *Y* to be constituted is for it to be constructed out of more basic concepts, the most fundamental of which comprise our ontology. The reverse of construction is analysis or reduction. If *Y* is a constructed object it is possible to analyse (reduce) talk of *Y* into assertions about experiences that a cognizing subject has of it (is 'given'). If *Y* is a barn, what makes barn talk *possible* (meaningful) is that such an analysis can be undertaken. Barn-talk will therefore be 'constituted' by more primitive concepts that can be related to what is given in elementary experiences through the reports that are given of those experiences.

Since the origin of all knowledge is subjective (constructed from the contents of individual experiences), Carnap's is a classically internalist account. It does however offer an apparent solution to the problem of a priori truths. When we undertake the semantic analysis of certain claims, their truth turns out to rest entirely with the meanings of the concepts used. The truth of 'a cat is a mammal', for example, follows from the meaning of 'cat'. If you know what a cat 'is' (that is to say, what the concept means; the conditions under which it is correct to use the term), you know that a cat is a mammal. More importantly still, it offers a way of dealing with Kant's 'usurpatory' concepts: if the condition of possibility of their meaning is reduction to experience, any concept which cannot be so reduced must be without empirical content (no observation links the conditions of its employment with the 'given') and therefore *meaningless*. This links up with the positivists' slogans about verifiability. According to the verificationist theory of meaning, the meaning of a sentence is the set of possible experiences that would tend to show that it is true. A variant is the more general verification principle, which avers that sentences are factually meaningless if there is in principle no method of verifying their truth. This link between empirical verifiability and meaningfulness inspired Schlick with positivistic fervour:

> Everything is knowable which can be expressed, and this is the total subject matter concerning which meaningful questions

can be raised. There are consequently no questions which are in principle insoluble ... The act of verification in which the path to the solution finally ends is always the same sort: it is the occurrence of a definite fact that is confirmed by observation, by means of immediate experience ... Thus metaphysics collapses not because the solving of its tasks is an enterprise to which human reason is unequal (as for example Kant thought) but because there is no such task. (1949: 56–7)

On the face of it this promises a ready response to the argument from ignorance. If doubt about the justification of my empirical beliefs rests on the ineliminability of sceptical possibilities like dreaming and the *malin génie*, it appears that it can't be meaningful precisely because they are ineliminable (i.e. insoluble, and therefore meaningless). Unfortunately, this quick fix comes with a familiarly heavy price tag. Schlick's talk of 'definite facts' 'confirmed by observation' takes us back to the problem of the criterion of truth, and the threat of the Agrippan argument. It seems entirely reasonable to ask how *S* knows that an assertion of experience is adequately representing what is 'given' in her experience. On the other hand, if with Carnap one adopts an internalist standpoint and supposes that subjective experiences are the building blocks of knowledge, it is not clear how one escapes solipsism and wins one's way to the objective (public) world. Does it even make sense to talk about immediate experience in this way? Can one use a simple observation language without already knowing a language that is public and therefore neither derived from nor reducible to simple experience?

In a sense these are criticisms of the sort Kant brought against the empiricists, but the Kantian contribution brings its own problems. In the last section I suggested Kant could be regarded as a sort of transcendental verificationist. Experience verifies applications of the categories in so far as they become meaningful only through constituting experience. For the positivists *constitution* is replaced by *construction*, and immediate experience becomes the test of meaning in so far as sentences can be reduced to it. Where for Kant experience serves as a criterion of meaningfulness because of the 'truth' of transcendental idealism, for the positivists it serves as a criterion of meaningfulness because of the 'truth' of verificationism. And like transcendental idealism, verificationism buys meaning at the expense of our concept of objectivity. Although our 'intuition' that the world is the way it is independent of our beliefs about it seems to fuel Cartesian scepticism, that recognition does not of itself seem sufficient to abandon it in favour of the world's reduction to experience. Similarly, Kant seems to oblige us to assent to the truth of transcendental idealism, a p-knowledge claim that itself stands in need of justification and yet which cannot be justified within Kant's system (it is not synthetic a priori). For their part, the positivists oblige us to assent to the truth of the verification principle, and yet since this divides statements into the meaningful (verifiable) and the meaningless (unverifiable), it is itself meaningless (being unverifiable). It is little wonder that the positivists found it impossible to express exactly what their principle was.[11]

To sum up, the problem with logical positivism is that to associate the a posteriori with standards of scientific evidence and the a priori with (in effect) logical truth fails on two counts. On the one hand, the distinction itself requires metaphysical resources it cannot justify (the verification principle), thereby inviting pk-scepticism in the form of the Agrippan argument. On the other hand, it does not answer to our experience in common life. More specifically, it fails to do justice to our concept of objectivity, and it does not explain why or how it is that features of our language (the sorts of concepts that Hume attacked and Kant defended) play the role they do in justifying our beliefs.

Carnap took a stab at these latter problems. In "Pseudoproblems in Philosophy", a piece written around the time of the *Aufbau*, he follows the logical positivist line and argues that one can pose meaningful questions regarding the existence of *particular* objects. Consider two geographers, S and R, who happen to have incompatible metaphysical beliefs and who disagree about the existence of a particular mountain. Since their disagreement about the mountain will be settled by the usual empirical methods, it is insulated from their philosophical beliefs: the "choice of philosophical viewpoint has no influence on the content of natural science" (1967a: 333). It is only when S and R remove themselves from the realm of experience (common life) and insist on giving "a philosophical interpretation of the empirical results about which they agree" (*ibid.*) that a dispute arises. Now S insists (say) that the mountain is *really* real (an objective feature of the external world), whereas R contends that it is only a dream mountain (and *S* only a dream companion). Since both these theses "go beyond experience and have no factual content . . . they have no meaning at all" (*ibid*.: 334).

In a later piece Carnap modifies his approach a little. When the geographers are deciding whether or not the mountain exists, they are addressing what he calls an 'internal' question of existence. Questions like this are only possible once one has "accepted the thing language with its framework for things", and the concept of reality used is taken to be "an empirical, scientific, non-metaphysical concept" (1967b: 73). These sorts of questions are contrasted with the 'external' question of existence, where the "reality of the thing world itself " is called into question (*ibid*.). Only philosophers raise this question. In this case *S* will give a positive answer to the 'external' question and *R* a negative one, neither appreciating that the question cannot be answered because it is *not real*.

For Carnap, then, both *S* and *R* fail to see that since what it is to be a 'thing' is determined by the possible verifiability of scientific-theoretical sentences, the question of a thing's reality can only arise *within* the system and not be applied *to* it. But if the philosophical question is not *real*, what is it? Carnap's suggestion is that it is a "practical question . . . concerning the structure of our language" (*ibid*.). We may, he says, make other *practical* choices (of other conceptual schemes); but since beliefs are theoretical items whose meaning relates to the verifiability of sentences, understood externally our commitment to the 'thing-world' (or any alternative) is not to be construed as a belief at all. Rather, it is the decision to accept of certain sort of rule-bound activity, like the decision to play chess rather than soccer. Like Hume, then, we cannot *justify* our commitment to talk of the external world because strictly speaking we don't *have* such a belief.[12]

Carnap's distinction between 'internal' (common life) and 'external' (philosophical) questions is thoroughly Kantian.[13] Whereas for Kant we cannot have experience without the categories, for Carnap we cannot reason empirically (including justify our claims) unless we commit ourselves to the framework of thing-constituting concepts, which are themselves answerable to pragmatic factors – their success or failure in dealing with experience. Our conceptual norms are legitimate because we cannot make sense of what it would be to question their justification (as criteria of justification come along with the acceptance of the framework). That seems to make Carnap's view impervious to an empirical version of the Agrippan argument. Similarly, since we do not, strictly speaking, have a belief in the external world, Carnap's position seems invulnerable to both the knowledge and the justification versions of the argument from ignorance.

Despite the promise, the problems are familiar. First, Carnap relies on verificationism to insulate the 'internal' realm of scientific activity from the 'external' realm of philosophical reflection and reserve the concept of belief for the former. But verificationism is itself a philosophical principle, in which case it must be a practical commitment and not a belief (if it were a belief it would of course stand in need of justification, and that would invite pk-scepticism). This may explain why it is difficult to say what it is, but it also makes it hard to know what it would be to commit oneself to it. One might have a good idea what the decision to play chess consists in, but it's not clear what it would be to become a thoroughgoing verificationist, or why one should strive to be one.[14]

If it's not clear how verificationism could be a practical commitment, as opposed to a theoretical belief, it's similarly difficult to imagine that thing-talk amounts to nothing more than a commitment – that we don't have a *belief* in the external world, and that nothing more than pragmatic success keeps us from trading in one conceptual scheme for another. It certainly seems to many philosophers that they do have a belief in an objective world of things, and that they think this belief is true. That's what motivates the desire to answer the argument from ignorance. Finally, one might add that the very idea of pragmatic success raises difficulties. As Kant might point out, pragmatic success does not amount to legitimacy – 'fate' and 'fortune' might be pragmatically successful concepts, but that does not make them the right one's for justifying our experiences.

Quine and normativity

Carnap hoped to show that our concepts are legitimate. He therefore acknowledged that epistemology is a normative enterprise. The attempt to demonstrate that we don't have a belief in the external world is part of that enterprise – drawing a line round what we do and do not have to justify. In the terms of Chapter 1,

Carnap's is a *heroic* response to the epistemological task. As we also noted, however, there is a *rejectionist* alternative, which denies that knowledge as such stands in need of a special kind of justification. The philosopher usually associated with this particular version of 'naturalism' is Quine. Unlike Carnap, Quine does *not* view philosophical questions as 'external', non-cognitive or 'practical' ones. Recalling Otto Neurath's figure likening science to a boat that must be rebuilt plank by plank, he asserts "the philosopher and the scientist are in the same boat" (1960: 3): "The philosopher's task differs from the others' . . . in no such drastic way as those suppose who imagine for a philosopher a vantage point outside the conceptual scheme that he takes in charge. There is no such cosmic exile" (*ibid.*: 275). Since philosophy is held to be continuous with, even if more general than, natural science, this has two immediate implications:

- We do have a *belief* in external objects. Like any other "positing", the "hypothesis of ordinary physical objects" (*ibid.*: 22; cf. 1975: 67) is open to empirical investigation, and therefore entitled to be called knowledge.
- Sceptical doubts constitute a threat to natural science that arises from *within* natural science: "scepticism is an offshoot of natural science . . . sceptical doubts are scientific doubts" (1975: 67–8).

Clearly, Quine's attempt to naturalize the problem of scepticism in this way could not answer the sceptical problems as traditionally conceived. Investigating how as a matter of empirical fact we come to believe in the existence of external objects, or how as a matter of empirical fact our sceptical doubts get off the ground ("the awareness of illusion, the discovery that we must not always believe our eyes" (*ibid.*: 67)), would never render the argument from ignorance or the Agrippan argument illegitimate. Being 'in the same boat' as someone is not *always* a source of consolation! The task is therefore to prevent scepticism presenting itself as a normative problem in the first place by offering an account of epistemology that is itself devoid of norms. In other words, the sceptic has to be denied the possibility of adopting the external standpoint of the 'cosmic exile'. This is the standpoint we have hitherto associated with the theoretical attitude, which allows the philosopher and the sceptic to take a purely reflective (non-practical) attitude towards our 'conceptual scheme' (concepts and practices of justification) and as a consequence generate doubts about its legitimacy.

As we've seen, Carnap aimed to insulate empirical (internal) practices against theoretical attitude doubt by denying the would-be philosophical exile anything other than a *practical* (external) perspective, and therefore denying that we have so much as a belief (a *theoretical* item) in the existence of the external world. Since Quine rejects an internal–external distinction, this option is not available to him. His proposal is therefore to eliminate the normative from epistemology – to 'naturalize' it – by presenting an alternative, 'naturalistic', conception of the nature of the knower. This is a conception that does not see a knower's claims as standing in need of a demonstration of their possibility, and therefore does not require the theoretical attitude. Instead Quine's naturalized epistemology "studies a natural phenomenon . . . a physical human subject" (1969: 82). This undergoes stimulation at its sensory surfaces and in response "delivers as output a description of the three-dimensional external world and its history" (*ibid*.: 83).

What emerges from Quine's account of this subject of knowledge is a strongly empiricist version of Kant's distinction between receptivity and spontaneity. Although the subject receives only a "meagre input" (1969: 83) of "surface irritations" (1960: 22), the result is a "world view" (*ibid*.: 5) that consists of a "torrential output" (1969: 83) of posited objects and projected theories. The enormous gap between the input and output "marks the extent of man's conceptual sovereignty" (1960: 5). Knowledge is therefore a composite of two distinct elements: the subject's receptivity relates to the world's contribution of uninterpreted "cues" (*ibid*.), and its spontaneity relates to man's interpretative scheme which sets to work on them and thereby *constitutes* the "torrential output". The naturalized epistemologist investigates the relation between the "meagre input" and the "torrential output" in order to determine "how evidence relates to theory, and in what ways one's theory of nature transcends any available evidence" (1969: 83).

Clearly the mark of success of Quine's approach to scepticism depends on the extent to which he can get us to abandon the idea that epistemology is a normative enterprise without violating what we called (in Chapter 1) the no-stipulations principle. There is no space to go into the details of Quine's argument, but here's one obvious problem. Imagine that S has the cognitive constitution described by Quine; that is, in response to a meagre sensory input she produces a torrential theoretical output. On the traditional view, we imagine a standpoint (adopting the theoretical attitude) from which the epistemic status of S's beliefs can be evaluated. Since this is the same (external) standpoint that the sceptic adopts when he suggests that S's experiences are consistent with her dreaming or being an envatted brain, Quine cannot sanction it. Of course, if that standpoint is closed, the only one that is open to the epistemologist is S's (internal); but S by definition doesn't know if her beliefs are true, since they are only part of that 'torrential output'. Pursuing this line, the episte-mologist is driven to the conclusion that any further theorizing he might engage in will itself be another projection from his sensory inputs, including his own original theory that knowledge is a combi-nation of a 'meagre' input and conceptual interpretation. In other words, the epistemologist who starts out by trying to investigate S's knowledge ends up in a position where his own theory makes it impossible to show that he has knowledge at all. The attempt to solve external world scepticism (the argument from ignorance) succumbs to the Agrippan argument.

The motivation for Quine's position is familiarly Humean: attacking the idea of cognitive responsibility (normativity) by taking 'knowledge' out of the hands of the knower (externalism). The prob-lem is that by retaining a theoretical distinction (p-knowledge) between what the world contributes to knowledge and what we contribute to knowledge, he allows the pk-sceptic to shift the idea of responsibility to the level of theory, and ask how the epistemologist knows that his theory is true (invoking the Agrippan argument). Quine's influence on contemporary philosophy has been enormous, and we'll encounter examples of his legacy in Chapter 6. Now it is time to return to take up the second strand of Kant's influence.

Transcendental arguments

Recall the argument from ignorance:

> S doesn't know that not-sp

If S doesn't know that not-sp, then S doesn't know that q

Therefore

S doesn't know that q

We could summarize Carnap's and Quine's approaches as attempts to demonstrate that the first premise is either false (Quine) or meaningless (Carnap). As presented, these attempts fail because they require certain p-knowledge claims that are themselves vulnerable to pk-scepticism (in the form of the Agrippan argument). As we've seen, Kant was not motivated by a concern with the problem of the external world, but by the threat of pk-scepticism. Nevertheless, he did offer an argument against the external world sceptic, the so-called 'Refutation of Idealism' (3). Kant recognized that the plausibility of something like the first premise of the argument from ignorance depends on presupposing a certain image of the relationship between the mind and the world (broadly, Cartesian), and it is this image that his attack on idealism seeks to rebut. What is distinctive about Kant's approach is that since he is aware that any argument against the idealist/sceptic requires p-knowledge, the refutation of idealism is foregrounded against his attempt to deal with pk-scepticism by showing that such knowledge is possible. To put it in a nutshell, Kant recognizes that any response to the argument from ignorance must show that the image of mind and world that makes the first premise seem true is incorrect, and it must do so while remaining invulnerable to pk-scepticism.

In contemporary terms the argument is something like the following. The Cartesian sceptic supposes that S has immediate and incorrigible access to experiences or thoughts with determinate content (e.g. that she is sitting at her desk in Chicago). Moreover, these 'inner' experiences or thoughts are epistemically privileged in so far as they are the basis on which S makes inferences to the existence of external objects. This account of the epistemic priority of S's experiences provides the backdrop to the first premise of the argument from ignorance, for S now discovers that although she cannot doubt that she is having a sitting-at-her-desk-in-Chicago experience, she can doubt that she's actually sitting at her desk in Chicago (dreaming, envatted brain etc.). It turns out that the 'subjective' evidence of inner experience is insufficient to warrant inferences to the existence of external objects and thereby bridge the gap between the mind and the world. Kant's proof aims to turn "the game which idealism plays . . . upon itself" (B: 274) by showing that "external experience is properly immediate" and "internal experience is itself possible only mediately" (B: 275) "through the existence of real things that I perceive outside me" (B: 274).

We can't consider the argument in detail, but a couple of points are worth noting. The aim is to show that a *specific* sort of scepticism is self-refuting since the condition of possibility of what the sceptic readily accepts – 'inner experience' – is something he denies. As such it aims to undercut the sceptic by showing that he cannot formulate his basic assumption: that S's thoughts could be the way they are (have the content they have) independently of the way the world is. In doing so it denies the sceptic the image of the relationship between the mind and the world that supports ontological internalism – the view that for S to be justified in believing that q, the grounds that justify her belief must be contents of her mind ('inner' experiences) – and gives the first premise of the argument from ignorance its plausibility.

In the 'refutation' Kant advances a variety of what is now called semantic or content externalism, the thesis that the 'content' of S's thoughts is at least partially determined by how things are in the world. The most influential recent use of a version of semantic externalism to respond to the first premise of the argument from ignorance derives from Hilary Putnam's attempt to prove that we're not envatted brains.[15] This has generated an enormous literature but I am not going to discuss it, for a very simple reason: the truth of semantic externalism has to be assumed before the thesis can be used against the sceptic's argument. What we are primarily interested in, then, are arguments for something like semantic externalism – the view that seeks to deny the sceptic the view of the mind that underpins the first premise of the argument from ignorance. This is what Kant's 'argument' aims to do, but like his other deductions its overall effectiveness is ultimately bound up with the details of his idealist response to the Agrippan argument. Since we've already dwelt on this, it is more appropriate to examine the contemporary interest in transcendental arguments. These are generally regarded as deriving from the 'deductions' that Kant offered in the *Critique of Pure Reason*. As Ralph Walker describes them, they are "anti-sceptical arguments which seek to justify their conclusions by exhibiting them as necessary conditions for experience, or knowledge, or language; or for experience, knowledge, or language of some general type" (Walker 1989: 56).[16] Their form is something like this:

P_1, If P_1 then C (or, P_1 *only if* C), *therefore* C[17]

where (P_1) is the "bare premise that . . . there is experience, knowledge or language of some very general kind" (*ibid.*: 59), which is *accepted by the sceptic*, and (C) is what the sceptic doubts. Applying this to the simple presentation of Kant's argument above gives us something like the following:

(P_1) One has first-person access to one's mental states ('internal experience is itself possible only mediately')

(P_2) It is a necessary condition of P_1 that one is able to describe public objects (C) ('external experience . . . of real things that I perceive outside me . . . is properly immediate')

Therefore

(C) One is able to describe public objects

The anti-sceptical force turns on the fact that the sceptic's doubts about (C) are 'unreal' because they constitute a rejection of a condition of possibility of the conceptual scheme within which alone his doubts *make sense* (P_1). The sceptic therefore cannot formulate the first premise of the argument from ignorance.

A number of sceptical objections have been raised against the legitimacy of these generalized, anti-sceptical transcendental arguments.[18] The historicist objection[19] is that in striving to identify what are claimed to be necessary features of *any* conceptual scheme, as opposed to just our own (and hence to justify them; that is, to answer the *pk*-sceptic), the 'method' of transcendental argumentation implies that we can step outside our scheme and compare it with others in order to see if these features are carried over to them. The criticism is that this could only be achieved by comparing the candidate necessity with all its conceivable competitors. But then we would need a criterion that would allow us to distinguish between identifying a genuine (justified) necessity and temporarily running out of interesting alternatives,[20] which invites the Agrippan argument.

The most influential objection to transcendental arguments is that they either establish the necessity of belief alone or tacitly rely on a version of the verification principle. If the former, they clearly fail to answer a sceptic since none need reject the claim that we have to *think* in certain ways. The problem is whether or not the ways that we have to think (the concepts we have to use) give us knowledge or justified beliefs. If transcendental arguments do indeed rely on some version of the verification principle, then we already have sufficient grounds for thinking that they will not work against the sceptic.[21] Barry Stroud originally raised the objection, but rather than examine one of his examples, let's look at a more interesting case, Wittgenstein's so-called 'private-language argument'.[22]

Verificationism and the private-language argument

The private-language argument can be fairly uncontroversially regarded as an anti-sceptical, transcendental argument against the Cartesian (ontologically and semantically internalist) image of the mind, according to which we have incorrigible first-person access to the contents of our mental states from which inference to the existence of external objects has to be made.[23] In Wittgenstein's terms this is to undermine the idea that there could be a language in which "the individual words . . . refer to what can only be known to the person speaking: to his immediate private sensations. So another person cannot understand that language" (1953: §243). Let P_1 be something the sceptic accepts – that S can 'meaningfully' talk about a private experience or sensation k. The aim of the argument is to establish that a condition of possibility of P_1 is something that the sceptic doubts – something along the lines that for S to mean something by 'k', someone other than S must in principle be able to determine whether or not she is having a k-experience or a k-sensation (that is to say, that ks exist as part of the publicly accessible world external to S's mind). We might then cast the argument as follows:[24]

(P_1) A sign 'k' is a word (has meaning) in S's language

Only if

(P_2) Its use is governed by a rule

Only if

(P_3) It is possible to misapply the rule

Only if

(P_4) It is possible to believe a thing k and it not be a k

Only if

(C) It is 'logically possible' (for someone else) to 'find out' that it is not a k

(P_2) expresses the view that when S calls something a k, a judgement (however unconscious) takes place, which suggests that a criterion of correctness (a norm) is being employed. (P_3) indicates that it is in the nature of judgements that they can go wrong, and (P_4) suggests what it would mean to 'go wrong' in such cases. The problem is that (P_4) is compatible with the *privacy* of S's sensations, and therefore with the idea that she could give the word 'k' meaning without recourse to a world external to the mind. In other words, (C) is not a *necessary* condition of (P_4) at all. And yet without it all the argument has demonstrated is that it is only if S has a criterion for identifying ks that is fulfilled that she can talk meaningfully about them; that is, that her *believing* that there are ks is necessary for k-talk. This is not a conclusion that any Cartesian sceptic needs to worry about. He needn't deny that S *believes* that external objects exist or that she has a pain in her leg (as opposed to a tickle under her arm). The problem is whether or not such beliefs are justified if S could have them even though (as a brain in a vat) she might not even have a leg to stand on!

According to this criticism, the only way to get from (P_1) to the anti-sceptical conclusion (C) is to rely on a version of the verificationist principle:

(P_5) 'k' has meaning in S's *language* only if it is possible to 'find out' whether or not a thing is a k

This is required to close the gap between belief and world, and thereby refute the sceptic by showing that meaning requires external criteria. This is not transcendentally *deduced* (as a condition of possibility); it is a *premise* requiring independent justification. If it were true, then the argument from (P_1-P_4) would become superfluous because (P_5) does all the required anti-sceptical work itself.

As we've seen, any attempt to justify (P_5) runs up against the Agrippan argument, and yet without it we're left in the position that the Cartesian sceptic who embraces (ontological and semantic) internalism wants us in – each of us might be a brain in a vat talking 'meaningfully' (to ourselves) about our vat-experiences and distinguishing all too successfully in rule-governed ways between pains in (vat-)legs and tickles in (vat-)arms. Each of us would be speaking a private language and none of our empirical beliefs would be justified claims about anything outside our vat environment.[25]

Rule-following and the private-language argument

Let's call the above presentation of the private-language argument/transcendental approach the 'sensation' interpretation. The 'sensation' model seems to lead to the conclusion that such an attempt to solve the argument from ignorance either fails (leaving us to contemplate our vat-pains and pleasures) or ends up readmitting the Agrippan argument. Is there another way of viewing the private-language argument that does not invite the *pk*-sceptic back into the fray? Let's call the alternative the 'rule' interpretation.[26] According to this the "'private language argument' as applied to *sensations* [§§243–75] is only a special case of much more general considerations about language . . . found in the sections *preceding* §243" (Kripke 1982: 3). These sections (§§138–242) deal with the intelligibility of private rule-following. Briefly, the argument is as follows: if the criteria, norms or rules that S uses to make judgements have to be applied, a question arises concerning what the rule might be for the application of the rule. To take an example, a rule of chess is that one can advance a pawn one or two squares the first time it is moved, and only one square thereafter. When S moves a pawn in chess, then, she might be said to play in accordance with this rule. It is natural to think that in order to do so, S has to be able to interpret the rule; and this is where the problem arises. The sceptic asks how S knows that she is applying the *right* rule, or interpreting the rule correctly, which suggests that in order to interpret correctly S has to know some further rule, which in turn requires interpretation (and so on).

This generates the regress of justification we associate with the Agrippan argument. The sceptical problem appears to be that if language (meaning) requires rules, and rules have to be applied, there is no sense in which a rule is ever knowingly (justifiably) applied correctly. And yet . . . we go on. That is to say, with respect to common life (talking; playing chess) we continue just as we did before. According to Wittgenstein this shows that "there is a way of grasping a rule which is *not* an *interpretation*, but which is exhibited in what we call 'obeying the rule' and 'going against it' in actual cases" (§201). Rules, then, are habits of action; parts of social and institutional practices; ways of going on that human beings are trained into, and which hook up with salient features of the world (like chess pieces and other people). Since to obey a rule is not to *think* anything, but to *do* something (even when that doing *is* thinking), one cannot obey a rule 'privately': obedience is exhibited in the successful (public) performance of an action. On the 'rule' interpretation Wittgenstein's position is often associated with Hume's 'solution' to the sceptical problem of what justifies reasoning from cause and effect. As we saw in Chapter 3, Hume invokes our natural (habitual) disposition to respond to regularities in our experience in order to undermine the sceptical force of the Agrippan argument. It should be noted, however, that Wittgenstein's account is not merely causal. The norms constitutive of practices are precisely that: *norms*. Like Kantian categories, these rules are present 'in' *public* experiences, and their imperviousness to sceptical doubt derives from the pull of common life.

The significance of this is that (P_4) is only a necessary condition of (P_3) if *private* rule-following is possible. That is to say, (P_4) is only a necessary condition of (P_3) if the Cartesian (internalist) image is *presupposed*. Since the aim of the 'sensation' interpretation of the private language argument is to rebut this image, something has clearly gone wrong. On the 'rule' interpretation, then, (P_3) is possible *only if* reference to membership of a wider community is (always already) made. In other words, we cannot make sense of a *private* model of rule-following if we adopt a standpoint from *within* the practical activities of a community of language users (as opposed to the Cartesian standpoint 'inside' our minds). Since (P_4) is not an intelligible position on the 'rule' interpretation, (P_5) – the verification principle – is not required to ensure that beliefs hook up to the world.

With this alternative account of the private language argument in mind it's worth noting a remark of Kripke's to the effect that "the demand for 'outward criteria' is no verificationist or behaviourist *premise* that Wittgenstein takes for granted in his 'private language argument'. If anything, it is deduced, in the sense of deduction akin to Kant's" (Kripke 1982: 100). Kripke does not elaborate on what he takes a deduction in Kant's sense to be, but the reference to Kant is instructive. For Kant a *private* language of whatever could meaningfully be termed 'sensation' is impossible. As we saw when we looked briefly at the 'refutation of idealism', the possibility of inner experience ('private' sensation) is outer experience: experience *is* knowledge and it necessarily exhibits obedience to certain constitutive rules; namely, the categories. Since there can be no 'private' rule-following for Kant, he too would hold something like (P_4) to be unintelligible. Kant's verificationism is *deduced*; it is a 'transcendental verificationism'. As we saw above, however, Kant's 'verificationism' is bought at the cost of his transcendental idealism. Without that, Wittgenstein's *deduced* verificationism can have none of the anti-sceptical consequences that Kant intended. Considerations of rule-following do not therefore amount to a refutation of scepticism, because they cannot prevent the sceptic (insisting on the internalist perspective) from adopting the theoretical attitude and taking a standpoint outside our practices (community) and claiming that they all fail to hook up to reality in the appropriate way.

Mitigated scepticism

We seem to have good reasons for concluding that the argument from ignorance cannot be refuted. I have suggested that what gives it its plausibility is a certain internalist (Cartesian) image of mind and world that arises in response to *pk*-scepticism and the Agrippan argument. If this is true, a refutation of the argument from ignorance involves having to show that this image is wrong, and this seems to require the sorts of p-knowledge claims that stand in need of justification themselves and which are thus vulnerable to the Agrippan argument.

The point of advancing the 'rule' interpretation of the private language argument was not, however, to present an argument which is explicitly in Wittgenstein's text and which is specifically intended as a refutation of scepticism. The fact that we have not managed to discern a refutation of the argument from ignorance does not therefore mean that this interpretation achieves nothing. We have already encountered examples where an 'argument' may be entered 'dialectically' and not be intended as a *direct* refutation. It is in this spirit – the spirit of *mitigated* or 'therapeutic' scepticism – that I suggest the private-language argument be viewed. Recognizing the sceptical threat to p-knowledge claims, it invites us to think about language and meaning in a way that discourages us from making the internalist assumption that underpins the argument from ignorance. It encourages us to reject the temptation to adopt the theoretical attitude and to embrace the engaged standpoint of common life (where we find that our norms/rules stand in need of no theoretical justification).

Our discussion of transcendental arguments offers ample evidence of how direct responses to scepticism can fail. These aim to show that the condition of possibility of the sceptic's doubts being meaningful is the truth of something she denies. If that is the case, the sceptic's doubt – expressed, say, in the first premise of the argument from ignorance – is meaningless. But if it is meaningless, there isn't really a problem of scepticism in the first place: there's nothing for the epistemologist to respond to since there's nothing for him to make sense of. This is why transcendental philosophy tends towards verificationism. It is the quick fix for demonstrating the meaninglessness of philosophical problems.

As we've seen, this approach cannot avoid the Agrippan argument. But it also presents a new concern: the simple, seemingly intuitive problem that the sceptic's doubts do in fact seem to make sense (a lot more sense than the verificationist principle, for example!). Even if these doubts presuppose an internalist image of the mind, that does not rule out the possibility that that image arises naturally from reflecting on our basic intuitions about objectivity and justification. In Chapter 5 we'll consider accounts of sceptical problems that accept that they are not meaningless (because they arise 'naturally' when we reflect on our knowledge claims) and that they are not open to theoretical rebuttal. For some philosophers this means that they stand in need of diagnosis – some understanding of how they come about that will wean us off them. For other philosophers they reveal something about the kinds of creatures we are that suggests we might never rid ourselves of them.

5 Un/natural doubts

Scepticism, intuition and the Humean Paradox

In common life we all have lots of beliefs, many of which are true and the majority of which amount to cases of knowing. I know that New York is east of Chicago, my car is parked in front of the house and that Karen is afraid to wear a hat. If asked why I think I know these things (by myself or another), I have a pretty clear idea how to respond: grab an atlas; point to the dilapidated Ford outside; explain the strange circumstances attending Karen's upbringing. Pushed for evidence beyond a certain point I'm likely to become either bemused or irritated ('because that is what it means to be *east* of something'). Practical attitude doubts operate within a limited ambit of reason-giving, and do not bear on our entitlement to the concept of knowledge.

S1   From the engaged standpoint of common life we have an ability to reflect on our beliefs and ask if we are justified in believing/know them to be true (practical attitude doubt)

As we have we have seen, however, practical attitude doubt does not appear to exhaust the possibilities. For example, contemplating an empirical claim q, it seems quite natural to press the question of how we know that q is the case in a different sort of way. We now find ourselves making a general observation about the dependence of our empirical beliefs on experience. In bracketing out the particular in this way we adopt the theoretical attitude and discover that while experience seems to justify empirical claims on the basis of its objectivity, we as yet have no evidence for the objectivity of experience. If we are not to beg the question, any potential evidence cannot involve a logically anterior commitment to the existence of external objects. That would be circular, and the Agrippan argument has taught us to beware of circular reasoning! We therefore conclude that our empirical knowledge claims can only be held justified to the extent that we can identify an epistemically secure or privileged evidential base from which to subsequently infer the existence of external objects. Our own (subjective) sensory beliefs seem to be the best candidates for these items. Finally, we come to realize that if we were dreaming or an envatted brain, our experiences could be just the way they are independently of whether or not external things *do* exist. That is to say, nothing in subjective experience explains *how* we can know what we claim to know, and therefore how empirical knowledge is possible. Starting from (S1) we arrive 'naturally' at:

S2 Reflecting in this way seems to lead us naturally to take up a philosophical standpoint on our epistemic concepts and generates philosophical sceptical doubts about their legitimacy (theoretical attitude doubt).

The naturalness of the transition from (S1) to (S2) confronts the non-sceptic with what I'll call the *Intuition Problem*; namely, showing why this seemingly intuitive outcome of our attempts to evaluate our epistemic practices is not as compelling as it appears. After all, it is this transition that makes the argument from ignorance possible. Here it is again:

S doesn't know that not-*sp*
If S doesn't know that not-*sp*, then S doesn't know that *q*

Therefore

S doesn't know that *q*

This is only the start, of course. Once the sceptic has raised this possibility, we find ourselves on the 'subjective' side of the gap that has opened up between our beliefs and the world. The problem now is what sort of evidence is available to us to effect the sort of inference we need from the former to the latter? Consider the following arguments:

I believe there's a barn in front of me
Whatever I believe is true

Therefore

There's a barn in front of me

The fact that the second premise is false is not important. The point is that if we take the first premise as a typical example of what we *can* assert, and the conclusion as the corresponding knowledge claim, what we need are propositions like the second premise to complete the inference. But the second premise is not a statement *about* experience, and not something we can get from experience as formulated: it is a p-knowlege claim of the sort we found Descartes attempting to elucidate.[1] Two related features of these claims stand out. On the one hand they raise the question of how to justify p-knowledge claims given the array of possible (and conflicting) solutions that have been offered. This gestures towards the Agrippan argument and pk-scepticism. On the other hand, these metaphysical recommendations arise in response to theoretical attitude doubts that carry no conviction from the standpoint of our practical dealings with the world, and therefore offer no constraint on possible solutions.[2]

In this sceptical narrative a seemingly natural concern with justification (of the sort radicalized in the Agrippan argument) gives rise to an obligation to secure a set of epistemically secure commitments, which in turn leads to the argument from ignorance. Attempts to solve this risk the reintroduction of the Agrippan argument and the implication that none of our empirical beliefs are justified. Finally, this theoretical 'discovery' must confront the plain fact that the practical attitude remains unaffected. To summarize, both sceptical doubts and any putative anti-sceptical solution to them are 'insulated' from our everyday concerns. And yet because of the force of the Intuition Problem we nevertheless feel that a conflict exists between the theoretical attitude that leads to sceptical doubt and the practical attitude of 'common life':

S3   Sceptical doubts raised from the philosophical standpoint carry
no conviction at the level of common life. Although we feel the
lack of conviction *ought* to carry with it some theoretical basis
for rejecting the sceptic's doubts, we cannot seem to find one.
And yet without a rejection the suspicion is that the sceptic is
picking up on some feature of (S1) that we are not entitled to.

This is an elaboration of the Humean Paradox. In this chapter we'll
be focusing largely on attempts to dissolve this by preventing the
transition from (S1) to (S2). What unites these is their 'naturalistic'
commitment to doing so by affirming the epistemic priority of
common life. This approach is in sympathy with the non-scientific
version of naturalism we encountered in Chapter 4, and at its most
sophisticated it contributes to the tradition of what we have called
'therapeutic' (or *mitigated*) scepticism. Not surprisingly, then, our
investigation into this version of naturalism will lead us back to
Wittgenstein. The importance of Wittgenstein notwithstanding, it
is Moore's attempt to offer a common-sense defence against scepticism that will be our starting-point, as it was for those whose views
we will go on to examine. Numbered among these is Thompson
Clarke, whose work has inspired somewhat divergent accounts of
the significance of philosophical scepticism. We'll end by looking at
a recent debate over whether sceptical doubts can be rejected
without abandoning our belief that the world is the way it is independently of how it appears to be to creatures like ourselves.

You need hands

We are interested in the sceptic's role in establishing a conflict
between the use we make of epistemic terms in common life (where
we have a sort of default entitlement) and their vulnerability in the
context of reflective, theoretical or philosophical (re-)evaluation.
This concern is brought to the fore by looking at G. E. Moore's
contribution to the problem of scepticism; most notably in his
"Defence of Common Sense" (1925, in 1959) and in the perplexing
"Proof of the External World" (1939, in 1959) that followed it.
In the former Moore lists a number of propositions that he takes
to be known to be true: for example, that the earth has existed
for many years, that he has never been far from it and that objects

were and still are to be found on it, some of which are people like ourselves with the same sorts of feelings and experiences. For Moore there is nothing 'private' about these items of knowledge; they are merely the kind of common-sense beliefs that lots of people, philosophers included, hold and are fully entitled to hold. Since we just presuppose the truth of such beliefs when we reason empirically, they are the kind of practical attitude commitments that mark the limits of any ordinary challenge to justify our beliefs. Of course, as key features of our conceptual scheme they are precisely the kind of beliefs whose legitimacy the sceptic challenges when he takes up the theoretical attitude and deploys the Agrippan argument.

If Moore is correct in asserting that we know with certainty that (say) material objects exist, then the argument from ignorance appears to have been refuted. In his "Proof of an External World" Moore explicitly takes up Kant's 'embarrassment to philosophy' and disputes his claim to have discovered "a strict demonstration – the only one possible".[3] Indeed, he goes on to assert that "so far from its being true . . . that there is only one possible proof of the existence of things outside us . . . I can now give a large number of different proofs, each of which is a perfectly rigorous proof" (1959: 145). The variety of proofs is generally reduced to one memorable example: "I can prove now, for instance, that two human hands exist. How? By holding up my two hands, and saying, as I make a certain gesture with the right hand, 'Here is one hand', and adding, as I make a certain gesture with the left, 'and here is another'" (*ibid*.: 145–6). This is, he argues, a "perfectly rigorous proof" (*ibid*.: 146) of the existence of external things. Recalling the argument from ignorance, Moore's 'Proof' amounts to a rejection of the first premise. Since he accepts the truth of the second premise (the conditional), he in effect proposes the following emendation:

S knows that q
If S doesn't know that not-sp, then S doesn't know that q

Therefore

S knows that not-sp

The striking feature of this proof as an argument against scepticism is of course that Moore takes as a truth standing in need of no justification precisely what the sceptic aims to *demonstrate* is false; and yet, Moore declares, "How absurd it would be to suggest that I did not know it, but only believed it, and that perhaps it was not the case!" (*ibid.*: 146).

By simply denying the sceptic's conclusion Moore is held by many (and far too quickly) to have missed the point altogether. Nevertheless, it's quite clear what he is getting at. If one accepts the conditional, the direction the argument goes in depends on what one takes as the premise. The sceptic insists that knowing that external objects exist or that one has two hands is the pressing concern because we do not know that (for example) we are not dreaming. Moore, on the other hand, is avowing that if right now one sets the belief that one might be dreaming alongside the belief that one is holding up a hand it is the latter that we will take as a paradigm case of knowing, not the former. Given the asymmetry it is clear for Moore that knowing that one has two hands should be the relevant premise, from which it follows that one is not dreaming. Moore pitches the *knowing* that characterizes the practical attitude against the theoretical reflection *on* such knowing (theoretical attitude) that seems to lead to the conclusion that one doesn't know that one is not dreaming. In doing so, he directly opposes the temptation to search for the foundations of knowledge in our own minds (ontological internalism) and thus affirms the epistemic priority of the engaged standpoint of practical life.

By giving us an argument for the existence of the external world that rationally foregrounds the primacy of the practical attitude, Moore dissolves the tension in (S3) by refusing to countenance the transition from (S1) to (S2). But this is only because the sceptic is not allowed to engage fully the apparently natural or intuitive force of this transition (because his doubt is restricted to the practical attitude where it seems unmotivated). The sense that Moore fails to take full account of the theoretical attitude and the corresponding *philosophical* challenge of scepticism (to meet it on its own territory) has become an important criticism, even among those who would support his defence of common sense. In the next few sections we will look at attempts to extend Moore's thinking about the status of knowledge claims paradigmatic of the practical attitude.

Austin and the relevant possibilities objection

Moore's attempt to confront the sceptic on the grounds of his own choice – common sense – receives a more nuanced treatment in the hands (!) of John Austin. Both maintain that when the philosopher's finding conflicts with the dictates of ordinary life, the former gives way to the latter. However, where Moore invokes the basic appeal of certain experiences or beliefs, Austin's focus is much more specifically on our use of language. In other words, he aims to prepare the ground against the (potential) sceptic by fleshing out the (as it were) phenomenology of common life through a detailed description of our linguistic practices. This allows Austin to do what Moore cannot: to diagnose the sort of misunderstandings of these practices that philosophers are apt to make, and the ramifications these have for their subsequent theorizing.

A relevant example of Austin's method is found in his "Other Minds" (1946, in 1970), where he discusses how challenges to our knowledge claims are customarily dealt with. Imagine, for example, that S claims to see a goldfinch in the garden. In response R might ask how she *knows* this[4] in one of two moods: first, as an earnest enquirer who assumes that S has a *default entitlement* to her knowledge and is interested in finding out more. Here S's answer might be that she's been a birdwatcher since she was 12, or that the bird has a red face. Alternatively, R might enquire as a *challenger* who questions S's judgement. If S's response to R's interrogation fails to satisfy, her entitlement will be removed: 'Pah,' R might declare, 'you clearly know nothing about ornithology!'

What interests Austin is the dialectic between claimant (S) and challenger (R): more precisely, when or how it comes about that an entitlement can be legitimately removed because the challenger does not consider the evidence adequate to sustain a claim to know. These circumstances fall into two broad categories: the evidence might be regarded as false ('That isn't red, it's brown'), or it might stand in an inappropriate relation to the claim, either by being factually inconsistent with it ('But Xs don't have red faces') or underdetermining the claim ('Yes, well, lots of birds have red faces'). It is the latter – call it the *relevant possibilities objection* – that is important. By *relevant* possibility I mean that a default claim can be challenged on the grounds that the evidence underdetermines the claim only if two conditions are fulfilled:

- There is some specific feature the lack of which motivates the possibility ('Having a red face is not enough; it has to have yellow and white wings as well').
- The possibility is appropriate ("within reason, and for the present intents and purposes" (1970: 84)) to the context in which the claim is made.

Regarding the second point, *S* doesn't have to show that, for example, "it isn't a *stuffed* goldfinch" (*ibid.*); but the presence in the area of other species of birds with red faces is relevant.

Before relating Austin's description to the problem of scepticism it should be noted that there is nothing general to say about what claims stand in need of evidence, nor about what sorts of claims will serve as evidence. As he notes in *Sense and Sensibilia*:

> Whether or not I have, or need, *evidence* for what I say is not a question of the kind of sentence I utter, but of the circumstances in which I am placed; and if evidence is produced or needed, there is no special kind of sentence, no form of words, by which this has to be done. (Austin 1962: 140)

There are no "*intrinsically* vulnerable" forms of words; indeed: "this procedure of representing forms of words as *in general* vulnerable is, of course, one of the major devices by which sceptical theses have commonly been insinuated" (*ibid.*: 138). This lack of *intrinsic* vulnerability derives from the above considerations about the *relevant possibilities objection*, and it suggests how one might respond to the argument from ignorance. To motivate a challenge to *S*'s claim to be sitting at a desk in Chicago, the sceptic needs to identify some *specific* (evidential) feature that shows her claim is lacking. A *general* concern about the unreliability of experience (certain vulnerable 'forms of words') is insufficient, and as such cannot provide a context for the introduction of a *relevant* possibility; namely, that *S* might be dreaming. The sceptic has simply failed to attend to the conditions that make a challenge genuine[5] and has therefore not mounted a coherent challenge to *S*'s (default) claim to know.

The Austinian 'default' conception of knowledge does not satisfy the *heroic* epistemologist who wants an answer to the question how knowledge is possible; and neither does it satisfy the sceptic. The former wants to take up a theoretical-philosophical standpoint on our ordinary practices of justification and subject them to critical evaluation. Likewise, the sceptic has no interest in remaining *within* the realm of the practical attitude, noting that once such an evaluation is undertaken we discover that we don't in fact know what we thought we did. Both insist upon what Austin is anxious to exclude: that there are circumstances that provoke general questions about *our* everyday concept of knowledge that cannot be answered in an everyday way.

Austin's insistence that the sceptic's possibilities be constrained by practical attitude talk of raising doubts 'within reason, and for the present intents and purposes' are held to have missed the point, even by those sympathetic to his desire to do away with both scepticism and traditional epistemology. In a criticism reminiscent of the charge of verificationism, Michael Williams concludes that Austin "fails to refute the sceptic" because to show that "what the sceptic says, or tries to say, is incoherent" is to "attempt too much" (1991: 166). In *Sense and Certainty* (1989), Marie McGinn voices a typical criticism:

> To start from the assumption that the assessment of judgements that we make from *within* the common-sense outlook is correct is implicitly to deny the possibility of the contemplative stance and the contrary, sceptical, assessment it yields. Without some philosophical motivation of this methodological assumption . . . Austin's position is . . . dogmatic.   (*Ibid.*: 64)

Her overall conclusion is decidedly negative: "We must conclude that the impression that Austin provides the sort of philosophical understanding needed to unravel the riddle of scepticism is in the end illusory" (*ibid.*: 66). Although there is no space to mount a full defence of Austin, an observation in "A Plea for Excuses" (1956, in 1970) gives us a clue: "ordinary language is not the last word: in principle it can everywhere be supplemented and improved upon and superseded. Only remember, it *is* the *first* word" (*ibid.*: 185). What McGinn and others assume is that Austin can be cast in the role of the *rejectionist*, but this fails to heed the supremely dialectical nature of his work. He does not engage with specifically sceptical arguments; on the contrary, his interlocutors are invariably 'dogmatic' philosophers[6] whose attempts to philosophically illuminate features of common life lead to scepticism. As with the Academic Sceptic, his starting-point is 'ordinary life' (ordinary 'language'). Where Carneades's fallibilistic, contextualist approach to epistemological concerns arose through an elucidation of the 'convincing' in response to the Stoic's search for certainty, Austin's 'default' model of knowledge arises through a more textured description of the everyday linguistic practices that constitute the practical attitude.

Returning to McGinn, then, Austin does not need a 'philosophical motivation' for his methodological assumption because it is not an 'assumption'. As anyone aware of the danger of *pk*-scepticism and the Agrippan argument might remark, the assumption is to think that there is anywhere else to start from that does not beg the question. Indeed, Austin might well respond that to start with ordinary language is a default entitlement and that any claim to cast doubt on it (to treat it *as* an assumption, and therefore as 'implicitly denying a possibility') must be motivated by some *relevant* possibility. The sort of 'philosophical understanding' that Austin is aiming at on this therapeutic interpretation is the kind that allows us to extend the practical attitude ('supplement, improve and supersede') *without* admitting either the dogmatist or the sceptic.

This is admittedly a positive reading and the suspicion remains that Austin does insufficient work to give us a "philosophically articulate understanding" (McGinn 1989: 66) of the practical attitude. Austinian claims are about *particular* objects in concrete situations, and have default status unless doubts about them are motivated. Since this image seems to build in a bias against the sceptic he may be regarded as making Moore's mistake – failing to show why we *ought not* to take the sceptic's evaluation of our epistemic concepts seriously (S3) by failing adequately to acknowledge the lure of scepticism (the transition from (S1) to (S2)). This emphasis on the *particular* also seems to neglect something that the sceptic wants to call explicitly into question: the epistemic warrant for the more *general* sorts of beliefs that seem to serve as evidence for empirical claims. These are the kind of propositions that Moore advanced as part of his 'defence' of common sense against what we are calling the Agrippan argument; paradigm cases of (practical attitude) knowing like 'the earth has existed for many years'. On Austin's account Moore's propositions would be *in*default*able*: it's hard to imagine any concrete context in which one would challenge someone who expressed them. And yet it is the *possibility* of a motivated (as opposed to unmotivated) challenge that seems to underwrite the default status of ordinary empirical claims. What is different about Moore's propositions?

It is at this point that the sceptic steps in. What is different about them, she argues, is that they are the class of claims for which the relevant context of evaluation *is* the theoretical-philosophical one. They are susceptible to the Agrippan argument precisely because they serve *as* the foundations for everyday empirical beliefs. If the inevitable sceptical conclusion that most of our beliefs are not justified is to be avoided, then, there must be some account of these beliefs that explains how they come to play the special role they do without leaving them vulnerable to the Agrippan argument. This takes us back to Wittgenstein.

Wittgenstein on certainty

In the last two years of his life Wittgenstein turned his attention to the two essays by Moore mentioned above. In their preface to the posthumous collection of his notes on these, *On Certainty*, Anscombe and von Wright note that Wittgenstein had long been interested in Moore's writings on the related topics of common sense and scepticism, and regarded the "Defence of Common Sense" as Moore's finest piece of work. Wittgenstein never completed the notes that comprise *On Certainty*, so it is impossible to offer an exhaustive account – not so much of *what* he was attempting to achieve but of *how* he was intending to achieve it. Nevertheless, it is clear that through an engagement with Moore's essays, *On Certainty* constitutes an attempt to respond both to the argument from ignorance, (Moore's 'Proof') and the Agrippan argument (Moore's 'Defence'). Quite how these responses are related is, however, less clear. The traditional view[7] is that *On Certainty* aims to demonstrate that while we must have basic certainties (like Moore's propositions) to guide our empirical enquiries, these are not foundational in the traditional sense and so are not susceptible to the Agrippan argument. On this interpretation Wittgenstein gives us a non-dogmatic, *philosophical* understanding of why practical attitude evaluations are legitimate. The response to the argument from ignorance emerges straightforwardly from this because one of those basic certainties is what the Cartesian sceptic challenges: the existence of external objects. Given the supposition that the argument from ignorance arises from a foundationalist response to the Agrippan argument, we will restrict our discussion to Wittgenstein's account of Moore's 'Defence'.

Wittgenstein (1969) gives several examples of the kind of proposition that Moore took to be examples of certain knowledge: I know that the earth existed long before my birth (§84), I know that that's a tree (§347), I know that I have never been on the moon (§111) or to China (§333). What intrigued Wittgenstein about these propositions is the peculiar role they play in our enquiries. While it seems odd not to think of them as true, their falsity is not a matter of *logical* impossibility; and yet unlike particular empirical claims ('lo, a goldfinch!'), they are strange things to announce as cognitive achievements. Wittgenstein's 'solution' is that they aren't cases of knowing at all: "I should like to say: Moore does not *know* what he asserts he knows, but it stands fast for him, as also for me; regarding it as absolutely solid is part of our *method* of doubt and enquiry" (§151). And again: "When Moore says he *knows* such and such, he is really enumerating a lot of empirical propositions which we affirm without special testing; propositions, that is, which have a peculiar logical role in the system of our empirical propositions" (§136). By stating that Moore's propositions 'stand fast' Wittgenstein is indicating the possession of a kind of certainty that puts them out of the game of giving and asking for reasons. In this sense Wittgenstein's account fits in well with the post-Kantian attempt to formulate some constitutive role for a priori principles. Unlike for Carnap, however, the semantic role these propositions play is not connected with epistemology as traditionally conceived (i.e. verifiable experience or, more generally, justifiable belief). S cannot doubt the 'truth' of (for example) 'I know that I'm a human being' because such propositions constitute the meanings of the words they employ. For S to say 'I am not a human being' is to demonstrate that she does not *understand* such sentences: "their truth . . . belongs to our frame of reference" (§83). To be unable to *use* such sentences is to be unable to take part in enquiry, because their 'peculiar logical role' is to serve as the framework *for* 'our method of doubt and enquiry': "their role is like that of rules of a game" (§95).

This talk of such propositions being 'like' rules should be famil-iar. As we saw in Chapter 4, the *Philosophical Investigations* makes a distinction between rules and moves made in accordance with rules. To take the traditional example, the rules of chess are not true or false, but the moves one makes in chess are either mistaken or correct depending on whether or not they accord with them. Although these framework propositions are 'like' rules, then, they cannot actually *be* rules because they are true. One of the most revealing comments Wittgenstein makes in con-nection with this is when he enquires of himself: "Is it that rule and empirical proposition merge into one another?" (§309). Like Kant's synthetic a priori principles these rules cannot be fully understood in isolation from empirical enquiry (experience) where the rule-proposition finds 'necessary' application (because of its constitutive role). Similarly, like Kant's principles they can be 'thought' in their pure 'categorical' form because their truth belongs to the framework of enquiry. The difference is that in the absence of Kant's idealism they cannot be 'deduced' transcenden-tally as the 'atemporal' conditions of possibility of experience because they are not demonstrable a priori to all rational crea-tures.[8] As we saw in our discussion of the private-language argument, these rules are embedded in practices or forms of life for which traditional ways of thinking about aprioricity are inap-propriate. Is it a priori that a pawn can move two spaces only on the first occasion of its use? Well, if you don't know that rule, you don't know how to play chess. Would chess be chess if we changed that rule? Well yes, we can imagine reforming the game of chess (and it clearly did not just pop into being in its present state); but it wouldn't be chess if we changed *all* the rules *at the same time*.

The fact that such propositions 'stand fast' does not mean that they are atemporal, then; but their temporality does not mean that they don't form the framework for our empirical enquiries. They are the grounds of our practices only in the sense that the rules of chess ground chess. But again, this talk of rules is only half the story: there is still the fact that unlike rules they are true, and it's their nature as the sort of truths that do not stand in need of justification that distinguishes them from other propositions. Instead of truths grasped in their self-evident purity, they serve to mark the posses-sion of certain abilities: "the end is not certain propositions' striking us immediately as true . . . it is our *acting*, which lies at the bottom of the language-game" (§204).

As we have seen, the Agrippan argument is driven by the idea that justification has an internalist element. Wittgenstein's account of framework beliefs aims to give us an understanding of certainty that avoids the internalist picture. Framework propositions are not appropriate items for psychological attitudes (like belief tradition-ally understood) because such attitudes invite the possibility of a demand for justification. The certainty that attends them is not therefore to be equated (internally) with an individual's grasp of a criterion of truth, but (externally) with the necessity of acting in a certain way. Recalling our investigation of the Ancient Sceptics in Chapter 2, these 'beliefs' constitute a kind of know-how that has normativity 'built in' (in the form of an ability to participate in enquiry) and which is therefore not vulnerable to the sceptic's doubt.

The details of the argument in *On Certainty* may remain obscure, but it is clear from the foregoing that Wittgenstein's approach to the Agrippan argument seems to concede a great deal to the sceptic. Indeed, it would seem that strictly speaking the scep-tic is correct: once we adopt the theoretical attitude we discover that we cannot justify beliefs that seem to play a crucial role in our epistemic practices. Of course, on the therapeutic interpretation the point is to try to get us not to see those apparent limitations *as* limitations, but rather as the result of an erroneous image of the mind. Let's look briefly at two positive views of what Wittgenstein is thought to have achieved.

Wittgenstein and *mitigated* scepticism

In *Skepticism and Naturalism* (1985), Peter Strawson offers some reflections on scepticism that link Wittgenstein with Hume. Acknowledging the naturalistic and sceptical strains in Hume's thought he articulates a version of what we've called the Humean Paradox:

> Hume . . . is ready to accept and to tolerate a distinction between two levels of thought: the level of philosophical and critical thinking which can offer us no assurances against

skepticism; and the level of everyday empirical thinking, at which the pretensions of critical thinking are completely over-ridden and suppressed by Nature, by an inescapable natural commitment to belief: belief in the existence of external body and in inductively based expectations.   (1985: 12–13)

The 'naturalistic' Hume acknowledges that sceptical doubts cannot be refuted, but claims that this does not leave reason with no role to play: within the framework laid down by nature it "leads us to refine and elaborate our inductive canons and procedures and, in their light, to criticize, and sometimes to reject, what in detail we find ourselves naturally inclined to believe" (*ibid*.: 14). This is reminiscent of Austin's reflections on 'supplementing, improving and superseding' ordinary language,[9] but it is the parallel with Wittgenstein that Strawson has in his sights. From Strawson's perspective Wittgenstein has as it were opened up the category of the natural to include the sorts of activities and practices that constitute the training regimes that make us competent language users. As a result the range of propositions that make up the frame-work of enquiry expands beyond the beliefs that Hume focused on (external world and inductive reasoning). The "profound commu-nity" (*ibid*.: 19) that Strawson identifies between them is the way this suggests for dealing with the sceptic: pointing out that since there is no such thing as the *reasons* for which we hold the 'frame-work' beliefs, both arguments for and arguments against scepticism are "idle, unreal, a pretense" (*ibid*.).

This transition from 'idle' to 'unreal' may be intended to solve the 'paradox' by preventing the transition from (S1) to (S2) and thus dissolving the tension in (S3), but it is the step the sceptic refuses to take. As we saw in Chapter 4, it marks the transition from a Humean to a Kantian perspective (from 'no conviction' to 'meaninglessness'). Given Strawson's earlier work on Kant (1966) and transcendental arguments (1959) it's not surprising that it is a step he finds 'natural'. Similarly it is not wholly inappropriate to ascribe it to Wittgenstein, since comparing him to Hume neglects the feature of his thinking that is most Kantian: that his framework propositions are not psycho-logical features of our thinking, imposed on the world by an overactive imagination, but logical features of language. On this account language is not to be understood as something that stands

over and against the world like (potentially) the empiricist's perceptions. No ontological distinction is being presupposed here. As Austin remarks, "When we examine what we should say when . . . we are
looking again not merely at words . . . but also at the realities we use
the words to talk about" (1970: 182). It may be understandable to
ascribe the anti-sceptical step to Wittgenstein, then, but if this is
regarded as a step he takes lightly it deprives his work of the diagnostic and dialectical resources required to show why the 'idle' might
become thought of as 'unreal' (resources required on a therapeutic
interpretation). Again, this is not an insignificant shift: it is the crucial
one. Unless it can be motivated, the Humean Paradox remains unre-
solved, and the sceptic will point out that the 'idleness' of their doubt
is beside the point. It is doubt raised when one adopts the theoretical attitude context, not that expressed with the practical attitude,
that is relevant. While such doubts remain unanswered our epistemic
concepts remain unvindicated.

Strawson's account of Hume and Wittgenstein emphasizes the
wrong connection and therefore fails to mount a criticism against
the sceptic in the right place. In separating out the 'naturalistic'
Hume from the 'sceptical' Hume he neglects the therapeutic–
dialectical aspect of Hume's philosophical method. By subsequently ascribing to Wittgenstein an updated, quasi-Kantian
version of the 'naturalistic' strain in Hume's thinking he makes it
appear that Wittgenstein has a *direct* answer to the sceptic, one that
charges him with an attachment to an 'unreal' problem. As we've
already had amply demonstrated, the charge of unreality or meaninglessness will leave the sceptic's 'withers unwrung'.

Given the association with Hume, an alternative reading of
Wittgenstein is of course possible: to see him as both a naturalist
and a sceptic, using the latter to advance the former. To this end it
should be noted that, as with Austin, Wittgenstein rarely mentions
scepticism in his later works. The targets of *On Certainty* are *heroic*
dogmatists who oppose scepticism, and whose thought is inclined
to lead to external world scepticism. In other words, his concern is
with the sort of philosophical thinking that, as Strawson says, is
equally idle: both arguments for and against scepticism; attempts to
both undermine and to redeem common life (to demand and to
offer justifications). This observation would lend some weight to
the suggestion that Robert Fogelin makes in *Wittgenstein* to the

effect that he be read as a Pyrrhonian, someone who aims to "eliminate . . . philosophy as traditionally practiced" (1987: 234) by (*pk*-)sceptically undermining any attempt to make of the beliefs of common life (those that 'stand fast'; that are like 'know how') things in need of justification.

In a later work Fogelin (1994) modifies this view somewhat and comes to regard Wittgenstein's thought as containing both Pyrrhonian *and* non-Pyrrhonian themes. The former involves an attack on both those who attempt to mount a defence against the Agrippan argument and those who would seek to utilize it. In this sense both the sceptic and the dogmatist are seen as captivated by the im/possibility of the task of justifying our beliefs (the 'justificationalist' project). The latter comes to the fore in Wittgenstein's talk of the public, contextualist, holistic framework of various rule-constituting language games. This element of his thought is held to be a *heroic* attempt to offer a coherentist response to the Agrippan argument. In other words, he is not attacking the whole justificationalist project but only the foundationalist reaction to it (one that issues in the argument from ignorance).

For Fogelin there is a "constant battle" (1994: 205) raging in Wittgenstein's later work between these two strands. He finds the following from the *Philosophical Investigations* to be exemplary of the neo-Pyrrhonian Wittgenstein:

> What we are destroying is nothing but houses of cards and we are clearing up the ground on which they stand (§118) . . . The clarity that we are aiming at is indeed *complete* clarity. But that simply means that the philosophical problem should *completely* disappear (§133) . . . Philosophy may in no way interfere with the actual use of language; it can in the end only describe it . . . Philosophy . . . leaves everything as it is (§124).
> (*Ibid.*: 220)

Fogelin's interpretation is plausible, and linking up Wittgenstein's metaphilosophical concerns with those of the Ancient Sceptic offers intriguing possibilities. The implication that (in our terms) Wittgenstein diagnoses that the argument from ignorance arises from a foundationalist response to the Agrippan argument, and attempts to block this by offering a coherentist alternative would fit in with a reading of *On Certainty*. It also accords well with the account of the Agrippan argument I gave in Chapter 1 and with our subsequent investigation of the relationship between the two forms of sceptical argument.

Notwithstanding these considerations, an alternative interpretation is possible. First, it should be observed that the above quotations are very un-Pyrrhonian things to say. Why would a Pyrrhonian feel motivated to hold forth about what philosophy can or cannot achieve? That would seem rather dogmatic to say the least. Philosophy may leave everything as it is, but that does *not* mean that one has no more understanding of *what* it is – no better description of what we do – when one has cleared the ground of the philosophical theories that distort our understanding. Rather than a conflict in Wittgenstein's thought, then, one might suggest an alternative: that it is not the neo-Pyrrhonians that are the model for his method but the Academic Sceptics. On this interpretation, Wittgenstein is a 'therapeutic' (*mitigated*) sceptic, offering an excavation of our concepts; dialectically playing off dogmatist against sceptic (the two strands) in order to draw out the public nature of our commitments in the way that Carneades brought out the idea of the 'convincing' in our thinking. In this sense, the non-Pyrrhonian elements are not dogmatically imposed on the space of philosophizing, but as it were revealed ('deduced', even) dialectically about common life as one 'returns' to it.

The legacy of Clarke

So far in this chapter we've been pursuing a line of thought that I've associated with 'therapeutic' scepticism. It is now time to turn to another strand of post-Moorean thinking which, although less dialectical in character, is no less concerned with the problem of how to prevent practical attitude reflection leading to theoretical attitude doubt. The *locus classicus* for this approach is Thompson Clarke's "The Legacy of Skepticism" (1972).[10] Clarke is widely regarded as having identified the basic question one should ask when attempting to explain why scepticism has the strange appeal it does:[11] what exactly is it that the sceptic is examining when she makes the transition from (S1) to (S2)? He suggests two possibilities:

(T1) "Our most fundamental beliefs," *or*

(T2) "The product of a large piece of philosophizing about empirical knowledge done before he comes on stage" (1972: 754)

At the beginning of this chapter I mentioned the Intuition Problem: that any response to scepticism has to deal with the fact that sceptical doubts seem to arise 'naturally' when we start to evaluate our epistemic practices (S1). In the light of this, the appeal of Clarke's dichotomy becomes apparent. If the sceptic is addressing our most fundamental beliefs about the objectivity of the world – that it is the way it is independently of our thoughts about it – the anti-sceptic has to confront the Intuition Problem head on, and this necessarily limits his options. He will have *heroically* to refute the sceptic, or show that their doubts are meaningless (or embrace Hume's position). If the sceptic's reflections are dependent on a set of *philosophical* commitments, however, a new option presents itself: to *diagnose* them in the hope that they can be shown to be disposable without cost to our understanding of ourselves as knowers (for whom knowledge is possible). The difference would be like that between trying to *prove* that God didn't exist (that the belief was false) and *identifying* the source of the belief, hoping thereby to demonstrate its irrelevance to an understanding of (for example) the nature of human existence.

Despite its appeal, (T2) raises another problem, which will be familiar, although we have yet to give it a name: the issue of theoretical burden. The natural or intuitive appeal of sceptical doubts derives not least from their slender elegance when contrasted with the bloated and nightmarish creations that *heroic* epistemologists have deployed to rebut them. This confronts the would-be diagnostician with what we'll call the *Quietist Dilemma*. According to this, philosophical diagnosis runs a double risk:

- It must avoid being so elaborate that it makes the appeal of (Cartesian) scepticism appear even more 'intuitive' in contrast (exacerbating the Intuition Problem).
- Any *p*-knowledge claims it makes will engage the attention of the (*pk*-)sceptic who will request a justification for the theory itself (raising the Agrippan problem).

With these in mind let's look at Clarke's paper. The first part of "The Legacy of Skepticism" comprises a dialectical defence of Moore against the charge that his own defences of common sense – in the form of assertions of propositions like 'there are external objects' – lack meaning. We've seen that for different reasons both Carnap ('external question') and Austin (no motivated challenge) might argue that Moore's claim to know that 'external objects exist' is meaningless or incoherent. Neglecting this debate, Clarke's main point comes out well in the context of the following example:

> Suppose a scientist is experimenting with soporifics, himself the guinea-pig. He is in a small room. He keeps careful records. Experiment #1. "1:00 P.M. Taking x dose of drug Z orally . . . 1:15 P.M. Beginning to feel drowsy. I am not focussing clearly on . . . 6:15 P.M. I've been asleep but am wide awake now, rested and feeling normal. *I know*, of course, *that I'm not dreaming now*, but I remember, while asleep, actually thinking I was really awake, not dreaming . . ." (1972: 758)

The problem, according to Clarke, is that because Moore's propositions are "virtually, perhaps entirely, context-free" (*ibid.*: 757) they can be understood in either a philosophical, or what he calls a 'plain' way – from the perspective of the practical attitude (S1). When Moore attempts his proof he is like the experimenter in the example, affirming a case of *plain* knowing against what he takes to be the *plain* doubts of the sceptic (one can imagine him holding up first one hand and then the other and then writing down his finding). What Moore refuses to countenance is the other way of understanding his propositions, which gives rise to the sceptic's *philosophical* doubts.[12] In the case of the dream version of the argument from ignorance, these *philosophical* doubts seemingly arise when the sceptic leaves behind the plain and points out that the experimenter does not in fact *know* that he's not dreaming (S2).

The contrast between *plain* and *philosophical* doubt comes out in the following way. If each of us were to pose to ourselves right now (at time t) the *plain* possibility that we might be dreaming, that would clearly present a challenge to our empirical claims. I for one would not in all likelihood be sat at this desk typing away if I were in fact asleep. Crucially, when we pose the possibility in this (plain) way we do so on the assumption *either* that we ourselves will awaken at some time later than *t* and discover (know, 'find out') that we were dreaming (like the experimenter), *or* if we are in a coma that someone could in principle know ('find out') what's going on in the world. In other words, a commitment to knowledge of the external world is built into the plain possibility. If we present it as a philosophical possibility, however, there is no future time at which we can imagine coming to know ('finding out') that we were in fact dreaming at time *t* because we can imagine confronting ourselves with the same philosophical possibility then.

What this gives us in effect are two versions of the argument from ignorance, one in which the sceptical possibilities are plain possibilities, and one in which they are philosophical possibilities. For Clarke, the plain possibilities are genuine and "of the utmost significance" (1972: 765) and it should be clear why this is the case: they promise to make sense of how we are able to *reflect* on our (plain) epistemic concepts. If Clarke can establish that the philosophical possibility (philosophical scepticism) is not a real possibility, he can elucidate a feature of the phenomenology of common life (S1) while showing that it does not lead 'naturally' to scepticism (S2). That would constitute a solution to the Intuition Problem and dissolution of the Humean Paradox – reflection without the theoretical attitude.

In response to his own basic question Clarke's approach is to argue that both philosophical defences *of*, and sceptical attacks *on*, the plain have a common theoretical backdrop (T2). That is to say, both arguments to the effect that we *don't* know what we claim to know (because we cannot rule out the philosophical possibility that we might be dreaming) and *heroic* responses to the effect that we *do* know (those that find Moore's response unsatisfactory because it does not present a philosophical defence of common sense, but only a 'plain' defence) are charged with presupposing that the "conceptual–human constitution is of a 'standard' type" (*ibid.*: 760).

The 'standard' type is a familiar one – it assumes in effect that there is some feature of experience (some *criterion*) that would allow us to rule out all the possibilities of error – that knowledge is the invulnerability of belief to doubt (certain). To see what happens when a *plain* sceptical possibility is converted into a *philosophical* possibility, consider the first premise of the argument from ignorance. To indicate that *S* doesn't know that she's not dreaming suggests that what she *needs* and what she *lacks* is a criterion in her experience that would allow her to determine that it is truthful. It presupposes the intelligibility of something (a criterion, drawn from the 'standard' model), the possibility of which it denies (since she will never know that we're not dreaming – never be able to rule out *all* possibilities of error): "The Philosophical [sceptical] possibility therefore, of necessity, calls in question (negates) the very knowing it presupposes" (*ibid.*: 765). If philosophical scepticism is self-defeating in this way, there is no genuine philosophical sceptical possibility. But if there is no such possibility, there can't be a problem for the *heroic* epistemologist who wants to say that we *do* know what the sceptic says we don't (because we might be dreaming). Both philosophical scepticism and philosophical defences of the plain turn out to be equally meaningless.

Where, then, does this leave the plain possibilities, which are based on the 'finding-out' model? Since these acknowledge that there is no criterion in experience capable of allowing us to know *now* (at time *t*) whether or not we're asleep (or in a coma), and yet they still make sense (as we saw with the experimenter), the concept of dreaming cannot itself presuppose the possibility of such a criterion. In other words, although it is integral to our (plain) concept of dreaming that we will later find out that we were dreaming (at time *t*), it will not be on the basis of *subsequently* being able to identify some feature of experience that was previously lacking (a criterion to rule out all possibilities of error). Clarke's conclusion is that since the (plain) dream possibilities cannot be conceived of on the standard model, the conceptual–human constitution (the plain) is not of the 'standard' type.

On Clarke's analysis, then, there is a way of decoupling the sort of reflection that is embodied in the *plain* sceptical possibilities from their *philosophical* counterparts. (S1) does not lead to (S2) of necessity: the latter only arises when one presupposes that the plain is constituted in a certain way (the 'standard'). To put it another way, it is a presupposition of the theoretical attitude that the plain is to be understood on the 'standard' model. The theoretical attitude has a theoretical commitment, and once one has diagnosed this commitment there should be no temptation to worry about (albeit self-refuting) sceptical challenges, or to construct (equally futile) defences of common sense. Again, to think that common sense stands in need of such a defence (or is vulnerable to such attacks) is to misunderstand it.

It may be repetitious to do so, but what Clarke can be inter preted as doing is offering what amounts to a dialectical defence of Moore: playing dogmatic sceptic off against dogmatic philosopher (both presupposing the 'standard' model) in order to show that one can only defend the plain in a *plain* way. However, when we return to the plain, aware of this, we do so with the plain possibilities still in view: we still have some account to give of their significance – what they tell us about our ability to reflect on our present practices: "Skepticism leaves us the problem of the plain, of its structure, the character and source of its relative 'non-objectivity,' and one major tool for unlocking its secrets, the plain skeptical possibilities" (1972: 769).

Although Clarke's strategy seems to fall into the 'large piece of philosophizing' (T2) category, the talk of 'relative non-objectivity' indicates why his work has inspired such a wide range of responses. As he notes, although on the standard model the motive for adopt- ing the theoretical attitude and reflecting philosophically is obvious (to seek out the invulnerable), that is not our conceptual constitu- tion. He acknowledges the force of the Intuition Problem:

> Certain intuitive philosophers I respect say that in philosophiz- ing we stand back and treat the world in its entirety as an object apart from us, whereas as plain men we are "inside the world" . . . the objectivity attainable within the plain is only skin-deep, *relative*. We want to know not how things are *inside* the world, but how things are, absolutely. And the world itself is one of these things.

To the extent that one acknowledges such intuitions one will agree that: "What *is* frustrating about Moore's plain questions is, it does seem, their not allowing us to ask how things *really* are objectively" (*ibid*.: 762). Clarke's bulwark against the Intuition Problem is of course his diagnosis of the sceptical possibilities. As we saw, this claims that philosophical scepticism imposes a restriction on the conceptual resources of the plain (as 'standard') that in fact renders it meaningless. Unfortunately, this way with the sceptic seems to fall foul of the Quietist Dilemma: not only do many philosophers continue to find the sceptical possibilities perfectly meaningful, but the theoretical motivation for what is in effect a verificationist ('finding-out') dismissal of such possibilities seems (in contrast) highly counter-intuitive, and itself standing in need of philosophical justification.[13]

Un/natural doubts: Williams and Stroud

The Quietist Dilemma suggests a reason why Clarke's paper has, to different degrees, been used to justify the view that any attempt to finesse sceptical problems involves the abandonment of a concept of objectivity (implicit in the plain, however that is to be construed) that captures a whole range of realist intuitions, spanning moral[14] as well as epistemological concerns. Few philosophers have done more to explore the apparently 'intuitive' appeal of sceptical doubt (and thus the *heroic* tradition in epistemology) than Barry Stroud. Although he continues to press the case against any perceived attempt to repress the full force of the Intuition Problem, his work in this area finds its fullest expression in *The Significance of Philosophical Scepticism* (1984a). This largely comprises a picaresque account of twentieth-century 'naturalistic' (*rejectionist*) philosophy's failure to ward of the spectre of philosophical scepticism, ranging from Moore's quixotic gesticulations, through Carnap's dismissive talk about idealist geographers, to Quine, threateningly brandishing the 'big stick' of naturalized epistemology.

Stroud's contention is that attempts to understand human knowledge in a natural or scientific way leave the problem of scepticism wholly unintelligible. Adopting the *rejectionist* perspective of (say) Quine (or Moore), we simply cannot see *how* the philosophical problem could ever arise. That would of course be fine if there weren't a strong presumption in favour of the 'reality' or meaningfulness of scepticism. The problem is that whilst "Almost nobody thinks for a moment that scepticism is correct", it appears to be "the inevitable outcome of trying to understand human knowledge in a certain way" (Stroud 1989: 32); that is to say, philosophically: "in philosophy we want to understand how *any* knowledge of an independent world is gained on *any* of the occasions on which knowledge of the world is gained through sense-perception" (Stroud 1996: 354–5). The predicament derives from the familiar Cartesian image underlying the argument from ignorance, according to which our sensory experiences have epistemic priority over the objects that we hope they are experiences of: "The difficulty in understanding how sense-perception gives us . . . knowledge of anything at all about the world . . . is that it seems at least possible to perceive what we do without thereby knowing something about the things around us" (Stroud 1984b: 549). The significance of philosophical scepticism is the threat it poses: "that once we really understand what we aspire to in the philosophical study of knowledge, and we do not deviate from the aspiration to understand it in that way, we will be forever unable to get the kind of understanding that would satisfy us" (Stroud 1989: 32). If global sceptical doubt is rooted in a rather traditional and intuitively appealing concept of objectivity, and nothing the *rejectionist* epistemologist has to say counts against it, then scientific epistemology cannot give us the understanding we aspire to. Alternatively, if the *rejectionist* is right, then we cannot even formulate the sceptical problem and that traditional conception and its attendant aspiration must be rejected as erroneous.

In short, then, Stroud accepts what is in effect Clarke's conditional: *if* the traditional concept of objectivity is fully intelligible, *then* philosophical scepticism is correct and we cannot show how knowledge is possible. Since the intelligibility of the traditional conception rests on that of the (philosophical) sceptical possibilities, we are confronted with the following disjunction:

Either We *can* imagine Descartes's dreaming scenario without presupposing the 'finding-out' model (entailing that either I will wake up or that someone is around, and therefore that some knowledge is presupposed by the possibility), in which case we *can* pose the philosophical possibility and scepticism is true (we cannot show that knowledge is possible; *heroic* epistemology fails).

Or We *cannot* conceive of the sceptical possibilities as other than plain, in which case dreaming presupposes knowing and the traditional conception of objectivity is false (and we cannot make sense of *heroic* epistemology).

Where Clarke inclines towards the second disjunct, Stroud goes for the first. For the latter it is *philosophical* scepticism and not *plain* sceptical doubts that function as the condition of possibility of the 'traditional conception' of objectivity. Stroud does not hold that a more elaborate version of Clarke's attempt to show that philosophical scepticism presupposes a self-defeatingly restricted account of the plain will work. As a result, no such approach will halt the reflective progression from simple intuitions about objectivity (S1) to philosophical scepticism (S2).

Although Stroud agrees that (T2) is the focus for diagnosis, he does not think that philosophical scepticism arises because the sceptic presupposes a theory in order to exploit the 'relative non-objectivity' of the plain (as with Clarke). The target for Stroud's response to Clarke's basic question is the concept of objectivity itself. The Intuition Problem can only be 'solved' by directly "reveal[ing] the incoherence of the traditional conception" – the one that leads naturally to scepticism – by "find[ing] some way in which the philosophical reflection goes wrong or misleads us" (Stroud 1996: 248) "and perhaps even supply[ing] an alternative we can understand" (Stroud 1984a: 274).

It's not very clear what kind of relationship Stroud envisages exists between objectivity and philosophical reflection: how the 'incoherence' of the former equates with the latter 'going wrong' or 'misleading' us. It is similarly obscure what 'an alternative' account of objectivity will give us in the way of an insight into the disjunction just outlined. Since there is no room to take up this issue directly, let's turn instead to an alternative interpretation of (T2). The moral seems to be that the Quietist Dilemma arises quite 'naturally' from attempts to respond to the Intuition Problem. Correlatively, then, an adequate response to the Intuition Problem and the Quietist Dilemma is the key to 'dealing' with scepticism. No one has argued more forcefully in this spirit than Michael Williams, who recognizes both the seriousness[15] of what he calls the 'New Scepticism' of Nagel, Stroud *et al.*, and shares Clarke's and Stroud's apparent resolution that the correct approach will involve the identification of a 'large piece of philosophizing'.

To this end, Williams distinguishes between 'constructive' and 'diagnostic' responses to external-world scepticism. The former "takes the sceptic's questions more or less at face value" and aims to show that we do in fact know what the sceptic says we don't; the latter "suspects that there is something drastically wrong with the way the questions are posed" (p. xvi). Williams maintains that the 'New Sceptics' have been successful not only in undermining confidence in the 'constructive' approach, but also in casting doubts on the plausibility of much that would pass as 'diagnostic'. In order to clarify matters, Williams makes a further differentiation. The 'therapeutic' diagnosticians aim to dissolve sceptical claims by showing that they are "defective in point of meaning" (*ibid.*). The objective of his own preferred 'theoretical' diagnosis[16] "is to show that sceptical arguments derive their force, not from commonsensical intuitions about knowledge, but from theoretical ideas that we are by no means bound to accept" (p. xvii). As a response to 'New Scepticism' this is promising. If the sceptic's doubts can be shown to arise not through the ingenuous interrogation of our everyday epistemic concepts, but as a result of invidious theoretical presuppositions, the Intuition Problem is solved and the playing field is at least levelled with respect to the Quietist Dilemma. Moreover, if the sceptic's theoretical burden turns out to be even more monstrously unwieldy than the anti-sceptic's once did, we might very well find ourselves with a response to what Kant so famously found embarrassing to philosophy and human reason (a response to the argument from ignorance that does not itself invite the Agrippan argument).

Williams's analysis recognizes a crucial constraint on any attempt to address the Intuition Problem: the rejection of "tendencies to dismiss traditional philosophical problems, particularly sceptical problems, as not real problems at all" (p.: xiv). Rather, since an attachment to a background theory is sufficient to render a line of argumentation meaningful, he can disdain the theoretical burden of attempting to demonstrate the converse and, subject to the details of 'theoretical diagnosis', take "the sceptic's questions more or less at face value" (p. xvi). In doing so he comes down decisively in favour of (T2), where the 'large piece of philosophizing' is construed explicitly as a 'commitment to a philosophical theory'. In doing so he is intimating that Clarke's error was to mix an unfortunate 'therapeutic' element (trying to show that philosophical scepticism is 'meaningless') with the otherwise admirable 'theoretical' diagnosis (claiming that the sceptic presupposes the human conceptual constitution is the 'standard type').

Unlike Stroud, then, Williams holds that a correct formulation of the sceptic's theoretical commitments allows us to decouple intuitions about objectivity (S1) from philosophical scepticism (S2). Moreover, it will facilitate this without any consequent loss of the sense that the world is importantly independent of us. As a result, it will not leave us with Clarke's 'relative non-objectivity' and some lingering feeling that we have not fully addressed what generates the Intuition Problem. There is considerable depth and detail to Williams's diagnosis,[17] but in brief the claim is that what he calls the "objectivity requirement", the view that:

(OR)   [The] knowledge we want to explain is knowledge of . . . a world that is the way it is independently of how it appears to us to be or what we are inclined to believe about it (p. 91)

is epistemologically neutral; it expresses "[The] simply logical point that our experience could be just what it is and *all our beliefs about the world could be false*" (p. 74). That 'gap' between experience/ appearance and reality, or mind and world may well, Williams concedes, be a "necessary condition for there being a threat of scepticism" (p. 248), but it is not sufficient. Something else is needed to generate the sort of radical scepticism we associate with the argument from ignorance.

The excavation of that supplement is the mainstay of Williams's diagnosis. What the reflective movement from objectivity (S1) to philosophical scepticism (S2) presupposes in the way of substantial theory is something he calls "epistemological realism" (a more fundamental analysis than the "foundationalism" that presupposes it (p. 115)). The 'epistemological realist' holds that:

(ER)   There are "underlying epistemological structures or princi-ples" that exhibit "unity" (p. 108), a Cartesian 'order of reasons' "cutting across ordinary subject divisions and operat-ing independently of all contextual constraints" (p. 117).

This leads us into thinking that we can "step outside all directed inquiries, however theoretical" (p. 200) and undertake "a *detached* examination of the *totality* of our knowledge . . . that there is such a thing as *the totality* of our knowledge of the world" (1988: 423). This is what Williams calls the 'totality condition'. With these pieces in place we have the following story. Traditionally, the argument from ignorance arises when common-sense (plain) reflection on our beliefs (S1) leads the sceptic to discover that what we need is a set of epistemically privileged beliefs that can be used to justify other sorts of beliefs. This is the doctrine of epistemic priority and in empirical matters it is our sensory beliefs or experiences that are taken to be self-certifying (I can't doubt I believe I'm typing) and the basis of inferences to facts (whether I'm *really* typing or not). As Stroud puts it, "the first sort are knowable without any of the second sort being known, but not *vice versa*" (1984a: 141). The final step is that epistemically prior items turn out not to warrant inferences to the existence of external objects because we don't know we're not dreaming. On Williams's account, then, the sceptic's 'discovery' of epistemic priority is not a discovery at all; rather, it is a *presupposition* of 'epistemological realism'. The argument from ignorance does not arise 'naturally' from interrogating our 'traditional concept of objectivity', but as a result of the fatal interaction of the 'totality condition' with the 'objectivity requirement' that occurs when 'epistemological realism' is presupposed (p. 91). Since the 'objectivity requirement' alone expresses a merely metaphysical belief, with no 'essential' relation to scepticism, the Intuition Problem no longer registers a substantive issue – it only motivates scepticism when 'epistemological realism' is presupposed. Finally, the "antidote" to 'epistemological realism' "is a contextualist view of justification" (p. 119). *If* we embrace the view that "there is *no fact of the matter* as to what kind of justification [a given belief] either admits of or requires" (*ibid.*) then we will never be tempted towards the kind of theoretical commitment ('epistemological realism') that makes philosophical scepticism an unanswerable problem.

Williams's contextualist recommendation should sound familiarly Austinian,[18] although he advances it in the context of a very non-Austinian style of enquiry. Rather than pursue this parallel, let us return to Stroud's account by examining his response to Williams's diagnosis. This involves two moves:

- the denial that 'epistemological realism' in particular is necessary to generate sceptical doubts, and
- the denial that *any brute* commitment to a philosophical theory is being revealed in the elaboration of philosophical scepticism.

Taking the particular first, Stroud acknowledges that the minimalist understanding of the 'objectivity requirement' (one that divines a "'logical gap' between 'statements about appearance' and 'statements about reality'" (1996: 353)) is not sufficient to generate the thesis about epistemic priority that leads to the argument from ignorance, but denies that this warrants the claim that only 'epistemological realism' could get us there. To this end Stroud recommends that one attend to what he holds is the true object of our enquiry: not "the logical relations . . . among abstract philosophical theses" like the 'objectivity requirement' and 'epistemological realism' (*ibid.*), but the *dynamic* process of reflection that leads to thoughts of epistemic priority (and thence scepticism). These occur when we subject "the 'truism' that knowledge of an independent world *comes from* particular occasions on which something is known through sense-perception . . . to . . . the special generality we seek in philosophy" (*ibid.*: 357, 355, emphasis added). Williams glosses that 'comes from' as a 'causal' truism that has no sceptical force (1991: 69) and thus no 'distinctively philosophical character' until it is supplemented by 'epistemological realism'. Stroud on the other hand emphasizes its "anthropological" suggestion of 'dependency': if it is indeed true, then it is an *observed* truth "about human beings . . . in the world as it is" (1996: 357). As such, the claim of 'dependency' has nothing to do with *presupposing* epistemic priority.

For Stroud, then, 'epistemological realism' is certainly not *the* correct theoretical diagnosis; but his doubts extend to *any* such account. Even if Williams could elucidate the sceptic's necessary theoretical presuppositions, we would still have to arrive at some sort of reckoning regarding that theory. We certainly couldn't state that because it leads to scepticism it must be false; but then, he argues, to what extent does giving us grounds for rejecting a theoretical presupposition differ from giving us reasons to think we've refuted scepticism? This brings us to the heart of the matter. As previously noted, Stroud and Williams think of themselves as trying to make good on Clarke's basic question, and opting for (T2). For Williams the theory and the activity of 'philosophizing' are in effect packaged together in the form of 'epistemological realism': it is the presupposition of 'epistemological realism' that motivates the *philosophical reflection* (S2) that in turn leads to scepticism (the theoretical attitude comes from having made a theoretical commitment). Without it we would be left with the 'merely logical gap' described by the 'objectivity requirement'. For Stroud, however, the philosophical standpoint (S2) is not coextensive with a *theoretical* commitment. The 'product' of the philosophizing is a "way of thinking about ourselves" or "a wish to think of ourselves, in a certain way" (*ibid.*: 359). For Stroud, reflecting on the kind of philosophical reflection that leads to scepticism aims to "reveal something interesting and deep about human beings, or human aspirations"; if not "human beings in general" at least "certain traditions or cultures" to which "all of us [here] belong" (*ibid.*: 348). The philosophical reflection that leads to scepticism may indeed 'go wrong', but that doesn't mean that 'the large piece of philosophizing' in question is a (disposable) *theory*.

In conclusion, it is not clear where Williams's diagnosis leaves us with regard to scepticism. On first impressions it goes to the heart of our investigation. If the argument from ignorance does arise from a foundationalist response to the Agrippan argument, and foundationalism itself presupposes 'epistemological realism', the possibility emerges that 'epistemological realism' may be a presupposition of the Agrippan argument itself. In other words, 'epistemological realism' is the source of the 'justificationalist' (aiming to justify our beliefs) project *and* scepticism.[19] However, this shifts attention to the status of Williams's diagnosis. If it were intended as a theoretical refutation, the intuitively minded 'New Sceptic' will reject the analysis on the grounds that it does not capture *their* intuitions[20] (which will always *appear* more immediate than the attribution of a theory that they do not accept: the Quietist Dilemma). At the same time, it is not clear what bringing someone to confess that they were committed to a theory actually achieves, given that theories do not arise *ex nihilo*, but in response to the desire to explain phenomena. Finally, on its own theoretical terms Williams's account does not side-step the problem of justification (and thus the Agrippan argument), in so far as his own contextualism includes an (albeit externalist) justificatory element.[21] Even if the latter weren't a problem, one can imagine the Ancient Sceptic contemplating the dispute between the 'diagnostician' and the 'New Sceptic' (the mode of Dispute) and reapplying the Agrippan argument in the sevice of *pk*-scepticism.

The moral seems to be that any attempt to wean philosophers off their intuitions must not convict them of holding a *theory*, but dialectically engage them so that they come to reflect 'naturally' on common life in a way that does not lead to scepticism. This approach has fallen out of favour with contemporary philosophers who have returned to the search for a quicker fix (although one informed by the findings of their more 'therapeutically' inclined forebears). In Chapter 6 we'll examine some contemporary attempts to solve the argument from ignorance (and avoid the Agrippan argument) by returning to the concept of knowledge itself.

6 Internalisms and externalisms

Therapy, diagnosis and intuition

We ended Chapter 5 with a contrasting pair of evaluations of the problem of Cartesian scepticism. According to the 'intuitive' account of the 'New Sceptics' theoretical attitude doubt arises 'naturally' as a result of a special sort of reflection on our epistemic concepts. Although it has no effect on the everyday use or application of these concepts, its formal truth nevertheless denies us a fully articulated grasp of what we take to be a central feature of our conceptual scheme: a full-blooded concept of objectivity (of the world being in some respects the way it is independently of our thoughts about it).[1] In contrast, on the 'diagnostic' account theoretical attitude doubt is what you get when you presuppose a certain sort of theory. Once this theory is exposed, talk of a special sort of reflection is expected to fade and sceptical problems become relics of the past. Both the 'intuitive' and the 'diagnostic' accounts can be regarded as responses to the perceived failure of the 'therapeutic' approach associated with Austin and Wittgenstein. Although they draw contrasting conclusions, both the 'intuitionist' and the 'diagnostician' regard the 'therapist' as having failed satisfactorily to address what we have called the Intuition Problem by dismissing sceptical problems as unreal.

In the foregoing I hope to have shown that this dismissal is premature and that 'therapeutic' scepticism is, despite the initial air of paradox, a plausible response to sceptical problems. Nevertheless, these three possible approaches do not so much exhaust the field of contemporary approaches to scepticism as determine different parts of its perimeter. As is customary, most of the activity is in the middle;

in this instance where mainstream epistemology is being done, and where we started our enquiry. Recall, then, that at the end of Chapter 1 I argued that *heroic* epistemology confronts two problems. The first is that demonstrating that knowledge (or justification) is possible requires a response to the Agrippan argument. To see the force of this problem, recall that *heroic* epistemologies are internalist–evidentialist and accept the *KK* principle. If knowing that *q* requires having adequate grounds in the form of evidence that one recognizes *as* evidence, it follows that if you know, you know that you know. Internalists agree, then, that for *S* to be justified in believing that *q*, *S* must recognize what it is that justifies her belief that *q*. Finally, reflections on the sources of justification of empirical claims seem to push us towards seeking an epistemic foundation in sensory experience; but this shift from methodological to ontological internalism leaves us vulnerable to the argument from ignorance.

The second problem is of more recent provenance: that the internalist's analysis of knowledge in terms of justified true belief is anyway inadequate to our Gettier-induced intuitions relating to the ascriptions of knowledge (and which in turn raises broadly sceptical concerns about our consequent *right* to the concept). It is the inter-action of these two problems that gives scepticism its contemporary flavour, and which makes the *rejectionist*'s key intuition clear: that rejecting the *heroic* demand for a legitimating account of knowledge involves the theoretical formulation of an externalist alternative that avoids *heroism*'s two problems. The anticipated result is that the alternative conception of knowledge will also provide a solution to the argument from ignorance. In short, answering Gettier and the sceptic go hand in hand!

At the end of Chapter 1 I argued that *rejectionist*–externalist theories cannot avoid the Agrippan argument. Rather than pursue this line of criticism directly we will spend the first part of this chapter investigating whether or not externalist theories are successful in responding to what is their more frequently chosen target,[2] the argument from ignorance, and see what if anything this tells us about their suitability for avoiding the Agrippan argument. Thereafter we will reverse the direction of enquiry and focus on the Agrippan argument. The chapter will conclude with Donald Davidson's attempt simultaneously to solve the Agrippan argument and provide an answer to Cartesian scepticism.

Internalism externalized

The feature shared by all versions of epistemic externalism is an antagonism towards the idea that the adequacy component of knowledge can be satisfactorily analysed using only a *purely* internalist conception of justification. The motivation is easy to see: what Gettier examples appear to point to are cases where S's belief that *q* is not adequate to the fact that *q*, despite being true and well reasoned (justified). It is as it were only *accidentally* true. What this has suggested to many epistemologists is the need for a term that tightens the link between belief and fact by taking the responsibility for that link away from the knower herself (in the sense of something she has to know she knows). This still leaves a wide variety of options, however. Consider the position referred to as *inferentialism*. With regard to knowledge, an inferentialist maintains that the epistemic justification of a belief is a function solely of its inferential relations to other beliefs. Inferentialism in this sense seems to suggest an internalist picture, but this neglects the fact that an inferentialist holds the view that mental capacities are necessarily constitutive of experience. As we saw in Chapter 4, this insight was the basis of Kant's so-called 'Copernican Turn' away from a passive to an active image of the knower, which suggests that experience (as phenomena) is both conceptually articulated (the categories are involved) and has 'external' content.

For a modern inferentialist, then, justificatory relations are inferential and their *relata* are beliefs, but that does not mean that the contents of the latter are fixed by (internal) facts about the knower alone.[3] Inferential justification can therefore be reconstructed along lines that aim to incorporate an external element. Nevertheless, in its 'purest' forms externalism detaches inferential justification from knowledge altogether and looks for an alternative account of adequacy, customarily in terms of truth-reliability. Again, although the details can be fleshed out in a variety of ways, the motivation is clear: if a true belief is to amount to knowledge in the absence of an adequate justificatory story, the slack has to be taken up elsewhere. According to reliabilists it's taken up by the method or process by which S comes to arrive at the (true) belief that she has. In other words, in order to have knowledge a knower just has to stand in an adequate (that is to say, reliable) relation to the facts that make her belief a true belief. She does not have to know that the method or process by which she arrived at her belief (or rather, by which she came to acquire her belief) is reliable.[4]

There are numerous versions of reliabilism around, and not all their proponents have been interested in scepticism. In one of the earliest responses to Gettier, Alvin Goldman (1967) argues that in order for a belief that q to amount to knowledge, the fact that q has to be causally linked to the belief in the appropriate sort of way. In other words a claim would fail to be knowledge if it were not the case that the fact that q caused the belief that q. Not surprisingly this worked well against Gettier's original examples, since that was the intention. Recall the case of Smith and Jones from Chapter 1: Smith came to (truly) believe that the person who would get the job had 10 coins in their pocket because her reasoning (accidentally) happened to apply to herself. If she hadn't hurriedly shoved that change into her pocket before rushing off to the interview, her belief would have been false. Her reasoning failed to track the link between the belief (the person with 10 coins will get the job) and what made it true (Smith having 10 coins in *her* pocket). On Goldman's analysis, the reason we are disinclined to see this as a case of knowing is the recognition that her belief was not *caused* by the fact that made it true.

It is the business of epistemologists to come up with counter-examples to putative analyses of knowledge (even their own), and these were not long in coming. Indeed, the second example from Chapter 1 works against Goldman's original account, for in the case of the barn Smith's belief *is* caused by the relevant fact. What could be more felicitous than a barn, spotted in natural light by a sober and employed woman with 20:20 vision causing the belief that there's a barn there? She has thoroughly reliable belief-forming mechanisms (what more could we expect of her?), and yet we would not say that she knew. Why not? Because there's that accidental feature again: if it *had* been a barn-façade Smith would *still* have thought (although now falsely) that it was a barn. Evidently, the 'true' account of knowledge has to rule out *that* possibility, and this is the task Goldman sets himself in a later work (1976). His conclusion, in brief, is that "A person knows that q . . . only if the actual state of affairs in which q is true is *distinguishable* or *discriminable* by him from a relevant state of affairs in which q is false" (1976: 774). Accordingly, Smith doesn't know that it's a barn because she can't tell the real thing from a façade in the context where the existence of barn-façades makes such a possibility a *relevant* possibility. There's a "relevant counterfactual situation[s] in which the same belief would be produced . . . and in which the belief will be false" (*ibid.*: 790). In this case the relevant counterfactual situation would be Smith looking at a barn façade. This raises a crucial issue: when is a (counterfactual) possibility that could defeat a knowledge-claim a *relevant* possibility? Or more to the point, recalling the sceptical possibilities deployed in the argument from ignorance, when is a (counterfactual) possibility an *ir*relevant possibility? Since this is not a book on epistemology we will leave Goldman's (bottom-up) attempts to answer this question to one side and approach the problem of knowledge (top-down) in a way that is externalist and seems to have obvious implications for the argument from ignorance.[5]

(Ir)relevant alternatives and the closure principle

Goldman's revision of his causal theory of knowledge is similar to a position assayed in Chapter 5 in connection with Austin. According to what I called the *relevant possibilities objection*, challenges to default claims can be mounted only if the challenger has a *specific* and *contextually appropriate* lack of evidence in mind. To make the parallel explicit, imagine that S lacks the ability to discriminate between birds of type A and birds of type B. Out with her twitcher chum, a distant relative of Austin, she cries 'Lo, an A!' Austin's relative knows that the presence of Bs in the area is a relevant possibility and therefore concludes that even if she is correct S doesn't *know* that it's an A because if it were a B she'd say the same.[6]

Contemporary developments of this 'relevant alternatives' account of knowledge are particularly associated with the work of Fred Dretske (1970, 1971). Apart from the post-Gettier milieu in which it circulates, what distinguishes it from Austin's approach[7] is that it seems to offer a specific (and original) response to the argument from ignorance. Simply stated, the position we'd like to win our way to consists in the recognition that whilst knowing or being justified involves ruling out all the *relevant* possibilities, it doesn't involve ruling out all the *logical* possibilities. More specifically, we want to be able to show that we don't need to rule out the sceptical possibilities, that they are irrelevant possibilities – irrelevant, that is, to whether we know or are justified or not. The problem is that according to the second premise of the argument from ignorance, *if S* doesn't know that she's not dreaming – if she can't rule out that possibility – then she doesn't know many of the things she takes herself to know. The key, then, is to deny that the second premise is true. How might one do that? Let's begin by looking at one of Dretske's examples:

> You take your son to the zoo, see several zebras, and, when questioned by your son, tell him they are zebras. Do you know that they are zebras? Well, most of us would have little hesitation in saying that we did know this. We know what zebras look like, and, besides this is the city zoo and the animals are in a pen clearly marked "Zebras".   (1970: 1015–16)

So far so good. However, "something being a zebra implies that it is not a mule and, in particular, not a mule cleverly disguised by the zoo authorities to look like a zebra" (*ibid.*: 1016). Do you know that they're not cleverly disguised mules? One's 'Moorean' intuition is perhaps to say that one does indeed know that they are not mules; but clearly one hasn't checked. Might it not be the case that a bunch of over-zealous Gettierians have taken over the running of the zoo, painting mules with stripes and (heaven forfend) heaping unspeakable cosmetic humiliation on other animals? Of course, it's unlikely; but now one thinks about it, it is *possible*. And staring into the pen, son by your side, feeling the burden of parental responsibility, you don't *know* that it's not true, do you? The pattern is familiar:

> *S* doesn't know that the animals are not carefully painted mules (not-*sp*)
> If *S* doesn't know that that the animals are not carefully painted mules (not-*sp*), then *S* doesn't know that the animals are zebras (*q*)

Therefore

> *S* doesn't know that the animals are zebras (*q*)

At this point, note that the second premise is thought by many philosophers to rely on the validity of what is called the 'Principle of Closure' for known implication. In Dretske's example:

1 *S* knows that the animals are zebras (*q*)
2 *S* knows that the animals being zebras (*q*) implies that the animals are not carefully painted mules (not-*sp*)

Therefore

3 *S* knows (or can come to know) that the animals are not carefully painted mules (not-*sp*)

Like all of us, *S knows* that it follows from the fact that the animals are zebras that they are not mules (2). If *S* does indeed know that the animals are zebras (1), then, she must know or at least be in a position to come to know that they are not mules. But according to the first premise of the zebra–mule version of the argument from ignorance she doesn't know that they are not mules. So it is not the case that she knows that they are zebras. In the more general case we have:

1' *S* knows that *q*
2' *S* knows that (*q* entails not-*sp*)

Therefore

3' *S* knows (or can come to know) that not-*sp*

According to the first premise of the argument from ignorance, (3') is false; but like everyone else *S* acknowledges that the truth of her empirical beliefs entails that she's not dreaming or an envatted brain (2'), so (1') is false. For Dretske, "Almost all skeptical objections trade on" (1970: 1011) this pattern of reasoning, so if the key to the argument from ignorance is the second premise, the solution is clear: to reject the 'Closure Principle' (at least as holding in general) by showing that the *falsity* of (3) and (3') is consistent with the *truth* of (1) and (1'). In other words, demonstrate that one *can* know (say) that one has two hands even though one *cannot* know that one is not dreaming or an envatted brain.

Denying closure II: Nozick

The best-known attack on closure is to be found in Nozick's *Philosophical Explanations* (1981: Ch. 3). In part this attempts to deal with Gettier examples by replacing the 'J' of the traditional analysis of knowledge with two counterfactuals, which cash out the adequacy condition by ensuring that knowing involves belief 'tracking' the facts:

(Nozick) S knows that q iff (S believes that q) & (q is true) & (if q weren't true, S wouldn't believe that q) & (if q were true, S would believe that q)

Thinking back to the barn example, Smith has a true belief but it does not amount to knowledge because it violates the third condition: she would still believe that there was a barn in front of her (q) even if it were only a barn-façade. The argument against closure rests primarily on the same condition. To take Dretske's example, it would seem that the reason we are inclined to deny that S *knows* that the animals are zebras, even if it is true that they are, is that she would continue to believe they were zebras if they were in fact painted mules. On Nozick's analysis, then, S's failure to be able to discriminate between the two possibilities – like Smith's inability to discriminate between barns and barn-façades – would seem to rule her out as a knower[8] on the grounds that she too violates the third condition. This is not, however, the case: "The subjunctive [the third condition] . . . does not talk of all possible situations in which q is false . . . It doesn't say that in all possible situations where not-q holds, S doesn't believe that q . . . What the subjunctive speaks of is the situation that would hold if q were false" (Nozick 1981: 173). Crucially, the truth-conditions of the subjunctive are not determined by all the logically possible situations in which q is false. That is to say, we are not to consider all the situations that are entailed by q. That the animals are zebras does entail that they are not painted mules, and their being painted mules is therefore one of the logical not-q possibilities. If this possibility were one of those that fixed the truth-values of the subjunctive, then clearly S would violate the third condition for knowledge. For Nozick, however, a range of restricted possibilities determines the truth-values of the subjunctive. When evaluating the third condition it is only the "not-q neighborhood of the actual world" (*ibid.*: 176) that is of interest. In other words (taking the example), the condition restricts the range of possible alternatives to S's observing zebras in a zoo and asks what would *then* be the case respecting her belief that she was. For example, that the animals are zebras implies that they are not giraffes. If S would believe that she were seeing zebras even if she were seeing giraffes, then the third condition is violated and she would not in fact be said to know (she lacks the discriminatory ability to track the fact in this case – the ability to identify zebras).

The argument against closure then goes as follows. S knows that q if the third condition is true in the 'not-q neighbourhood of the actual world'. In the case of the zebras, that does *not* include the possibility that they are painted mules, and so S knows that the animals are zebras (1). S also knows (as do we all) that the animals being zebras implies that they are not painted mules (2). If closure holds, then on the basis of (1) and (2) she should know (or be able to come to know) that the animals are not painted mules (3). However, according to the third condition, for S to know that the animals are *not* painted mules it must be the case that if they were she would believe they were. But since she identifies zebras on the basis of their black-and-white stripes and so on (good enough in the 'actual world' where she needs to discriminate between them and giraffes, for example), she would in fact believe that they were zebras even if they were painted mules. So (3) is false, and closure fails.

Generalizing this point gives us a response to the argument from ignorance. S knows an empirical fact such as that she has two hands (q) if the third condition is true. Since that does not include among its possibilities the idea that she might be an envatted brain, S knows that q (1'). Like all of us, S also knows that having two hands implies that she isn't an envatted brain (2'). If closure holds, then, she should know (or be able to come to know) that she isn't an envatted brain (3'). However, since all her experiences would be the same even if she were an envatted brain, she would continue to believe that she wasn't even if she was, and therefore her claim does not satisfy the third condition. Since S can know that q and not know that not-sp, closure fails. Or to put it more positively, while the first premise of the argument from ignorance is true, the conclusion is false: none of us knows that we're not envatted brains (or dreaming), but that *doesn't* mean that empirical knowledge is not possible.

Nozick's analysis relies on using the semantics of possible worlds to specify truth-conditions for the third condition, the notions of close (neighbouring) and distant worlds fixing the range of relevant possibilities. Since this is a much-disputed area[9] it offers grist to the *pk*-sceptic's mill. Nozick's approach also contributes little to addressing the Quietist Dilemma, with its related concerns of theoretical burden and the Intuition Problem. As Dretske pointed out above, however, it is the attack on closure that promises to do all the anti-sceptical work, and that can be undertaken without utilizing the obscure work of philosophical logicians. Indeed, Dretske formulated such an attack in work that pre-dates Nozick's[10] and has the advantage of being closer to the tradition of Austin and Wittgenstein in drawing on ordinary-language distinctions (which in principle offers the possibility of showing how the sceptic leads us astray in our thinking). Let's return to his account, bearing in mind that the comments about relevance apply equally to Nozick's position.

Denying closure I: Dretske

Dretske's elaboration of a relevant alternatives account of knowledge is intended to warrant a (at least partial) rejection of closure. We don't need to get too bogged down in the detail, but the argument in outline is as follows. It is uncontroversial to state that if *q* entails *p*, and *q* is true, *p* is true. There are certain operations that work across this entailment and others that don't. For example, *the fact* that *q*, *it's true* that *q*, and *it's necessarily the case* that *q* all 'penetrate' to *p*: "If *p* is a necessary consequence of *q*, then the statement that we get by operating on *p* with one of these . . . operators is a necessary consequence of the statement that we get by operating on *q* with the same operator" (1970: 1007). On the other hand, *I fear* that *q*, *I hope* that *q* and *it is strange* that *q* do not 'penetrate' to *p*. 'Manchester United will win the league next year' entails that 'some team will win the league next year', but I can fear the former without fearing the latter. Similarly, 'Lois bought Tim the new Radiohead CD' entails that 'Lois bought Tim the new Radiohead CD or the new Spice Girls CD', but Tim can hope for one without hoping for the other! Where the first set of operators "penetrate to every necessary consequence of q" (*ibid.*), the latter, and others like them, "fail to penetrate to some of the most elementary consequences of a proposition" (*ibid.*: 1008).

The operator of concern relates to *S knows* that q. If *S* knows that q, does she know all the things that she knows that q entails? That is to say, is 'knowing' the kind of operator that penetrates to 'every necessary consequence of q'? If it is, then closure holds and the second premise of the argument from ignorance remains intact. In short, Dretske's suggestion is that knowing is *semi*-penetrative. Knowing that q penetrates only as far as a set of consequences of q that constitute its *relevant* alternatives. His analysis of knowledge is something like the following:

(Dretske)   *S* knows that q iff (*S* believes that q) & (q is true) & (*S* is in a position to rule out all the *relevant* alternatives to q).

How does Dretske rule out the irrelevant alternatives without relying on 'close' and 'distant' worlds? Well, there are certain presuppositions that are entailed by q and which rule out the *irrelevant* consequences, but which knowing that q does not penetrate to. Rather like Wittgenstein's view of Moore propositions, then, these presuppositions are rules of the game that cannot be brought into question by the game itself.[11]

To make this clearer, let's go back to the zoo example. *S* knows that the animals being zebras implies that they are not carefully painted mules (2). She also knows that their being zebras implies that they are not giraffes. We would all presumably agree that the second implied possibility is relevant – that if *S* knows that they are zebras and knows that their being zebras implies that they are not giraffes, then she knows that they are not giraffes. If the first implied possibility were relevant, however, *S* could not be said to know that the animals were zebras unless she ruled out the possibility that they were painted mules (which we are assuming she can't do just by looking). Dretske's thought is that it is a presupposition of animal-viewing in zoos that they are honestly run – one of the background conditions without which the activity as presently practised would make no sense (although that may objectively change). Since it is a presupposition, you don't have to *know* it in order to identify zebras, although it does of course have to be true. Since you don't have to know it, you don't have to rule out its alternatives – you don't have to *know* that animals are not being painted. Presuppositions like the honest running of the zoo rule out the painting possibility as irrelevant to the knowledge claim (1), although they do not of course rule out the giraffe possibility as irrelevant. The alternatives relevant to (3), however, are rather different – they would include animatronics, sculptured animals, holographic projections and the like. Since S doesn't know that these aren't true, she doesn't know that they are not painted mules. Since (1) is true but (3) is false, closure fails.

First it should be clear that the relevant alternatives approach is intended to deal with something like the argument from ignorance, where our inability to discriminate between actual and possible (although irrelevant) states of affairs is at issue.[12] Even if it is judged successful, then, it has nothing to say in response to the Agrippan argument, which we have been taking as the more basic of our two sceptical problems. Putting that to one side, it is clear that at the level of description of our ordinary practices there is something *obviously* right about Dretske's account. The avid bird-watcher does not contemplate the possibility that stuffed birds have been placed in her vicinity any more than Carnap's geographers worry that the world may have been created only 5 minutes ago. It does indeed seem to be the case that we presuppose certain things when we undertake certain activities, and it is by highlighting this feature or our practical attitude engagements that Dretske's account scores points over Nozick's for intuitive plausibility.

Unfortunately, the sceptic is not interested in denying that we do make such presuppositions, and on the accounts of Dretske and Nozick the sceptic is held to be correct in one important respect: we don't know that we're not envatted brains, the victims of crazed Gettierians, or dreaming. Since the response is that we don't need to know these because they are not relevant, these accounts offer scant resources for dealing with the Intuition Problem – they don't explain why the 'plain' sceptical possibilities seem to lead so naturally to the 'philosophical' sceptical possibilities. They deny that they do, of course, but that falls well short of weaning us off the kind of reflections that lead to the Humean Paradox.

Objections to 'relevance' are not restricted to the charge that it fails to give us an adequate insight into how the argument from ignorance arises, however. There are at least two further problems. First, note that Dretske is what one might call a 'relevance-invariantist': the alternatives that are relevant to any knowledge claim are fixed by what is and what is not relevant in the actual situation. Whatever new possibilities the sceptic or *S* herself might come up with are irrelevant to whether or not she knows that *q*; although if sceptics had the courage of their convictions and really went around painting mules, then that would become relevant to the *objective* situation (and assuming that *S* doesn't stop believing that *q* as a result of her *ir*relevant doubts). There are two related concerns here. On the one hand, the idea that what is and what is not relevant is *objective*, and therefore wholly independent of what human beings think and do, seems like an abuse of the term given its close ties to the activities of interpretation and judgement.[13] It is very difficult to get a grip on a concept of relevance that is severed from what we as human beings value. On the other hand, I suggested at the end of Chapter 1 that in order to count as knowledge a belief must be reasonable from the knower's own point of view and not just objectively reliable. On Dretske's account, as long as *S*'s belief is true and the relevant alternatives are ruled out, it doesn't matter if it is otherwise inconsistently held – she knows. But now it looks as if talk of relevance is trying to do two jobs at once – capturing the intuition about rational consistency but liberating it from the subject and locating it in the objective situation that she occupies. One could argue for this if one were an inferentialist and believed that mental capacities are necessarily constitutive of experience, but this is not a suggestion that Dretske would be amenable to.

I don't want to press this criticism too far, so here's the second problem. As we've seen, the relevant alternatives analysis of knowledge warrants a rejection of the principle of closure. However attractive the anti-sceptical results of this conclusion may be, many philosophers find it highly counter-intuitive and are inclined to think that it is an excessively high price to pay to rid oneself of the Cartesian sceptic. Indeed, it might be thought to mark a victory for another kind of sceptic, for once we have conflicting intuitions like this in play the dispute necessarily attracts the attention of the *pk*-sceptic who suggests that the opponents might try to justify their respective claims.[14]

Invariantism and contextualism

Dretske's relevance-invariantism is not the only option open to the relevant alternatives theorist. The majority hold that determinations of relevance have a *contextual* element. According to what I'll call 'relevance-contextualism', what counts as the relevant alternatives is sensitive to the context of utterance, even when these alternatives are not present in the objective situation.[15] If S presents to herself the possibility that the animals might be painted mules, then that becomes a relevant alternative. More dramatically, the relevance-contextualist will allow that the conversational context of the *attributor* of knowledge to S can have a bearing on what the relevant alternatives are. If, discussing S, R and P introduce the possibility that the animals might be mules, then that too becomes a possibility that must be ruled out before S can be said to know that the animals are zebras.

This invocation of context ameliorates one of the problems with Dretske's account by relating what is relevant or irrelevant to the human activities of reasoning and judging. Nevertheless, the relevance-contextualist response to the argument from ignorance is in effect the same as Dretske's: there is a mismatch between the alternatives relevant to S knowing that q and S knowing that not-*sp*. The former (1′) can be true while the latter (3′) is false because the context of utterance determines what the relevant alternatives are, and the alternatives relevant to the practical attitude claim to know that q differ from those relevant to the theoretical attitude claim to know that not-*sp*. As a response to the Humean Paradox it comes down to saying that we ought not to worry about our inability to show that the sceptic is wrong (as indeed we can't according to the relevance theorist) because the failure of closure 'insulates' our practical attitude beliefs from *philosophical* doubt. But trying to address the Intuition Problem by advocating the anti-intuitive rejection of the principle of closure does not seem like a very promising line to take.

In recent years there has been an attempt to address some of the shortcomings of relevance-contextualism. More specifically, there has been a tacit recognition that a satisfactory response to the argument from ignorance must involve a fuller diagnosis of why it seems so compelling – one that does not make dealing with the sceptic more difficult by necessitating a rejection of closure.

According to the contextualist proper,[16] the truth-conditions of attributions of the form 'S knows that q' and 'S doesn't know that q' vary according to the context in which they are uttered. These contexts determine the epistemic standards that S must meet if her true belief is to amount to knowledge, and as with versions of relevance-contextualism the context is one in which those *ascribing* knowledge are situated. Where the invariantist[17] proper maintains that the epistemic standards that govern any knowledge claim are insensitive to situational variation, the contextualist holds that while R might truly assert that S knows that q, that does not necessarily contradict P's assertion that S *doesn't* know that q (if R and P are in contexts where different epistemic standards apply).

One of the advantages of the contextualist approach to knowledge is that it highlights a feature of our ordinary-language use. Although we are ordinarily quite promiscuous when it comes to ascribing knowledge to people, we are inclined to make more stringent judgements when more is at stake. Of course, the contextualist does not *just* think that the conditions for when people actually *do* ascribe knowledge to people vary with context – the invariantist will happily acknowledge that if R is ignorant about quantum physics he is more likely to ascribe knowledge to someone who appears authoritative than P, who is an expert. Rather, it is the case that in R's context S really does know and in P's she doesn't (even if what she believes is true). Another advantage is that indexing the truth-conditions to context gives the epistemologist an option for dealing with the argument from ignorance that does not involve rejecting the principle of closure.

To see how this goes, consider R, who in the context of everyday life (adopting the practical attitude) asserts (truly) that S knows that q. Since S knows that q, then applying the principle of closure S knows that not-sp. Now consider P, who establishes an epistemic context with a higher standard by introducing the possibility that S doesn't know that not-sp (thus adopting the theoretical attitude). Since S does not know that not-sp, P applies the principle of closure and concludes that S doesn't know that q. The conclusion is that what the sceptic P concludes is true when evaluated according to their epistemic standard and false when evaluated according to R's, and that closure holds relative to any particular epistemic standard. The key to the Intuition Problem, then, is the recognition that in moving from the practical to the theoretical attitude the sceptic is exploiting a perfectly natural feature of our everyday use of language that allows for the fact that the *meaning* of knowledge attributions are context-sensitive.

Contextualist approaches to scepticism are in their infancy, historically speaking, although they do have much in common with the tradition of Austin, Moore *et al*. Like Williams, the contextualist does not reject the sceptic's doubts as meaningless and therefore avoids a host of familiar problems. Moreover, the emphasis on the way we use language in common life also promises certain advantages over Williams's anti-intuitive suggestion that the sceptic is presupposing a certain theory in order to generate the argument from ignorance. Of course, according to the contextualist the sceptic is in some sense correct and that will always appear to some philosophers like an acknowledgement of failure.[18] The invariantist, for example, will simply deny that knowledge attributions are context-sensitive and press the point that the sceptic is not exploiting a feature of ordinary usage but pointing out what we have to know (not-*sp*) if we are to demonstrate that knowledge is *possible*.

What the invariantist's epistemological *heroism* implicitly picks up on is the suspicion that the account of knowledge that relevance theorists and contextualists offer is not really the kind of knowledge we're actually interested in. In other words, they violate the no-stipulations principle by failing to offer any way of linking up knowledge with justification. Of course, that is largely the point – getting rid of that problematic element. But as we've seen, it is scepticism about justification that presents the main challenge to our cognitive self-image. Thus whilst it might be true (according to the contextualist) that *S* does know that *q* and *R* truly says that *S* knows that *q*, *S* may not be able to justify her belief that *q* (because, for example, Hume is right that we can't *justify* inductive inference), and *R* might not be able to justify his statement. Since contextualists say nothing about justification, they offer no response to the Agrippan argument.[19]

Interlude: getting a grip again

In this chapter I've suggested that externalist theories of knowledge can be regarded as combining an attempt to solve Gettier problems with a desire to answer the argument from ignorance. No one has yet offered an account that succeeds in doing this, and at the end of Chapter 1 I suggested that there are reasons for thinking that even if one were successful it could not, *qua* theory, avoid *pk*-scepticism.[20] This way of describing the situation may be slightly misleading, however. Perhaps externalist theories have not been successful because by attempting to avoid the Agrippan argument they violate the no-stipulations principle and fail to acknowledge the intuitions that make knowledge something we value.[21] On this understanding, externalist treatments of the argument from ignorance give the impression of ignoring what troubles us because they 'change the subject' of knowledge. In doing so they provide no understanding of *how* we know what we think we do that allows us to see that what we have is knowledge that the world is a certain way.[22]

The intuitions that drive this reaction to externalism might of course be 'wrong', and we have encountered several ways in which that 'wrongness' could be elucidated. If one regards the intuitions as deriving from a set of unconscious theoretical commitments, one will aim to identify those commitments. If, on the other hand, one thinks that sceptical problems arise from a certain style of thinking, then one will aim to cure oneself and others of that style of thinking by taking up the standpoint of the therapeutic sceptic. If the intuitions are not 'wrong', however, the *heroic* epistemologist has been right all along and we have to *legitimate* our account of knowledge by showing how it is possible. But a legitimating account comes in the form of reasons and arguments, and these demand in their turn that the reasoner *justify* their reasonings. Since this takes us back to the Agrippan argument, we will spend the remainder of this chapter examining attempts to respond to it.

Internalism revisited I: coherentism

We'll structure our discussion of internalist responses to the Agrippan argument around a discussion of BonJour's "The Dialectic of Foundationalism and Coherentism" (1999). This offers a defence of an epistemically internalist foundationalism[23] against an epistemically internalist coherentism. The value of this piece for us derives in part from the fact that BonJour's earlier book, *The Structure of Empirical*

Knowledge (1985), contains both an incisive critique of externalist accounts of justification and knowledge and one of the most influential statements of internalist coherentism. Since coherentism and foundationalism are the traditional options for responding to the Agrippan argument, reinterpreting BonJour's rakish progress from *internalist* coherentist to *internalist* foundationalist will serve as a good opportunity to reflect on the likely success of either against the sceptic.[24] We'll start with the coherentist picture.

As we saw in Chapter 1, the foundationalist response to the threatened regress of justification is to deny that all assumptions are dogmatic:

(Fo) There are some beliefs that do not stand in need of further justification, and which serve as the grounds for other claims.

The coherentist is sceptical about the linear account of justification that this presupposes. Any coherence theory of empirical justification must therefore initially satisfy the following (related) desiderata:

(Co_1) Offer an account of justification that does not invite the regress problem.
(Co_2) Make the concept of coherence intelligible.

As BonJour points out (1999: 123), the most plausible response to (Co_1) is due to Bosanquet:[25] to think of justification in holistic terms, with beliefs considered as parts of a mutually supportive system or network. This gives us our original definition:

(Co) Beliefs are linked together in a complex system and lend one another mutual evidential support.

Crucially, then, no belief can be evaluated epistemically in isolation, only in the context of the coherent system of which it is a part. The fact that justification *per se* applies only to the whole is the key to responding to the Agrippan argument. To assert that a belief is justified is to ensure that no further justificatory challenge *could* be raised because *ex hypothesi* there is nothing 'outside' the coherent system to serve this function.

The success of (Co) clearly hinges on the plausibility of the response to (Co$_2$). What exactly is coherence and when can one tell when a system is coherent? In *Structure* BonJour notes the various standards that a coherent system has to satisfy. It must, for example, be logically consistent (1985: 95), involve a high degree of inferential connectedness[26] (*ibid*.: 98) and exhibit probabilistic consistency (*ibid*.: 95). As he later comes to realize, however, even the demand for logical consistency sets an implausibly high standard that no human cognitive constitution could seriously be expected to realize. On this account, any belief that S had that was inconsistent with another – no matter how 'distant' in terms of inferential connections – would be sufficient to render all her beliefs unjustified.

This demand for consistency might stir vague memories of Chapter 2. To see why, consider the following. Coherentism is intended to block the regress of justification by giving us a *reason* for thinking that a particular belief is justified. According to our definition of methodological internalism, a belief's being justified requires that the believer has access to a reason for believing it is true. If S is to reject the regress of justification on the grounds that her belief that q coheres with her other beliefs, she must have a grasp or representation of that coherent set of beliefs – a belief or complex of beliefs to the effect that her beliefs are coherent. Since the higher-order belief (or beliefs) that constitutes such a grasp is not itself part of the system, however, the question naturally arises as to how we know that it (or they) is (are) justified. This return of the repressed regress led the coherentist BonJour to make what he calls the 'Doxastic Presumption': to treat the higher-order belief that one's system of beliefs is coherent as "an unjustified hypothesis in relation to which issues of justification are *conditionally* assessed, yielding results of the general form: *if* my representation of my system of beliefs is correct, then such-and-such a particular belief is justified in the sense of being likely to be true" (1999: 126–7). The obvious problem with this is that it gives the game away to the sceptic without so much as a word of reproach. After all, an 'unjustified hypothesis' is just the Dogmatist's 'mode of Hypothesis', and the claim that *if* my assumption is true *then* there is no regress is not going to cut the mustard with the sceptic. What I want to get at here is a more structurally revealing point, however. In Chapter 2 we saw that the Stoic, under pressure to make good on the idea of a cognitive impression, was forced into a position according to which one would know anything *only if* one knew everything. To have knowledge proper *S* must have a stable cognitive economy and exercise the maximal level of cognitive responsibility. I described such an *S* as satisfying the Full Competency Requirement and argued that one would only *know* that one satisfied this requirement *if* one were a wise man.

To make the parallel clear, then, note that no wise man could have inconsistent beliefs (no matter how 'distant' the inferential connections) because that would leave open the possibility that he might later come to reject something that he had earlier assented to. And we've seen that only a wise man knows that he is a wise man and therefore knows anything. What I'm suggesting is that this is a necessity the coherentist has tried to transform into a virtue by ensuring that justification only operates at the level of the whole system. BonJour's 'unjustified hypothesis' serves the same function that the concept of the wise man or sage did for the Stoics. Where the 'Doxastic Presumption' states that *if* my representation is correct, *then* a belief is justified, a Stoic brought up to speed with developments in logic might well say *if* I am a sage, *then* I have knowledge![27]

Let's call the problem for which the 'Doxastic Presumption' was the unsuccessful attempt at a solution the 'problem of internalism':

- *The problem of internalism.* If justification requires coherence, what justification does *S* have for believing that her beliefs are coherent?

Any internalist coherentist is clearly going to have to do a better job at answering the problem of internalism than BonJour did. In addition, any coherence theorist has to offer plausible responses to the following:

- *The problem of content.* If justification is just coherence, it would seem that *S*'s beliefs about (say) everyday objects could be adequately justified despite being out of contact with those objects. How does 'empirical content' get into the system?
- *The problem of uniqueness.* On any plausible account of what constitutes coherence, any number of internally coherent but incompatible systems of belief is possible. This leads to the

possibility that *any* belief can be justified in *some* coherent system.

• *The problem of truth.* What reason is there for thinking that coherence leads to truth, and therefore is apt to serve as the basis for epistemic justification?

We don't have the space to discuss the internalist response to all these problems. They are, however, closely related, and the problem of truth is perhaps the most important. Historically speaking, philosophers have responded to the charge that justification on the model of coherence might not be truth-conducive by arguing for an epistemic account of truth. In other words, the temptation has been to make both truth and justification matters of coherence. This presents considerable problems given that we have strong intuitions that a belief can be justified and yet not be true, but the case has been made.[28] Nevertheless it should be clear that relying on a coherence theory of truth makes it more difficult to see how the problems of uniqueness and content might be dealt with. In any event, we're now looking at BonJour's early work and he expressly disavows such an approach.[29]

For early (and later) Bonjour, then, truth is a matter of correspondence, not coherence. In order to establish that the coherent system is objective (legitimate), he therefore needs to provide a reason for thinking that it is. The problem this introduces is similar to that which required the 'Doxastic Presumption'; namely, that a reason is just another belief, and a belief is just part of the coherent system. BonJour's "metajustification" (1985: Ch. 8) aims to offer an a priori argument to the effect that the *truth* of a persistently coherent set of beliefs is the *best explanation*[30] of their coherence; that is, he tries to establish the claim that the correspondence of coherent beliefs to the world is a better explanation for the coherent and stable course of experience than (for example) being an envatted brain. The obvious sceptical response to this is that whilst it might well be the best explanation given what we *think* we know about the world and our experience of it, we don't in fact know that what we think we know is true. An envatted brain might come to the conclusion that the best explanation for the coherence of its beliefs is that they are objective, but that doesn't mean that it knows that it's not an envatted brain! In short, it appears that BonJour's internalist coherentist response to the Agrippan argument opens up a gap between mind and world that leaves us vulnerable to the argument from ignorance.

Internalism revisited II: foundationalism

With such problems awaiting resolution, it is perhaps not surprising that BonJour has come to the conclusion he has concerning "the untenability of the central coherentist view" (1999: 130) he once held. Nevertheless, as someone committed to his earlier criticisms of externalism it is equally unsurprising that he has turned instead to an internalist version of foundationalism. Recalling (Fo), a foundationalist theory of justification confronts two basic questions:

(Fo$_1$) What is the nature of the basic (foundational – epistemically prior) beliefs such that they serve the role that they do?
(Fo$_2$) How do the basic beliefs justify the non-basic beliefs?

Any answer to (Fo$_2$) will clearly depend on (Fo$_1$). If, for example, one could demonstrate that such basic beliefs extended to beliefs about external (publicly observable) objects, one would have an easier job showing how such beliefs warrant further beliefs (and a ready response to both sceptical arguments). If, however, such beliefs are restricted to internal states of the subject (ontological internalism), the critical task becomes one of identifying inferential links between such states that overcome the gap between mind and world by warranting conclusions about the latter (otherwise we have the argument from ignorance again).

Turning to (Fo$_1$), we can follow John Pollock's (1986) useful distinction between 'doxastic' and 'nondoxastic' theories. A doxastic theory holds that "the justifiability of a belief is a function exclusively of what beliefs one holds" (Pollock 1986: 19); a nondoxastic theory insists that "other considerations also enter into the determination of whether a belief can be justified" (*ibid*.: 21). Applying this to foundationalism,[31] we have two options: for the doxastic foundationalist the peculiar nature of foundational beliefs is that they are self-certifying or self-justifying, the obvious example being Descartes's 'clear and distinct' ideas. Since we're focusing on empirical justification, what is of interest to us now are nondoxastic theories, according to which the favoured beliefs are justified because they stand in relation to something that is not a belief. For the internalist foundationalist this something is a subjective state; for the externalist foundationalist it is something in the world.

We've encountered examples of externalist foundationalism in the form of reliabilism; the traditional forms are internalist and exploit the empiricist intuition that knowledge derives from subjective and introspectively available experience of the world (ourselves included in it). To take the example of perception, the problem with this is that if a sensory experience *e* is to serve as a *justification* for *S*'s basic belief that *q* that is available to *S*, *e* must have a specific feature *f*, the possession of which *S* grasps as a reason for believing that *q*. This presents a dilemma. On the one hand, if *S*'s grasp of *f* comes in the form of a belief-state *r*, it means that the candidate basic belief in fact depends on *r* for its justification, and that invites the charge of regress. On the other hand, if *S*'s grasp of *f* comes in the form of a something less than a propositionally contentful belief state, it's hard to see how *S* is *justified* in believing that *q* on the basis of *e* at all.[32] Scepticism looms from both directions.

This does not of course mean that internalist versions of foundationalism have not been forthcoming. Perhaps the most formidable is presented by Roderick Chisholm in the successive editions of his *Theory of Knowledge* (1989).[33] Rather than delve into the mysteries of Chisholm's work, however, we'll stick to BonJour's (1999) more tentative version. His view is something like the following. As I stare down at my desk (the "perceptual experience" (1999: 133)) I acquire the belief that there's a fair-trade chocolate bar in front of me (the "occurrent belief" (*ibid*.: 131)), and arrive thence at the belief that I have such a belief (the "metabelief" (*ibid*.)). The internalist wants to see the metabelief as the available *justification* for the 'foundational' occurrent belief. As we saw, the problem is that if the metabelief is a contentful belief it invites the regress, and if it falls short of having content it cannot serve as a justification.

BonJour's suggestion comes in two parts. The first addresses the relation between the occurrent belief and its justifying ground, claiming that the occurrent belief has awareness of its content 'built in to' it – that consciousness of content is *constitutive* of these beliefs.[34] Such beliefs are therefore self-justifying, and the "constitutive awareness of content is strictly *infallible*" (1999: 132). In other words, *S* cannot be wrong about having a belief with the specific content *q* because what it is to have such a belief is to be 'aware' of having a belief with that content. To make good on this foundationalist response to the Agrippan argument BonJour must of course develop an account of occurrent beliefs that makes it possible to link their infallibility to the world. Since it is empirical beliefs and not Descartes's a priori beliefs that he is dealing with, this requires rather more effort.[35] The second part of BonJour's account therefore addresses the relation between perception and occurrent belief. The perception is held to be nonconceptually or nonpropositionally contentful.[36] However, when *S* has an occurrent belief she "conceptually characterizes" (*ibid*.: 134) that content, constituting it *as* the belief it is, and of which she is (infallibly) aware.

First, it should be noted that a great deal here rides on the intelligibility of the conceptual–nonconceptual distinction. This is hotly disputed and it is quite clear that the *pk*-sceptic would have a field-day with it, but let's focus on something specific. As BonJour points out, the most natural way to describe how we 'conceptually characterize' the non-conceptual content is "in terms of the physical objects and situations that we would be inclined on the basis of that experience, other things being equal, to think we are perceiving" (1999: 135). One obvious response to this is to ask whether I am *really* inclined to think that I'm observing a physical object when I look down at my chocolate bar. Do I actually find myself declaiming 'Lo, a physical object! Thank heavens it's physical and not immaterial, or my appetite would never be satisfied'? As Austin (1962: 6–19) might say, other things being equal I'm *not at all* inclined to think any such thing.

Putting ordinary-language considerations to one side, the whole point of course is that the Cartesian sceptic is not at all inclined to take all things to be equal! *Au contraire*, one might add. Bonjour recognizes this of course, and acknowledges that one needs a *reason* to believe that one's characterizations, which strictly speaking are held to be "physical-object *appearances*" (1999: 136), are indeed 'correlated' with *real* physical objects. His response is underwhelming, to say the least:

> My own fairly tentative suggestion would be that the basis of
> the inference between sensory appearance and objective fact is
> to be found in two further fundamental facts about such
> appearances . . . their involuntary, spontaneous character, and
> . . . the fact that they fit together and reinforce each other.
>
> (*Ibid.*: 138)

In other words, BonJour the foundationalist continues to accept
some version of *explanationism*: the view that an objective domain
of physical objects is the best explanation of our experience being
the way it is. In response to this the Ancient and Cartesian sceptics
happily join forces: the former asks why we are justified in thinking
that spontaneity and coherence justify claims about (recalling Hume)
matters of fact and existence; the latter points out that an envatted-
BonJour brain has spontaneous and coherent experiences too.

Davidsonic

It is not surprising that externalists reject internalism and aim to
replace legitimating accounts of knowledge with causal-reliabilist
alternatives. Nevertheless, internalists seem to have something over
externalists in so far as they recognize that some role for justification
is required if we are to retain contact with what we require from an
understanding of how knowledge is possible. Unfortunately, both
internalist– coherentist and foundationalist responses to the
Agrippan argument make it difficult to see a way of avoiding the
argument from ignorance. We'll therefore reverse the direction of
BonJour's 'dialectic' and conclude by looking at an attempt to offer
an externalist coherentism. In work spanning nearly forty years
Donald Davidson has elaborated an understanding of language and
agency that promises an alternative to the theoretical attitude:[37] a
standpoint on our activities that aims to satisfy the qualms that
motivate the internalist while warding off the temptation to fall in
with the sceptic. It also links up in interesting ways with the work of
Wittgenstein that we encountered briefly in Chapters 4 and 5. For
want of space, we will on the whole restrict our attention to
Davidson's "A Coherence Theory of Truth and Knowledge" (1983).

Take an example of any proposition q. For S to *know* that q on
the traditional view q must be true and S must be justified in

believing that q. The question is, what is the source of justification and is it available to the knower? As we've seen, the nondoxastic foundationalist looks to avoid the epistemic regress by seeking justification in something that marks the interface between the beliefs of the knower and the world they are about. For the traditional empiricist this is captured by the idea that some basic perceptual beliefs are justified by the sensations that cause them and which they in turn 'resemble' (Fo_1). These then provide the justificatory building-blocks for the more complex beliefs (Fo_2).

Philosophy of language raises a related question: to believe that q, S must know what q means, which indicates that S must recognize what it takes to be justified in asserting that q. This raises a parallel question: what is the source of the justification, and is it available to the speaker? As we saw in Chapter 4, this 'linguistic turn' in philosophy was part of Kant's legacy, when it appeared that attention to semantics could give philosophers the constructive edge they needed in epistemology. Following in the empiricist tradition, the nondoxastic foundationalist bit the ontological internalist bullet and sought for a source of justification in "experience, the given, or patterns of sensory stimulation, something intermediate between belief and the usual objects our beliefs are about" (Davidson 1983: 126).

Semantic versions of foundationalism like that found in Carnap's *Aufbau* and the work of Quine aim to pin the meanings of some sentences directly to observation or patterns of sensory stimulation. These then constitute the meanings and therefore the assertion conditions of more complex utterances (that is to say, determine what is to count as justified assertions). As we saw with Carnap and Quine, this approach seems to lead to the argument from ignorance, since in both cases it is open to the sceptic to adopt the theoretical attitude and to point out that sensations, perceptions or patterns of sensory stimulation could all be exactly the way they are while the world remains (in)different. In other words, the semantic approach has done little to overcome the ontologically internalist structure of traditional empiricism. Since it still seeks to locate a source of justification in the subjective realm of experience, meaning itself – which was supposed to help overcome the subjective–objective split – becomes subjective: "Trying to make meaning accessible has made truth inaccessible. When meaning goes epistemological in this way, truth and meaning are necessarily divorced" (Davidson 1983: 126). This is of course the philosophical state of affairs that Wittgenstein diagnosed: the idea that ontological internalism leaves envatted brains babbling away to themselves in a private language. As we saw in Chapter 4, this is why proponents of the version of naturalism we associated initially with Wittgenstein (and subsequently with Austin) turned towards an investigation of ordinary language (common life). In other words, this variety of naturalism sought to purge philosophical reflection on the nature of justification of the (theoretical attitude) prejudices that had been imported from the (ontologically internalist) empiricist tradition – purge semantics of epistemology, one might say. What the account of language use in terms of rules and practices seeks to achieve is an understanding of justification (normativity) that links it to public meaning (non-internalist). On this account, to know the (public) meaning of *q just is* to be justified in using it, without having to invoke 'intermediates' as justificatory items. Moreover, this understanding of language is achieved from *within* the standpoint of common life (the practical attitude), not by adopting a theoretical attitude *towards* it.

As we'll see, this position is close to the one Davidson holds, although as a student of Quine his journey was rather more complicated. The moral he draws from the above quotation is two-fold. First, "that nothing can count as a reason for holding a belief but another belief" (1983: 123). Whatever test we have for justifying our beliefs, it cannot involve their 'confrontation' with something non-doxastic; it must be a question of their *coherence* with other beliefs. Secondly, if the problems of 'uniqueness', 'content' and 'truth' are to be addressed, that test must be one that links our beliefs, not to the ontological internalist's epistemic intermediaries, but directly to the world itself. In other words, if meaning is to be the link between belief and world, meaning must be given by *objective* truth conditions.

It is important to note that for Davidson truth is a 'primitive' (unanalysable) concept. That 'primitivity' is partly captured by the disquotational feature of language conveyed by Tarski's Convention T, which declares sentences like the following true:

[T] 'Snow is white,' spoken by an English speaker, is true if and only if snow is white.

This Tarskian insight is the backbone of Davidson's approach to semantics, and underpins his claim that meaning is to be understood in terms of objective truth conditions: "the truth of an utterance depends on just two things: what the words as spoken mean, and how the world is arranged" (1983: 122). On this account, for *S* to be justified in asserting that *q*, *S* must have a test for ensuring that the objective truth conditions of *q* are in fact satisfied, and that test is coherence. As Davidson points out, however, coherence itself cannot ensure that any *particular* belief is true or not. All it can establish is that "most of the beliefs in a coherent total set of beliefs are true" (*ibid.*: 121). Or, as Davidson adds,

> since there is no useful way to count beliefs, there is a presumption in favour of the truth of a belief that coheres with a significant mass of belief. Every belief in a coherent total set of beliefs is justified in the light of this presumption . . . So to repeat, if knowledge is justified true belief, then it would seem that all the true beliefs of a consistent believer constitute knowledge.
> (*Ibid.*: 121–2)

Before continuing, it's worth noting two things: first, that Davidson conditionally accepts the standard (pre-Gettierian) analysis of knowledge; secondly, that on this account some of our false beliefs would be justified. The second point reminds us that although coherence is the *test* for truth, it is not constitutive of truth. This allows Davidson to situate his own brand of realism: on the one hand, since truth is not analysable in terms of coherence (is not 'epistemic'), the independence of belief and truth is maintained (in line with our intuitions about objectivity); but, on the other, truth is not wholly divorced from belief (is not *radically* 'non-epistemic'): "*each* of our beliefs may be false. But of course a coherence theory cannot allow that all of them can be wrong" (Davidson 1983: 123). This brings us to the crux of the matter, for as Davidson recognizes, one (familiar) version of scepticism suggests that although our beliefs might hang together in a coherent and consistent fashion, that does not mean that they might not all be false. The task, then, is to answer 'the problem of truth' and give such a sceptic a *reason* for thinking that a coherent set of beliefs is true. Since the coherentist rules out any other source of justification but another belief, that reason cannot be a form of evidence (*ibid*.: 127). This is no more (or less) than Descartes attempted to do. Where his 'reason' was that God would not systematically allow us to be misled, Davidson takes a rather different approach. The argument therefore proceeds in two stages:

CTTK(1) Establish that a correct understanding of a person's propositional attitudes shows that most of what they believe must be true (the 'presumption' above is legitimate). This constitutes the response to the problems of 'uniqueness', 'content' and 'truth'.

CTTK(2) Anyone who concerns themselves with the thoughts about the objectivity of their thinking must know what a belief is, and will be led to conclude that most of anyone's beliefs – their own included – are true. This aims to capture the intuition in the problem of 'internalism'.

Central to the argument of CTTK(1) is the idea of a 'radical interpreter' confronted with the task of trying to understand a language with which they are unfamiliar, and for which no translation manual exists. The problem, as Davidson notes elsewhere, is that "Meaning and belief play interlocking and complementary roles in the interpretation of speech" (1984: 141). The attribution of beliefs and the interpretation of sentences are interdependent aspects of interpretation: we cannot imagine making sense of a speaker's utterances without knowing a great deal about what his beliefs are, any more than we can imagine finely individuating his beliefs without knowing what many of his words mean (*ibid*.: 195). What the radical interpreter needs, then, is some way into the system that avoids the putative circularity of presupposing access to either. Davidson's suggestion, following Quine, is the plausible idea of 'prompted assent': looking at those occasions when what the speaker says seems causally linked to worldly saliences (saying 'that's a rabbit' in the presence of rabbits, for example).

Applying this method, we have to suppose that the speaker is expressing a genuine desire to communicate, and not fooling around (saying 'that's a rabbit' in front of one rabbit and 'there's a horse' in front of another); that is, holding true the sentences they assent to. This does not in itself help much, however, because it tells us nothing specific about the attitudes the speaker expresses, nor about his beliefs. If, for example, I know in advance that the speaker believes that rabbits are brown, have long ears and go hoppety-hop, I can hazard that when, in the presence of a brown, long-eared hoppety-hopper they say 'that's a rabbit', I should interpret their sentence accordingly. The fact that they say 'there's a rabbit' with a sober and sincere look on their face doesn't advance the radical interpreter's project.

So what does? In short, the answer is that one must interpret using the so-called principle of charity. In the first instance, this

> directs the [radical interpreter] to translate or interpret so as to read some of his own standards of truth[38] into the pattern of sentences held true by the speaker. The point of the principle is to make the speaker intelligible, since too great deviations from consistency and correctness leave no common ground on which to judge either conformity or difference.   (1983: 129)

Put simply, the claim is that to make "even a first step towards inter-pretation" (1984: 196), we must assume general agreement on beliefs. An important extension of charity (applying principally to the prompted assents) is thus that from the point of view of the radi-cal interpreter, he cannot make the speaker largely wrong about the world, but must "interpret sentences held true (which is not to be distinguished from attributing beliefs) according to the events and objects in the outside world that cause the sentences to be true" (1983: 131). This is not, then, an option, but a condition of possi-bility of interpretation. Crucially, it expresses Davidson's externalist (casual) semantics (and his response to the problem of 'content'): the content of our beliefs and what we say is determined in part by the relations between our assertions and the features of the world that the radical interpreter identifies as their causes. To put it more force-fully, it is from the standpoint of the radical interpreter that we discover *all there is to know* about what makes a speaker's beliefs about, and their words mean, what they are and do (*ibid*.: 129).

There is an obvious problem with the argument as it stands: "the appeal to charity turns out to involve the idea of unproblematic access to certain causal relations between speakers and objects in the world" (Williams 1991: 313). We have a position where the radical interpreter is identifying the causal relations that constitute prompted assent as if access to (justified true beliefs about) worldly saliencies were unproblematic – and that in an argument that is supposedly anti-sceptical! Davidson is aware of the possibility: "Why couldn't it happen that speaker and [radical interpreter] understand one another on the basis of shared but erroneous beliefs?" (Davidson 1983: 131). His response, and what concludes CTTK(1), is the less-than-divine idea of an 'omniscient interpreter'. The omniscient interpreter is a non-radical version of the familiar figure – non-radical because she has access to anything in the world that bears on what does and would cause a speaker to assent to any of the sentences they do. Crucially, then, the omniscient interpreter applies in an optimal way the same method as the radical inter-preter. Unlike Descartes's deity (or malevolent demon), she is every bit as constrained in her attribution of content as the radical inter-preter. When the omniscient interpreter turns her attention to the speaker, then, she finds that he is mostly true by his own lights. But since, by hypothesis, that is *objectively* true, he is mostly true *simpliciter*. Similarly, when the omniscient interpreter looks upon the radical interpreter, she finds that he too has mostly true beliefs. To conclude, the radical interpreter can't share mostly false beliefs with the speaker because they both have mostly true beliefs accord-ing to the only opinion that matters!

Now it will come as no surprise to learn that many philosophers have found this suggestion somewhat less than fully convincing.[39] Before discussing it, however, let's conclude Davidson's argument. With CTTK(1) in place the question is, what reason do you or I have to believe that our beliefs are mostly true? The answer comes swiftly: when I reflect on the nature of belief, and with it the related concepts of objective truth and causality, I realize that "most of [my] basic beliefs are true, and among [my] beliefs, those most securely held and that cohere with the main body of [my] beliefs are most apt to be true" (Davidson 1983: 133). Of course, whether one finds this plausible as a straight *theoretical* response to the sceptic will depend entirely on whether one is well disposed towards the externalist semantics it presents in 'pure' form. In "Afterthoughts, 1987" (1987) a response to Rorty's (1986) suggestion that he should not have presented himself as refuting the sceptic, but as telling him to get lost, Davidson acknowledges as much: "If one grants the correctness of this account, one *can* tell the sceptic to get lost" (Davidson 1983: 136). This is reminiscent of BonJour's 'Doxastic Presumption', and the response is similarly familiar: if the Cartesian sceptic won't grant the account and the *pk*-sceptic asks for the justification for its purported correctness (the fact that it 'refutes' scepticism being deemed inadequate), neither will consider themselves inclined to obey the command.

In more recent work Davidson (1991, 1992) has focused less on the technicalities attending the elaboration of a theory of meaning and more on the metaphor of 'triangulation'. In this we are invited to think of a speaker, his linguistic community and the world as the three vertices. None of these elements can be eliminated from an understanding of human agency, and the relationship between no two has priority. Reminiscent of Wittgenstein, the account aims to deny the sceptic the purchase required to prise the three apart and claim that language as a whole fails to latch on to the world, or that individuals can constitute private meanings. As even Davidson's most vociferous advocates would concede, however, this does not amount to a refutation of the argument from ignorance. Rather, it should perhaps be read as continuing the therapeutic sceptic's work of opposing the view of the human subject that *invites* such scepticism.

It is in this dialectical spirit that we return to the much-maligned image of the omniscient interpreter. What Davidson is trying to suggest is that if we want to take up an, as it were, 'outside' perspective on our dealings with the world (as we surely do) then we should not conceive of it along the lines of the theoretical attitude. In other words, we should resist envisaging it as a standpoint from which beliefs can be 'read off' such that they are the way they are independently of the way the world is – the presupposition, in other words, of the ontological internalist. Davidson wants to deny the very possibility of articulating the internalist standpoint by refusing to countenance such a view of content: where Descartes's defence against scepticism hinges on God's not mis*leading* us, Davidson's omniscient interpreter cannot see us as mis*led*.

In concluding, it must of course be stressed that the therapeutic sceptic cannot sanction Davidson's claim to have shown that the theoretical attitude is impossible to adopt – the sceptic's dream is not an *impossible* dream, and to insist that things are otherwise is to risk the Agrippan argument. Nevertheless, it does allow us to think about how we reflect on the practices of others and ourselves without inviting us to disengage theoretically from those practices. Consider a context in which we are contemplating someone's epistemic performance. It may be a real situation or merely a thought-experiment, like those used in Gettier examples. Adopting the standpoint of the omniscient interpreter, we may discover that Smith's belief in this or that is unjustified, but it will still be the case that most of her beliefs are true, and since the pattern of justification follows the pattern of truth, most of her beliefs will be justified as well. Of course this won't tell us which particular beliefs are justified, nor give us conditions for justification that hold across the board, but then only a dogmatist would come up with such a strange idea in the first place. With the idea of the omniscient interpreter, 'therapeutic' sceptics have one more weapon to wield dialectically against the dogmatists of their own time.

Notes

Chapter 1: Scepticism and knowledge

1. This is not to suggest that *rejectionists* need think that philosophy has nothing to say to the sceptic. Rather, they think we can rightly regard ourselves as knowers without first having to show that sceptical doubts are unfounded.
2. Another famously 'Cartesian' sceptical position – not one Descartes himself advances – is the so-called 'Problem of Other Minds' (how do we know that creatures that look like us have minds?).
3. It is supposed, then, that we have intuitions regarding the extension of the concept, and use that to arrive at its intension. For a powerful critique of this approach to epistemology, see Craig (1990).
4. Sometimes misleadingly called the 'infinite regress' or 'epistemic regress' problem; or the problem of 'epistemic circularity'. For the source of the name see Chapter 2.
5. Adapted from Gettier (1963).
6. Adapted from Goldman (1976).
7. It would be odd to maintain that what makes it true that I have a headache is something wholly independent of 'me', but the thought is that the meaning of the word 'headache' is not wholly dependent on what I take it to mean.
8. The 'fourth term' in an indefeasibility theory is meant to rule out the possibility that S's justification for believing that q could be undermined by her acquisition of new beliefs. In Gettier example 2 Smith is not indefeasibly justified precisely because if she came to learn that she was in barn-façade country she would no longer consider herself to *know* that the barn was a barn and not a barn-façade.
9. Adapted from BonJour (1985). For a more detailed discussion see Fogelin (1994).

Chapter 2: The legacy of Socrates

1. The Delphic oracle is said to have described Socrates as the wisest Athenian on the grounds that only he knew that he knew nothing.
2. Sometimes translated under the title *Outlines of Pyrrhonism* and generally referred as *PH*, which abbreviates the Greek title *Pyrr. Hypotyposis*.

References to this work are to the book number and section of the Annas and Barnes edition (Sextus Empiricus 1994). All other references in this chapter are to sources translated in Long and Sedley (1987).

3.   *Technē* (expertise).
4.   For so-called 'eliminativist' theories see Stich (1983) and Churchland (1984).
5.   He was succeeded as head of the school by Cleanthes (d. 232 BCE) and Chrysippus (*c.* 280–207 BCE), who along with their contemporaries are collectively referred to as the 'Old Stoa'.
6.   Socrates' method is called *elenchus* – the testing of people's views through questioning.
7.   See Couissin (1929). See also Hankinson (1995: 77–8).
8.   From a contemporary perspective, if one's belief that q satisfies the criterion of truth, one knows that q. In this sense, that one recognizes that the criterion has been met constitutes one's justification for believing that q. In the terms of Chapter 1, this suggests that any Dogmatism will be methodologically internalist. It should, however, be kept in mind that knowledge here is not to be understood as straightforwardly propositional.
9.   We'll neglect the discussion of feelings in what follows since it is reasonable to view them as of a kind with sensations.
10. For the Stoics, to know the meaning of q is to know the truth-conditions of q. When I assent to q, I judge that those conditions are satisfied. The criterion of truth is my indication that the conditions are in fact satisfied. We'll look briefly at truth-conditional semantics in Chapter 6.
11. While remaining rational, that is.
12. Note that this use of the term is different from Plato's, for whom *doxa* are true opinions.
13. If the matter becomes 'weightier' because for some reason S decides that the barn might in fact be a barn-façade, she might consider it to be irresponsible not to rule out the possibility by 'thoroughly exploring' the situation.
14. In contemporary parlance, truth has been 'deflated'.
15. There are also the 'two modes' (I. 178–9).

Chapter 3: Demons, doubt and common life

1.   Popkin (1979).
2.   Luther, *De Servo Arbitrio*, quoted in Popkin (1979: 6–7).
3.   Of course, the *pk*-sceptic can respond to the putative member of the 'elect' in the same way they did to the putative sage: by asking him how he *knows* that he is a member of the elect.
4.   L'Abbé François du Phanjas, quoted in Popkin (1979: 172).
5.   All page references are to the twelve-volume edition of Descartes's works by Adam and Tannery (*AT*). The translations are from Descartes (1988).
6.   As with the Stoics, I can 'read' the book of my mind, even though none of the propositions (thoughts) may be true.
7.   This was first published in 1641 and bundled with six sets of objections and replies from leading thinkers of the day.
8.   To continue the book parallel, the result of inspecting q_1 is to note that the criterion is that odd-numbered sentences are true.
9.   Descartes adds that he "can never be quite certain about anything" until the

possibility that "there is a deceiving God" is eliminated (*AT* VII: 36). The suggestion is that while one is fully focused on a clear and distinct idea one cannot doubt its truth, but when one focuses on the possibility that God might be a deceiver, that former intuition is undermined. The obvious parallel is with the Stoic distinction between *katalepsis* and *episteme*: only those who possess the latter will find that they never have to re-evaluate their assents to the cognitive. Similarly, only he who has demonstrated that God is veracious will be confident that a remembered intuition of a clear and distinct idea cannot be doubted. In Descartes's terms, the possessor of knowledge is he who has undertaken the reflective–theoretical task of working through the *Meditations*.

10. For it to be *my* walking it has to be *my* body; but given the sceptical possibilities we do not even know that bodies exist, let alone that this one walking is *mine*.

11. The fundamental assumption of ontological internalism is – one might argue – that there is an original unity between thinker and thinking such that the thinker has incorrigible access to the content of their thoughts. This in turn suggests that we are in possession of a criterion after all – one that allows us to identify a thought as *our* thought, just as Luther supposed that one could discriminate between the 'true' reading of scripture and a 'false' one. We'll return to the question of whether or not Descartes's sceptical thought-experiments and variations thereupon are 'natural' or 'theoretical' in Chapter 5.

12. Hume (1978). Henceforward *T*.

13. Confusion as to how they were related might well have contributed to the failure of the *Treatise*; "It fell dead-born from the press, without reaching such distinction, as even to excite a murmer among the zealots" ('My Own Life' in Hume 1987).

14. Most notably Smith (1941) and Stroud (1977).

15. The *Treatise* is subtitled "An Attempt to introduce the experimental Method of Reasoning into MORAL SUBJECTS".

16. Hume (1975). Henceforward *E*. First published in 1748, this was intended as a more popular presentation of some of the themes from Book I of the *Treatise*.

17. Hume's analysis is widely regarded as the first statement of the so-called 'problem of induction'.

18. Or any other relevant feature: we don't think the future will be like the past in *all* respects, but the basis of our reasonings about matters of fact and existence relate to those that will be. The only way to distinguish between relevant and non-relevant features is on the basis of past experience, but their *continuing* relevance is what is in question. Supposing continuing relevance on the basis of past relevance is of course to beg the question. Incidentally, this shows that Nelson Goodman's (1983) so-called 'New Riddle of Induction' is just the old Humean one.

19. Note that this is where Descartes would invoke God's veracity.

20. In the twentieth century this has focused on the derivative distinction between 'analytic' and 'synthetic' truths.

21. Note the way Hume reverses Descartes's method of enquiry. Where the latter uses scepticism to exclude the practical from the realm of the theoretical in the pursuit of certainty, Hume uses scepticism to exclude the theoretical from the practical in the pursuit of the probable.

22. Strictly speaking, with regard to the so-called problem of the external world we do not *really* have such a belief, given that it can play no part in reasoning

from cause and effect. We cannot *really* doubt it, and even when we pretend to (become overcome by sceptical reasoning), it remains insulated from our everyday life.

Chapter 4: Transcendental meditations

1. It is standard practice to refer to this text using the page numbers of the first (A) and second (B) German editions (1781 and 1787 respectively). The translations are from Kant (1993).

2. Kant confesses that it was Hume who "interrupted" his "dogmatic slumber" and gave his philosophical investigations "a quite new direction" (1977: 260).

3. These are examples of what Kant calls 'antinomies' (A: 405–566/B: 432–594).

4. Not all contemporary philosophers regard all and only a priori judgements as necessary, and a posteriori judgements as contingent. See Kripke (1980).

5. Like those of geometry and claims like "Different times are merely parts of one and the same time" (A: 31/B: 46).

6. Space and time are not concepts but the "two pure forms of sensible intuition" (A: 21/B: 35).

7. There is a great deal of scholarly debate about what exactly Kant meant by this distinction. He sometimes writes as if *noumena* really are "objects in addition to the objects of possible experience . . . though it is impossible for us to know the slightest thing about them"; at other times as if the same objects are presented to us in different ways, "on the one hand as appearances; on the other hand, as things in themselves" (quoted in Coffa 1991).

8. These included Otto Neurath (1882–1945), Moritz Schlick (1882–1936) and Hans Reichenbach (1891–1953). Wittgenstein (1889–1951) attended the meeting of the circle upon his return to Vienna in 1926. The work of the 'logical positivists' was popularized in England by A. J. Ayer (1910–89) in his *Language, Truth and Logic* of 1936 (by which time the circle hadn't met for four years).

9. Translated as *The Logical Structure of the World* in Carnap (1967a).

10. "The word 'object' is . . . used . . . for anything about which a statement can be made . . . not only things, but also properties and classes, relations in extension and intension, states and events, what is actual as well as what is not" (1967a: 5).

11. Ayer claims that it was a convention, "a definition of meaning which accorded with common usage in the sense that it set out the conditions that are in fact satisfied by statements which are regarded as empirically informative" (1959: 15).

12. The 'success' of 'thing-talk' could therefore never offer evidence for the *reality* of the thing-world.

13. Indeed, his charge of meaninglessness against the philosophical question goes with a diagnosis of a certain sort of illusion: confusing the 'material' and 'formal' modes of speech, and thereby supposing that the 'thing-world' is a 'thing'.

14. As with the Stoics, perhaps only the wise man 'knows'!

15. See Putnam (1981: Ch. 1).

16. Cf. Kant: "The transcendental deduction of all *a priori* concepts has . . . a principle according to which the whole enquiry must be directed: to show that these concepts are a priori conditions of the possibility of all experience" (A: 93/B: 125).

17. This can be iterated regressively, as in: 'P_1 only if C_1; C_1 only if C_2; C_2 only if C_3 . . .' and so on.

18. For recent work on transcendental arguments see Stern (1999, 2000). Interesting collections include Schaper & Vossenkuhl (1989) and Bieri et al. (1979).

19. Usually associated with Körner (1967, 1971: Ch. 13) in the English-speaking world, but also made by Collingwood (1940).

20. Cf. Rorty (1979: 83).

21. The fact that transcendental arguments are associated with the verification principle should not be that surprising given that the logical positivists introduced it as part of the 'naturalization' of Kantian philosophy. Similarly, I suggested that Kant himself could be viewed as a kind of transcendental verificationist, and transcendental arguments are related to Kant's deductions.

22. Stroud (1968) raises the criticism against Strawson (1959) and Shoemaker (1963), whose work in the 1960s revived this form of argumentation in Anglo-American philosophy. The verificationist interpretation of the private-language argument is to be found in, among others, Hacker (1986), Budd (1989) and Grayling (1985).

23. This image was shared by Carnap and the positivists, who took it that what was 'given' in experience was 'private'.

24. The following is adapted from Malcolm (1954) and Thomson (1966). The former claims to find an argument in the *Philosophical Investigations*, and the latter criticizes it as being 'verificationist'. There is no argument like this in the *Investigations*, but at this stage we are interested if such an argument could work.

25. This is the conclusion to be drawn from Putnam (1981: Ch. 1).

26. See Kripke (1982) and Fogelin (1987).

Chapter 5: Un/natural doubts

1. For Descartes the equivalent would be something like 'God would not allow most of my beliefs to be false'.

2. As we've seen, Kant tries to avoid this problem by showing that properly (transcendentally) understood, experience does constrain the solution.

3. B xxxvii (fn). Kant is of course referring to his 'Refutation of Idealism'.

4. Or why you *believe* it. Austin describes both cases, but for the sake of brevity we'll restrict our discussion to knowledge claims alone.

5. In *Sense and Sensibilia* Austin also avers that the claim that dreams are qualitatively indistinguishable from waking experiences is "perfectly extraordinary" (1962: 48).

6. Ayer, Price and Geach in *Sense and Sensibilia*; Wisdom in "Other Minds".

7. See for example McGinn (1989).

8. If the term has any meaning one might say that they are *quasi*-transcendental.

9. It also resonates with the 'therapeutic' interpretation of Hume, according to which the sceptical and naturalistic aspects are united to elaborate features of common life.

10. Clarke's only publication on the subject. Barry Stroud, Stanley Cavell, Thomas Nagel and Marie McGinn are not alone in testifying to the influence of his unpublished writings.

11. Stroud describes it as the "ground-floor question" (1996: 359).
12. As Clarke notes, "he is not a philosopher's philosopher, but a philosopher's plain man" (1972: 758).
13. Recalling the discussion of transcendental arguments in Chapter 4, one might conclude that what Clarke shows is that the plain possibilities require only that one must *believe* that (in effect) the world exists, not that it does.
14. Thomas Nagel (1971, 1986) takes what we've called the Intuition Problem to be expressive of the human condition. For Stanley Cavell it is an expression of "want[ing] to know the world as we imagine God knows it. And that will be as easy to rid us of as it is to rid us of the prideful craving to be God" (1999: 236–7).
15. It is, he says, "one of the most important movements in contemporary philosophy" (Williams 1991: xiv). All references are to Williams (1991) unless noted otherwise.
16. This taxonomy can obscure more than it illuminates, and Williams is now apt to play down its probative force. As is apparent from this and earlier chapters, the distinctions are ill drawn and not at all suited to evaluating dialectical responses to scepticism. It is not even clear where one would situate Hume or Kant, for example.
17. For a shorter version of the argument of Williams (1991) see Williams (1988).
18. Compare the quotes from *Sense and Sensibilia* above, where Austin talks about the need for evidence depending on circumstances, and the fact that no claims are *intrinsically* vulnerable to doubt.
19. See Williams (2001) for a development of this thought. This would put it in competition with the *mitigated* sceptical approach I ascribed to Wittgenstein above.
20. Other non-intuitive philosophers have been equally 'sceptical'. Cf. DeRose (1993); Vogel (1997); Rorty (1997); Fogelin (1999).
21. Cf. p. 295.

Chapter 6: Internalisms and externalisms

1. In other words, if scepticism is intuitively rooted in our traditional concept of objectivity, and epistemology either fails to answer it or to make it intelligible, epistemology is inconsistent with that traditional conception.
2. See Sosa (1994) for an externalist response to the Agrippan argument, and Stroud (1994) for an 'intuitionist' reaction. A *pk*-sceptical response to Sosa's argument would follow the line taken at the end of Chapter 1.
3. Indeed, in its most sophisticated versions, inferentialism rejects the internal–external dichotomy altogether and therefore doesn't feel the need to find a new term to close the gap between belief and fact. See for example Robert Brandom's (1994) attempt to avoid Kant's phenomena–noumena distinction by adopting a more Hegelian position. For a dialectical attempt to overcome the internal–external division see Part I of Fogelin (1994).
4. Note that even though externalism aims to eliminate the knower's need to know they know, the lesson of Gettier examples is not to eliminate cognitive responsibility (why else would the examples strike us as unacceptable cases of accidental belief?). The normative component is passed over (promissorily) to the cognitive scientist, who is charged with the task of finding out the appro-

priate truth-reliable processes. This enthusiasm for scientific method is the legacy of the Quinean naturalism we briefly examined in Chapter 4.

5. It should be clear from the description that *rejectionist*–externalist theories of knowledge like reliabilism are broadly foundationalist in character. That is to say, they aim to identify a set of beliefs that do not stand in need of justification and are capable of justifying other beliefs in a non-inferential way (Fumerton 2002). Note that on this interpretation externalist analyses do aim to provide an account of knowledge that offers a response to the Agrippan argument and so *rejectionist* responses might well be described as *heroic*–externalist! Of course, that the *heroic* and *rejectionist* responses are opposite sides of the same coin is what the *pk*-sceptic has claimed all along since they both engage in theory and not 'therapy'.

6. It's worth noting the difference as well as the similarity: for Austin the relevant possibility motivates a challenge to *S*'s claim, whereas for his distant (post-Gettierian) relative it issues in the judgement that *S* doesn't in fact know.

7. Unlike Dretske, Goldman and Nozick (see below), Austin does not for example trade in subjunctives, being neither inclined towards philosophical logic nor having at his disposal the relatively recent developments in possible-world semantics.

8. A familiar way to put this is that her criterion of judgement – a black-and-white-stripy-animal perception – is not a criterion of truth; or, in Nozickian terms, it fails to ensure that her belief tracks the truth. Recall Zeno's recourse to a counterfactual analysis in response to Arcesilaus's criticism of the Stoic account of the criterion.

9. Kripke himself warns of their misuse (1980).

10. Although Nozick's book came out quite a while after Dretske's work, he records in a footnote that he wasn't familiar with it at the time of composition.

11. Note that in Carnap's terms these are the rules that divide the questions that can be raised ('internal') from those that can't ('external'). This parallel with Wittgenstein might support Williams's suggestion (1991: 186–7) that since Wittgenstein's framework propositions aren't 'known' he is an advocate of closure-denial. However, this would not be so if it is the case that *S* can say of Moore (for example) that he knows that he has two hands even though Moore can't (reasonably) say this of himself. Contextualist accounts of knowledge attributions seem to capture something of this intuition. On the logic of presupposition see Collingwood (1940).

12. Note the similarity with Clarke: to suppose that a sceptical possibility is relevant would be to presuppose that experience might in principle have a feature that would allow us to discriminate between (for example) being awake and being asleep. That is to say, it presupposes what Clarke calls the 'standard' model of human conceptual constitution. See Chapter 5.

13. One might say the same about presuppositions, unless they are *conditions of possibility*, in which case we encounter the problems discussed in Chapter 4.

14. Note that although *S* knows that *q* just if her belief is true and she rules out the relevant alternatives, it may also be the case that the sceptic can lead her to doubt that what she thinks of as the relevant alternatives are in fact the relevant alternatives. That doesn't mean that she doesn't know, but it does mean that she'll never be in a position to determine what it is that she does and doesn't know (or when knowing 'penetrates' to what *q* implies). Since we at

least occasionally want to act on the basis of what we think we know, *that* might lead her to the conclusion that she ought to 'suspend belief' and go along with appearances. This sceptical conclusion may be one the relevant alternatives theorist is happy with.

15. See for example Goldman (1976), Stine (1976), Cohen (1988) and Heller (1999).

16. See for example Cohen (1988), Lewis (1979, 1996), Unger (1984) and DeRose (1992, 1995).

17. See Unger (1984).

18. I'm tempted to suggest that this sceptical *result* of contextualism could be exploited dialectically in the manner of the Academic Sceptic, but this latter style of thinking tends to be anathema to philosophers who engage in epistemology in the Anglo-American tradition.

19. I am not aware of any attempt at a contextualist solution to the problem so cannot prejudge the case. Nevertheless, it is difficult to see how one might *justifiably* draw the vital distinction between when R and P *will* hold that S is justified in believing that q and when R and P judge truly that S is so justified (for a defence of contextualism in the parallel case of knowledge ascriptions see DeRose 1999). Since it seems likely that it will be much more difficult to play semantic tricks with the concept of justification, this suggests that the contextualist will find the argument from ignorance (j) a tougher nut to crack.

20. Brandom (1995) regards McDowell (1995) as presenting "nothing less than a generalized argument against all possible forms of epistemological externalism" (Brandom 1995: 895). The 'therapeutic' sceptic needn't endorse Brandom's modal enthusiasm, merely note the argument for dialectical purposes.

21. As I note above (fn. 5), externalist theories can be regarded as foundationalist responses to the Agrippan argument, which lends support to this claim.

22. See Stroud (1994: 302).

23. Cf. BonJour (2001).

24. BonJour's definition of internalism is our methodological internalism: "roughly, that a belief's being epistemically justified requires that the believer in question have in his cognitive possession or be suitably aware of such a reason or adequate basis for thinking that the belief is true" (1999: 118).

25. See Bosanquet (1892).

26. Think of the neuronal structure of the brain as a model.

27. What I am suggesting here is that the foundationalist Stoics were driven to a form of coherentism by sceptical considerations.

28. It is familiar in post-Kantian idealist tradition (Cf. Hegel 1977), but see also the concluding section on Davidson.

29. Discussions of the relationship between truth and justification in the analytic tradition abound. Audi's (1993: Ch. 10) is useful.

30. Explanationism, or 'inference to the best explanation', as it is sometimes called. See Lipton (1991).

31. There is no place in Pollock's classification for BonJour's nondoxastic foundationalism, although his nondoxastic internalist 'direct realism' is similar (Pollock 1986: 24, 175–9).

32. For more on this see BonJour (1985: Ch. 4, 1999: 121–2).

33. For 'externalist' criticisms of this see Sosa (1999).

34. Note that this sounds like Kant's transcendental unity of apperception: the view that all intuitions must be connected in one consciousness and therefore attended by the 'I think' (Cf. B: 135–40).

35. As we saw in Chapter 2, the Stoics held that because beliefs are part of the rational faculty one cannot be mistaken about their contents (they are 'infallible'). *That* I perceive a chocolate bar in front of me is distinct from the judgement (assent) that there *is* such a bar in the world. To make that second claim requires the development of the cognitive impression, which invites the Agrippan argument.

36. 'Non-conceptual content' is a gerrymandered concept that aims to satisfy the intuition that the world affects us in a causal way that constrains our thinking about it. Since we can't, for example, legitimately believe what we want about the world, the world must therefore take a lead. If the world gave us 'conceptual content' it would suggest a curious coincidence – not to say dependence – that goes against our sense of the world's 'otherness'. It would also indicate that we could 'discover' a priori the sorts of interesting things that we ordinarily look to scientists for. The world therefore gives us content, but we have to do the work to organize/systematize it. See McDowell (1994) for the view that the world could constrain us without being 'non-conceptual'.

37. Useful introductions to Davidson's work are Evnine (1991) and Ramberg (1989).

38. It should be noted that Davidson does not think that one could read in the wrong basic concepts – what, according to Kant, renders our thinking legitimate – because he does not think that we can make sense of alternative basic concepts. The argument, in "On the Very Idea of a Conceptual Scheme", employs a similar combination of Tarski and radical interpreter.

39. Cf. McGinn (1986).

Bibliography

Annas, J. & J. Barnes 1985. *The Modes of Scepticism*. Cambridge: Cambridge University Press.

Audi, R. 1993. *The Structure of Justification*. Cambridge: Cambridge University Press.

Austin, J. L. 1946. "Other Minds". See Austin (1970), 76–116.

Austin, J. L. 1956. "A Plea for Excuses". See Austin (1970), 175–204.

Austin, J. L. 1962. *Sense and Sensibilia*. Oxford: Clarendon Press.

Austin, J. L. 1970. *Philosophical Papers*. Oxford: Oxford University Press.

Ayer, A. J. 1936. *Language, Truth and Logic*, London: Gollancz.

Ayer, A. J. 1956. *The Problem of Knowledge*. London: Pelican.

Ayer, A. J. (ed.) 1959. *Logical Positivism*. Glencoe, IL: Free Press.

Beck, L. W. 1965. *The Metaphysics of Descartes*. Oxford: Oxford University Press.

Beiser, F. C. (ed.) 1993. *The Cambridge Companion to Hegel*. Cambridge: Cambridge University Press.

Bennett, J. 1979. "Analytic Transcendental Arguments". See Bieri *et al.* (eds) (1979), 45–64.

Bieri, P. 1979. "Scepticism and How to Take It: Comment on Stroud". See Bieri *et al.* (eds) (1979), 299–307.

Bieri, P., R.-P. Horstmann, L. Krüger (eds) 1979. *Transcendental Arguments and Science*. Dordrecht: Reidel.

Bird, G. 1962. *Kant's Theory of Knowledge*. London: Routledge.

BonJour, L. 1985. *The Structure of Empirical Knowledge*. Cambridge, MA: Harvard University Press.

BonJour, L. 1999. "The Dialectic of Foundationalism and Coherentism". See Greco and Sosa (eds) (1999), 117–43.

BonJour, L. 2001. "Toward a Defense of Empirical Foundationalism". In *Resurrecting Old-Fashioned Foundationalism*, M. DePaul (ed.), 21–38. Lanham, MA: Rowman and Littlefield.

Bosanquet, B. 1892. *Knowledge and Reality*. London: Sonnenschein.

Bowie, A. 1993. *Schelling and Modern European Philosophy*. London: Routledge.

Brandom, R. 1994. *Making it Explicit*. Cambridge, MA: Harvard University Press.

Brandom, R. 1995. "Knowledge and the Social Articulation of the Space of Reasons", *Philosophy and Phenomenological Research* 55: 895–908.

Bubner, R. 1978. "Kant, Transcendental Arguments, and the Problem of the Deduction", *Review of Metaphysics* **28**: 453–67.

Budd, M. 1989. *Wittgenstein's Philosophy of Psychology*. London: Routledge.

Burnyeat, M. 1982. "Idealism and Greek Philosophy: What Descartes Saw and Berkeley Missed". In *Idealism Past and Present. Royal Institute of Philosophy: Supplement 13*, G. Vesey (ed.), 19–50. Cambridge: Cambridge University Press.

Burnyeat, M. (ed.) 1983. *The Skeptical Tradition*. London: University of California Press.

Carnap, R. 1967a. *The Logical Structure of the World and Pseudoproblems in Philosophy*, R. A. George (trans.). London: Routledge.

Carnap, R. 1967b. "Empiricism, Semantics and Ontology". See Rorty (ed.) (1967), 72–84.

Cavell, S. 1999. *The Claims of Reason*. Oxford: Clarendon Press.

Chisholm, R. 1989. *Theory of Knowledge*, 3rd edn. Englewood Cliffs, NJ: Prentice Hall.

Churchland, P. M. 1984. *Matter and Consciousness*. Cambridge, MA: MIT Press.

Clarke, T. 1972 "The Legacy of Skepticism", *Journal of Philosophy* **68**: 754–69.

Coffa, A. 1991. *The Semantic Tradition from Kant to Carnap: To the Vienna Station*. Cambridge: Cambridge University Press.

Cohen, S. 1988. "How to be a Fallibilist", *Philosophical Perspectives* 2, *Epistemology*, 21–123.

Collingwood, R. G. 1940. *An Essay on Metaphysics*. Oxford: Oxford University Press.

Couissin, P. 1929. "The Stoicism of the New Academy". See Burnyeat (ed.) (1983), 31–63.

Craig, E. 1990. *Knowledge and the State of Nature*. Oxford: Clarendon Press.

Dancy, J. 1985. *Introduction to Contemporary Epistemology*. Oxford: Basil Blackwell.

Davidson, D. 1983. "A Coherence Theory of Truth and Knowledge". See Malachowski (ed.) (1990), 120–34.

Davidson, D. 1984. *Inquiries into Truth and Interpretation*. Oxford: Oxford University Press.

Davidson, D. 1987. "Afterthoughts, 1987". See Malachowski (ed.) (1990), 134–8.

Davidson, D. 1991. "Three Varieties of Knowledge". In *A. J. Ayer: Memorial Essays. Royal Institute of Philosophy: Supplement 30*, A. Phillips Grifiths (ed.), 153–66. Cambridge: Cambridge University Press.

Davidson, D. 1992. "The Second Person", *Midwest Studies in Philosophy* **17**: 255–67.

DeRose, K. 1992. "Contextualism and Knowledge Attributions", *Philosophy and Phenomenological Research* **52**: 913–29.

DeRose, K. 1993. "Review of Michael Williams' *Unnatural Doubts*", *Philosophical Review* **102**: 604–7.

DeRose, K. 1995. "Solving the Sceptical Problem". See DeRose & Warfield (eds) (1999), 1–52.

DeRose, K. 1999. "Contextualism: An Explanation and Defense". See Greco and Sosa (1999), 187–205.

DeRose, K. & T. Warfield (eds) 1999. *Skepticism: A Contemporary Reader*. Oxford: Oxford University Press.

Descartes, R. 1988. *Selected Philosophical Writings*, J. Cottingham, R. Stoothoff, D.

Murdoch (trans.). Cambridge: Cambridge University Press.

Dretske, F. 1970. "Epistemic Operators", *Journal of Philosophy* 67: 1007–23.

Dretske, F. 1971. "Conclusive Reasons", *Australasian Journal of Philosophy* 49: 1–22.

Evnine, S. 1991. *Donald Davidson*. Stanford, CA: Stanford University Press.

Fogelin, R. 1985. *Hume's Scepticism in the Treatise of Human Nature*. London: Routledge.

Fogelin, R. 1987. *Wittgenstein*, 2nd edn. London: Routledge.

Fogelin, R. 1994. *Pyrrhonian Reflections on Knowledge and Justification*. Princeton, NJ: Princeton University Press.

Fogelin, R. 1999. "The Sceptic's Burden", *International Journal of Philosophical Studies* 7: 159–72.

Förster, E. (ed.) 1989. *Kant's Transcendental Deductions*. Stanford, CA: Stanford University Press.

Fumerton, R. 1995. *Metaepistemology and Skepticism*. Lanham, MA: Rowman and Littlefield.

Fumerton, R. 2002. "Foundationalist Theories of Epistemic Justification", http://plato.stanford.edu/entries/justep-foundational/ (accessed 25 April 2002).

Gettier, E. 1963. "Is Justified True Belief Knowledge?", *Analysis* 23: 144–46.

Goldman, A. 1967. "A Causal Theory of Knowing", *Journal of Philosophy* 64: 355–72.

Goldman, A. 1976. "Discrimination and Perceptual Knowledge", *Journal of Philosophy* 73: 771–91.

Goodman, N. 1983. *Fact, Fiction, and Forecast*. Cambridge, MA: Harvard University Press.

Grayling, A. C. 1985. *The Refutation of Scepticism*. London: Duckworth.

Greco, J. & E. Sosa 1999. *The Blackwell Guide to Epistemology*. Oxford: Basil Blackwell.

Guttenplan, S. D. (ed.) 1975. *Mind and Language*. Oxford: Clarendon Press.

Hacker, P. M. S. 1986. *Insight and Illusion*, 2nd edn (rev.). Oxford: Clarendon Press.

Hankinson, R. J. 1995. *The Sceptics*. London: Routledge.

Hegel, G. W. F. 1977. *Phenomenology of Spirit*, A. V. Miller (trans.). Oxford: Oxford University Press.

Heller, M. 1999. "Relevant Alternatives and Closure", *Australasian Journal of Philosophy* 77: 169–208.

Henrich, D. 1989. "Kant's Notion of a Deduction and the Methodological Background of the First *Critique*". See Förster (ed.) (1989), 29–46.

Hiley, D. R. 1988. *Philosophy in Question*. Chicago, IL: Chicago University Press.

Hookway, C. 1990. *Scepticism*. London: Routledge.

Hume, D. 1975. *Enquiries Concerning Human Understanding and Concerning the Principles of Morals*, 3rd edn, L. A. Selby-Bigge (ed.). Oxford: Clarendon Press.

Hume, D. 1978. *A Treatise of Human Nature*, 2nd edn, L. A. Selby-Bigge (ed.). Oxford: Oxford University Press.

Hume, D. 1987. *Essays: Moral, Political, and Literary*, E. F. Miller (ed.). Indianapolis, IN: Liberty Classics.

Kant, I. 1956. *Critique of Practical Reason*, L. W. Beck (trans.). New York: Macmillan.

Kant, I. 1964. *Groundwork of the Metaphysic of Morals*, H. J. Paton (trans.). New York: Harper & Row.

Kant, I. 1977. *Prolegomena to Any Future Metaphysics That Will Be Able To Come*

Forward As Science, J. W. Ellington (trans.). Indianapolis, IN: Hackett.

Kant, I. 1993. *Critique of Pure Reason*, Meiklejohn & V. Politis (trans.). London: Everyman.

Kenny, A. (ed.) 1981. *Descartes: Philosophical Letters*. Oxford: Basil Blackwell.

Körner, S. 1967. "The Impossibility of Transcendental Deductions", *The Monist* 51: 317–31.

Körner, S. 1971. *Fundamental Questions in Philosophy*. London: Penguin.

Kripke, S. 1980. *Naming and Necessity*. Oxford: Basil Blackwell.

Kripke, S. 1982. *Wittgenstein on Rules and Private Language*. Oxford: Basil Blackwell.

Lehrer, K. & M. Clay (eds) 1989. *Knowledge and Scepticism*. Boulder, CO: Westview.

LePore, E. (ed.) 1986. *Truth and Interpretation*. Oxford: Basil Blackwell.

Lewis, D. 1979. "Scorekeeping in a Language Game", *Journal of Philosophical Logic* 8: 339–59.

Lewis, D. 1996. "Elusive Knowledge", *Australasian Journal of Philosophy* 74: 549–67.

Lipton, P. 1991. *Inference to the Best Explanation*. London: Routledge.

Long, A. A. & D. N. Sedley 1987. *The Hellenistic Philosophers*, vol. 1. Cambridge: Cambridge University Press.

Mackie, J. 1976. *Problems from Locke*. Oxford: Clarendon Press.

Malachowski, A. (ed.), (1990) *Reading Rorty*, Oxford: Basil Blackwell.

Malcolm, N. 1954. "Wittgenstein's Philosophical Investigations", *The Philosophical Review* 63: 530–59.

Malcolm, N. 1958. "Knowledge of Other Minds", *The Journal of Philosophy* 55: 968–78.

Martin, R. 1989. "Collingwood's Claim that Metaphysics is a Historical Discipline", *The Monist* 72: 489–525.

McDowell, J. 1994. *Mind and World*. Cambridge, MA: Harvard University Press.

McDowell, J. 1995. "Knowledge and the Internal", *Philosophy and Phenomenological Research* 55: 877–983.

McGinn, C. 1986. "Radical Interpretation and Epistemology". See E. LePore (ed.) (1986), 356–68.

McGinn, M. 1989. *Sense and Certainty*. Oxford: Blackwell.

Moore, G. E. 1942. "A Reply to My Critics". See Schilpp (ed.) (1942), 535–677.

Moore, G. E. 1959. *Philosophical Papers*. London: Allen and Unwin.

Nagel, T. 1971. "Brain Bisection and Unity of Consciousness". In his *Mortal Questions*, Cambridge: Cambridge University Press (1979).

Nagel, T. 1986. *The View from Nowhere*. Oxford: Oxford University Press.

Nozick, R. 1981. *Philosophical Explanations*. Cambridge, MA: Harvard University Press.

Pollock, J. 1986. *Contemporary Theories of Knowledge*. Totowa, NJ: Rowman and Littlefield.

Popkin, R. H. 1966. "David Hume: His Pyrrhonism and His Critique of Pyrrhonism". In *Hume*, V. C. Chappell (ed.). London: Macmillan.

Popkin, R. H. 1979. *The History of Scepticism from Erasmus to Spinoza*. Berkeley and Los Angeles, CA: University of California Press.

Putnam, H. 1981. *Reason, Truth, and History*. Cambridge: Cambridge University Press.

Quine, W. V. 1960. *Word and Object*. Cambridge, MA: MIT Press.

Quine, W. V. 1963. *From a Logical Point of View*, 2nd edn (rev.). New York: Harper.

Quine, W. V. 1969. *Ontological Relativity and Other Essays*. New York: Columbia University Press.

Quine, W. V. 1975. "The Nature of Natural Knowledge". See Guttenplan (ed.) (1975), 67–81.

Ramberg, B. 1989. *Donald Davidson's Philosophy of Language: An Introduction*. Oxford: Basil Blackwell.

Reichenbach, H. 1938. *Experience and Prediction*. Chicago, IL: University of Chicago Press.

Reichenbach, H. 1965. *The Theory of Relativity and A Priori Knowledge*. Berkeley and Los Angeles, CA: University of California Press.

Rorty, R. (ed.) 1967. *The Linguistic Turn*. Chicago, IL: Chicago University Press.

Rorty, R. 1971. "Verificationism and Transcendental Arguments", *Noûs* 5: 3–14.

Rorty, R. 1979. "Transcendental Arguments, Self-Reference, and Pragmatism". See Bieri *et al.* (eds) (1979), 77–103.

Rorty, R. 1986. "Pragmatism, Davidson and Truth". See Rorty (1991), 126–50.

Rorty, R. 1991 *Objectivity, Relativism and Truth: Philosophical Papers*, vol. 1. Cambridge: Cambridge University Press.

Rorty, R. 1997. "Comments on Michael Williams' *Unnatural Doubts*", *Journal of Philosophical Research* 22: 1–10.

Rosenberg, J. 1975. "Transcendental Arguments Revisited", *Journal of Philosophy* 62: 611–24.

Schaper, E. & W. Vossenkuhl (eds) 1989. *Reading Kant: New Perspectives on Transcendental Arguments and Critical Philosophy*. Oxford: Basil Blackwell.

Schilpp, P. A. (ed.) 1942. *The Philosophy of G. E. Moore*. Evanston and Chicago, IL: Northwestern University Press.

Schlick, M. 1949. "The Foundation of Knowledge". See Ayer (ed.) (1959), 209–27.

Sextus Empiricus 1994. *Outlines of Scepticism*, J. Annas and J. Barnes (eds). Cambridge: Cambridge University Press.

Shoemaker, S. 1963. *Self-Knowledge and Self-Identity*. Ithaca, NY: Cornell University Press.

Slote, M. A. 1970. *Reason and Scepticism*. London: Allen & Unwin.

Smith, N. K. 1941. *The Philosophy of David Hume*. London: Macmillan.

Sosa, E. 1994. "Philosophical Scepticism and Epistemic Circularity", *Aristotelian Society Supplement Volume* 68: 263–90.

Sosa, E. 1999. "Skepticism and the Internal/External Divide". See Greco and Sosa (eds) (1999): 145–57.

Stern, R. (ed.) 1999. *Transcendental Arguments: Problems and Prospects*. Oxford: Clarendon Press.

Stern, R. 2000. *Transcendental Arguments and Scepticism: Answering the Question of Justification*. Oxford: Clarendon Press.

Stich, S. 1983. *From Folk Psychology to Cognitive Science: The Case Against Belief*. Cambridge, MA: MIT Press.

Stine, G. 1976. "Skepticism, Relevant Alternatives, and Deductive Closure", *Philosophical Studies* 29: 249–61.

Stout, A. K. 1929. "The Basis of Knowledge in Descartes". In *Descartes: A Collection of Critical Essays*, W. Doney (ed.), 169–91. London: Macmillan (1967).

Strawson, P. F. 1954. "Critical Notice of *P. I.*", *Mind* 63(249): 70–99.

Strawson, P. F. 1959. *Individuals*. London: Methuen.

Strawson, P. F. 1966. *The Bounds of Sense*. London: Methuen.

Strawson, P. F. 1985. *Skepticism and Naturalism: Some Varieties*. London: Methuen.

Stroll, A. 1994. *Moore and Wittgenstein on Certainty*. Oxford: Oxford University Press.

Stroud, B. 1968. "Transcendental Arguments". See Walker (ed.) (1982), 117–31.

Stroud, B. 1977. *Hume*. London: Routledge.

Stroud, B. 1983. "Kant and Skepticism". See Burnyeat (ed.) (1983), 438–45.

Stroud, B. 1984a. *The Significance of Philosophical Scepticism*. Oxford: Clarendon Press.

Stroud, B. 1984b. "The Allure of Idealism", *Aristotelian Society Supplementary Volume* 58: 243–58.

Stroud, B. 1989. "Understanding Human Knowledge in General". See Lehrer & Clay (eds) (1989), 31–50.

Stroud, B. 1994. "Scepticism, 'Externalism', and the Goal of Epistemology", *Aristotelian Society Supplement Volume* 68: 219–307.

Stroud, B. 1996. "Epistemological Reflection on Knowledge of the External World", *Philosophy and Phenomenological Research* 56(2): 345–58.

Thomson, J. J. 1966. "Private Languages". In *Philosophy of Mind*, S. Hampshire (ed.), 116–43. New York: Harper & Row.

Unger, P. 1975. *Ignorance: A Case for Scepticism*. Oxford: Clarendon Press.

Unger, P. 1984. *Philosophical Relativity*. Minneapolis, MN: University of Minnesota Press.

Vogel, J. 1990. "Cartesian Skepticism and Inference to the Best Explanation", *Journal of Philosophy* 87: 658–66.

Vogel, J. 1997. "Skepticism and Foundationalism: A Reply to Michael Williams", *Journal of Philosophical Research* 22: 11–28.

Walker, R. C. S. 1978. *Kant*. London: Routledge.

Walker, R. C. S. (ed.) 1982. *Kant on Pure Reason*. Oxford: Oxford University Press.

Walker, R. C. S. 1983. "Gassendi and Skepticism". See Burnyeat (ed.) (1983), 319–36.

Walker, R. C. S. 1989. "Transcendental Arguments and Scepticism". In *Reading Kant: New Perspectives on Transcendental Arguments and Critical Philosophy*, E. Schaper & W. Vossenkuhl (eds), 55–76. Oxford: Basil Blackwell.

Williams, B. 1978. *Descartes: The Project of Pure Inquiry*. Harmondsworth: Penguin.

Williams, M. 1971. *Groundless Belief*. Oxford: Basil Blackwell.

Williams, M. 1988. "Epistemological Realism and the Basis of Scepticism", *Mind* 97: 415–39.

Williams, M. 1991. *Unnatural Doubts*. Oxford: Basil Blackwell.

Williams, M. 1996. "Understanding Human Knowledge Philosophically", *Philosophy and Phenomenological Research* 56: 359–78.

Williams, M. 1999. "Skepticism". See Greco & Sosa (eds) (1999), 35–69.

Williams, M. 2001. *Problems of Knowledge*. Oxford: Oxford University Press.

Wittgenstein, L. 1953. *Philosophical Investigations*, G. E. M. Anscombe (trans.). Oxford: Basil Blackwell.

Wittgenstein, L. 1969. *On Certainty*. Oxford: Basil Blackwell.

Index